Built for a Better World

How **Seventh Generation** Pioneered a Movement That Changed the **Purpose of Business**

JEFFREY HOLLENDER

with GEOFF DAVIS

FC

FAST COMPANY *Press*

This book is a memoir reflecting the author's present recollections of experiences over time. Its story and its words are the author's alone. Some details and characteristics may be changed, some events may be compressed, and some dialogue may be recreated.

Fast Company Press
New York, New York
www.fastcompanypress.com

This work is being published under the Fast Company Press imprint by an exclusive arrangement with *Fast Company*. *Fast Company* and the *Fast Company* logo are registered trademarks of Mansueto Ventures, LLC. The Fast Company Press logo is a wholly owned trademark of Mansueto Ventures, LLC.

Distributed by River Grove Books

Design and composition by Greenleaf Book Group
Cover design by Greenleaf Book Group
Cover image ©Adobe Stock/domnitsky

Publisher's Cataloging-in-Publication data is available.

Print ISBN: 978-1-63908-174-5

eBook ISBN: 978-1-63908-175-2

First Edition

To my wife, Sheila Hollender,
without whom none of this would have been possible.

Contents

CHAPTER ONE

A Rude Awakening!

On a cold night in late October, I was sobbing hysterically in the Seventh Generation subterranean parking garage in Burlington, Vermont.

The tears alone were surprising. Crying has never been a go-to emotional response for me. And I'd certainly never shed a single tear over anything work-related. But this was not an ordinary night.

Minutes before, the Seventh Generation board of directors had adjourned. To say the meeting had not gone well would be a monstrous understatement. It had been a hot-button session of heated debate, and I was overwhelmed by the fear that the company I had fought so hard for was about to get seriously burned.

The trouble had been brewing for almost a year, and it all started when I made a deal with a benign devil.

After nearly twenty years of environmental trials and corporate tribulations, I was burned out. The daily grind of keeping a challenging business afloat had finally taken a toll I couldn't ignore. I needed to step back from my all-consuming, over-active role as Seventh Generation's Co-CEO lest my last surviving nerve fray beyond repair.

I had told the board, "I want to take a break and step back from my day-to-day responsibilities; I'd like to focus on writing and speaking. I can still be CEO and the public face of the company, but somebody else should actually run the show."

On the surface, nothing had to change. We'd just rejigger the chain of command behind the scenes and bring in a new set of hands to steer us into 2010 and the next chapter in the Seventh Generation story. Then I could catch my breath and promote our company's ideals without having to actually engineer them into an ever-complicated reality.

The board agreed and we hired the somewhat ironically-named Heidrick & Struggles, a fancy executive search firm, to find our next company president.

After a long national hunt through more corporate corridors than I cared to count, we landed on one of the nicest people I've ever met, a guitar-playing runner named Chuck Maniscalco. Chuck had been the CEO of PepsiCo's Quaker-Tropicana-Gatorade division. We believed his consumer products brand expertise was just what we needed to get Seventh Generation to our ultimate goal—a billion dollars in sales.

Just one small problem: Chuck didn't want to be president. He wanted to be the CEO. This proposition would take me much further out of the management loop than I wanted to go, both figuratively and literally. Such a change not only meant relinquishing influence, it would move me out of my longtime office, stuffed into an attic library sitting in a forgotten corner of the building. Too exhausted to argue, I agreed.

A fatal mistake.

My always-wiser wife, Sheila, tried to warn me. She thought it was a terrible idea and fought adamantly against the entire arrangement. She'd interviewed Chuck as part of the hiring process and was convinced he was not the best fit for Seventh Generation. Moreover, she urged me not to relinquish authority, to maintain ultimate control of the company to which we'd both dedicated our lives. But I wasn't looking for authority. I was dead set on finding a pressure relief valve. Chuck was it. That was that.

Chuck joined the Seventh Generation community shortly thereafter and plunged into the work of shepherding the company into the new decade. His hands were full from day one.

For one thing, over the previous year, the company had grown 50 percent and annual sales now stood at a benchmark record of $150 million. It was hands down our best year ever, but after years as a small, struggling, niche company, this explosive success had everybody juggling myriad challenges. The whole company—from human resources to product development—was working overtime.

Despite the upheaval and corresponding pressures, I was elated. At last, our long-term survival seemed assured. But we needed a new investment for the final lap, and Chuck's pedigree was part of our plan to secure the $30 million in funding we required. With his résumé on our team, we would create the investor confidence necessary to transform Seventh Generation from risky into a surefire bet.

It was a wild time of bursting at the seams, burning cash, growing pains, and corporate soul-searching. Two visionary women, Carol Sanford and Cheryl Heller, were instrumental in developing, "global imperatives," a set of eight ideals. More than ideals, these were commitments to creating a just and equitable world by promoting its health and wellbeing, and leading the world toward a higher consciousness.

After about six months into Chuck's tenure, the mistake became clear. Though he said all the right things, he wasn't internalizing Seventh Generation's global imperatives or nurturing the company culture. He understood how to sell pallets of dish liquid to grocery shoppers, but he couldn't get comfortable with the let's-go-fight-climate-change-and-all-get-arrested side of the business at its very core. As talented as he was, it turned out he just didn't have social responsibility woven into his managerial DNA, and at Seventh Generation, that was the most crucial leadership qualification.

There were other troubles simmering as well, such as the stock options. At the time, employees held about 20 percent of our stock, after having been distributed 1 percent of the company ownership each year for the past twenty years. I was pushing to get that number up to 30 percent to become an ESOP, an employee-owned company. For whatever reason, the board of directors hadn't been paying enough attention to my efforts with this and suddenly it became an issue. Out of nowhere, one board member freaked out that we were giving so much stock to employees. Not only did he want us to stop, he wanted them to give half of it back.

I did not have one problem with that . . . I had a whole lot of problems with it. First off, why on Earth would any employee agree to such a give-back? After all, it was their blood, sweat, and tears over many long years that had created all this tremendous value for our shareholders.

The argument was that we'd go out of business if employees didn't acquiesce. Not even Chuck's stellar résumé would be enough to overcome investor hesitation about such a large ESOP program, and their reluctance would prevent us from raising the money we needed to survive.

I disagreed. Vehemently. It was not only absurdly unfair, it was disingenuous. I wondered if their sudden concern was more about the dilution of the board members' own shares. Never mind that those shares had risen in value from about $1.75 to over $22.50 in ten years, a return of over 1,000 percent, meaning the board had already made a huge amount of money. The reason they had all profited so handsomely was thanks to the hard work of a Seventh Generation community motivated in no small part by their legitimate sense of ownership in the company. The idea that we would screw over the very people responsible for our collective wealth—retroactively, no less—was utterly revolting.

Then there was Terrible Tim (not his real name). He ran a venture capital fund and had been brought on board for some additional cash and to help with the new round of fundraising. Or so they said. In the summer of 2010, he'd planted an underling in the office to analyze our operation. Now suddenly there was all this talk about the total worth of the company—but why? A new valuation was completely irrelevant to anything we were doing. It was as useless as it was baffling.

Unless, of course, some of the board was secretly readying Seventh Generation to be sold. Such a move would put the company's values and vision at the risk of destruction. A move I had vocally sworn I would never let happen.

Which brings us back to that Friday night in Burlington, at a board meeting held after hours in our offices, where I laid all these collective concerns on the table.

I said, "Asking the employees to give back their hard-earned stock is the exact opposite of our company values. It is as grotesque as it is unfair. It is absolutely not a reflection of the company we have worked so hard to become."

What kind of company did we want to be? A marketable one? What's the real reason Terrible Tim and his minions are haunting our halls? What are you guys not telling me about your ultimate intentions? "What exactly is going on here?" I asked.

All this was before we even got around to the subject of our newish CEO. "Look," I said, "Chuck just doesn't get the company or its mission. It's not his fault. No hard feelings. I love the guy personally, but in the final analysis, he's not the right fit."

I laid out how hiring Chuck was regrettable and ultimately my mistake, but he had to go if for no other reason than the fact that fundraising on the basis of his résumé was completely unethical. "We can't take the money when we know he's the wrong person for the job. I don't care what we have to do," I said. "I don't want the cash if it has to come on his credentials."

The board wasn't having it. "If we let Chuck go, it will hurt our valuation," they argued. "It will look like we don't have our shit together, which will make it impossible to raise the funds we need."

"So what?" I replied. "That's not a reason to stay the course. It's wrong, and it's fraudulent, too. In fact, despite all the talk about how proud everybody here is of the company's values, it's starting to look like the money matters a whole lot more."

Poor Chuck. Even he knew he was in the wrong place, and he tendered his resignation to the board on the spot. If I didn't think he was the right person for the job, he didn't want it.

The board not only refused his offer, they collectively pushed back against me. Hard. No one supported even one of my positions. Other than my wife, nobody had my back.

So much tension filled the room, you would have needed a chainsaw to cut through it. And even then, it might have killed the chainsaw. No votes were taken. No decisions were made. I left the meeting in shock.

Suddenly, it was clear to me that despite being a company founder for the last two decades, despite all I had given to Seventh Generation in its quest for both principles and profits, I had nothing. No power. No board allies. No influence to persuade my adversaries. After years of giving seats to our big investors and giving up control with majority ownership, the money was all in, and Sheila and I were inexplicably on the outs—a minority of two fighting a united majority that, alarmingly, seemed to no longer understand the company they were charged with guiding.

It was a horrifying moment, one made all the more painful by the betrayal of an investment banker who was also a very close longtime friend, someone I'd known since the fifth grade. He had always assured me that our friendship was more important than business. He told me he'd always have my back. Now his promise felt like a Vermont-sized load of complete bullshit.

Alone. Abandoned. Tormented. The tears were bitter, and they flowed freely, salty acknowledgement that the dream I'd built was in danger of becoming a nightmare.

A good night's sleep helped. In the frost-clarified light of a bright Vermont autumn morning, with the last of the season's brilliant foliage rustling in the Lake Champlain breeze, the heavy emotional weight of the previous evening partially lifted, aided by Sheila's gentle assurances that everything would be all right.

Still, I knew I was in the middle of a real corporate shit show. Getting out of it wasn't going to be easy, but I believed eventually I'd find a reasonable path forward. Things would work out. As my crazy entrepreneurial career had taught me, compromise was usually the name of the game. You have to give a little to get something better. I could bend without breaking, and the board could, too. Together, we'd figure this out.

I mulled over these thoughts, watching Saturday's morning light glitter across Lake Champlain and the Adirondacks beyond, when the phone rang.

It was the company's attorney and mine, too. We'd worked together for years—his father had been on the board of one of my early companies—and I considered him a friend. It was a little weird that he'd call on a Saturday morning, but the previous night had been so heavy, it wasn't a complete surprise.

He asked me if Sheila was there and could I get her on the phone, too? I called her into the room and put him on speaker.

He was talking, but it wasn't really the friend I had trusted for so many years. He was all lawyer, speaking in legalese, and it was obvious he was reading from some kind of prepared script. The words fell out of the phone and tumbled into an ugly heap on the table.

Following our meeting last night, the board of directors had reconvened. A vote had been called. The company I'd taken from backwater niche business to national brand "no longer required my services." I would not be allowed to return to the office. Effective immediately, my role at the company was terminated.

I was terminated.

What happened next is a long, strange story. How I reached that brilliant Saturday morning in October is one that's longer and even stranger still. In between both stories dwells a major chapter in the history of corporate social responsibility and a world of lessons learned the hard way about starting and running businesses that want to evolve.

For over forty years, I've hammered away at a single idea in which I deeply believe: Business has the potential to become a force uniquely suited to making the world a better place. This idea is the one tool that contains the power and reach needed to get that job done with the urgency the world needs. We just have to rearrange how it works.

To get there, I've been obsessed with creating a different type of bottom line that puts people and the planet before profits. This bottom line marks its successes not just with plus signs but minus signs as well. And I've spent most of my adult life building a company that would put these essential ideals into actual viable practice and show the world the way. I know—it doesn't sound easy, and it's not as easy as it sounds. History will tell future generations whether or not I succeeded.

There is a whole lot to learn from this episode alone, much of which took years to figure out. Three lessons seem critical:

First, carefully select the people you place on your board. A big check is no reason to offer a board seat. Great care and due diligence are required, much the same work that would go into the due diligence required to hire a new leader to your senior management team. Ask for references. Get the names of three CEOs with whom the prospective board member has worked. Find out how they responded when a serious disagreement arose. Did they stand up for the purpose of the business? Or where the short-term stock price would benefit?

Second, pay great attention to governance. Important values and principles (like donating 1 percent of sales to not-for-profit organizations) don't belong on a poster—they belong in the company's charter. These ideals must be legally embedded in the way the company does business and not subject to change.

Third, make sure your board is on the same page as you are concerning the vision for the company. Reviewing the business results and strategy in board meetings is not enough. You must ensure board members are deeply aligned with your values and purpose. I clearly failed to communicate how critical employee ownership was to the company's brand and the financial results of the company. Or the fact that our purpose would be put into jeopardy if the business was sold to a large company who liked the brand but not all the crazy things we did to build it into the iconic organization that elicited warm and fuzzy feelings in our customers' hearts.

Seventh Generation was a leader in the corporate responsibility movement. That leadership required taking risks that many business owners would never be willing to undertake. Those risks, such as our partnership with Greenpeace, formed the personality of our brand in a manner that was as essential as it was delicate. And that's the story I want to invite you to now be a part of. Are you ready?

CHAPTER TWO

Training Wheels

You don't get to control Why, Where, When, or How you come into this world. But once you're here, you do have some say in Why, Where, When, and How you care for the world.

My journey to environmental entrepreneurialism didn't start with founding Seventh Generation. It started in the steel and concrete capital city of capitalism itself.

Like any new worker, I started on a Monday.

November 8, 1954, was a lovely late autumn New York City day by all accounts, and I made my debut in a delivery room at Manhattan's Doctors Hospital on the Upper East Side.

My father, Alfred L. Hollender, was a rising star in the advertising world, and my mother, Lucille, was a former actress from Chicago. Together, they had embarked on an industry-sponsored drama of their own, a real-life version of *Mad Men*, set in a fancy four-bedroom Upper East Side apartment. And unbeknownst to everyone, I had just been cast as Errant Son No. 1, something my mother welcomed but caused nothing but irritation for my dad.

I can't recall much of my first few years on Earth. There was a lot of smoking. A lot of drinking. Formal dinners with cigarette holders at every place setting and separate dishes for fish bones and artichoke leaves, and countless cocktail parties at which I would be trotted out for five minutes, shown off like a new puppy, and then promptly put back in my five-star crate to be ignored.

My father was a Napoleonic figure at a mere 5' 1", who had grown up on Chicago's South Side, just another scrappy, street-smart kid hustling for paydays that were always in short supply. Yet from a childhood marked by little hope and even fewer resources, he grew up into the kind of successful man from which the self-made American myth is wrought. He loved regaling my brother and me with stories of how he'd put himself through the University of Chicago by selling hot dogs at the University of Illinois Stadium. He was not the slightest bit shy about telling us both, ad nauseum, that the most important thing in life was to "make it on your own."

Yet I don't think he ever truly faced up to the fact that his was a mixed set of signals at best—his own success denied us the opportunity to ever make it entirely on our own. Thanks to his achievements, we sought our own success from an advantaged starting position. It was all more than a little paradoxical, but nevertheless, the injunction was there, and we never forgot it.

Somehow my father parlayed those hot dogs into a University of Illinois architecture degree, yet he never put pen to blueprint. Instead, he fell into an early career in the Chicago radio business, which boomed in the 1920s, and stayed strong well into the Depression. He broadcasted sports and played big band music before turning that passion and its accompanying skills into some valuable work for the United States Army. In less than a year, he rose to the rank of Lieutenant

Colonel and was put in charge of the all-important Counterintelligence Psychological Warfare Division during World War II. There he developed a close lifelong friendship with General-turned-President Dwight D. Eisenhower.

After the war, he landed in New York and married Lucille, whom he'd met on a vacation in Cuba. He pivoted from creating wartime disinformation to the biggest propaganda effort of them all: American advertising. Soon, he made his mark as president of Grey International, the global arm of Grey Advertising, a job that provided him with no end of power and prestige. With the privileges provided, he and my mother built a "respectable" upper-class life for their family.

Childhood was a gilded existence in a prosperous post-war era. The Hollenders were doing very, very well, including their two children—myself and my younger brother Peter. We had a life most other kids would have killed for. As the son of an ad man, I was encouraged to watch as much television as possible, and I enjoyed ridiculous perks like exclusive weekend cartoon focus groups. My father would troop me and my classmates into the office to preview the latest Saturday morning offerings, and we would tell him which ones we were sure to watch.

Yet amid all this physical plenty lay a core of emotional poverty—my father's job sat at the root of the trouble. He was tasked to scale his firm into an international giant, which was not a family-friendly assignment. To accomplish the task, he spent half his life traveling the world and buying up ad agencies wherever markets looked ripe. With corporate checkbook in tow, he and my mother were away for long stints, leaving me and my brother with no one but the nanny.

Every time they'd prepare for another departure, I'd get sick. With hindsight and sixty years of psychological progress, it's easy to see the connection. But the mid-twentieth century was a less enlightened time, and nobody back then put two and two together. In fourth grade, I was sent to a therapist to explore my constant bouts of illness, which started me on a lifelong journey through nearly every type of therapy you can imagine. A fitting end to my elementary school career.

After attending the Town School for kindergarten and the first grade, my parents decided to move me to the Allen-Stevenson School, an Upper East Side academy more befitting the Hollender family's rising social status. Upon enrollment, I was deemed insufficiently developed and forced to repeat first grade. The required haircut—a dramatic crewcut—revealed another deficiency in the form of my unusually big ears, which became the butt of endless jokes.

Meanwhile, my younger brother Peter was a beautiful child with long dark hair and the kind of charisma that enchanted even the most emotionally hardened teacher. He was as blessed with natural attributes as he was with personality. And he had no difficulties parlaying the two into endless, effortless trouble.

He was trusted to buy office supplies, pick up lunch from the deli, or make keys for a new teacher. Whenever he did the latter, he made sure to keep an extra copy for himself. Eventually, he ended up with access to the entire school, including the file cabinets holding all the student IQ scores, which he promptly sold back to the kids themselves for a significant sum. Brilliant but deviant, it wasn't the kind of success that'll win you an academic commendation. Where my brother was concerned, the consequences of such misadventures were just the beginning of what would be a rough arc through a tortured life.

Peter just could not stay clear of trouble, though I think it was largely a rebellion against my father. The two had had a complicated relationship nearly from birth. In a way, my dad claimed me as his, and my mother claimed Peter as hers. Yet my father was always jealous of the attention she gave Peter.

At some point, my parents made the decision to put some space between me and my unruly brother by sending me off to Riverdale Country School for the fifth grade.

Despite the nightmare of a daily bus ride to the Bronx, I found Riverdale to be the only school where I ever learned anything worth knowing, thanks to incredible teachers like Holland Fitz.

The unconventional Mr. Fitz thought we should possess the ability to question the nature of reality. He challenged us to be critical thinkers by not automatically accepting what we thought we knew. And that, too, was a pretty big concept to learn.

Around eighth grade, I started to have serious doubts about the true worth of wealth. As I became more aware of the world around me, awakened by a growing counterculture movement, I felt increasingly uncomfortable, if not embarrassed, by my family's affluence.

During the late '60s and early '70s, cultivating this kind of moral conscience in their overprivileged children was par for the course for many upwardly mobile post-war parents. And yet those same parents were shocked to suddenly find their own kids intent on denigrating and destroying the very systems that had provided their privilege, a foundation the previous generation had spent its lifetime building.

In my own case, the irony of that circumstance is not lost on me. And the lifelong guilt hasn't been either.

I grew receptive to more subversive notions about success, namely that what my father did was not only unfortunate but possibly even corrupt. I devoured Vance Packard's *The Hidden Persuaders*, a best-selling exposé of subliminal manipulation within advertising, and I peppered my father with questions that often led to screaming matches. What were the social outcomes, I asked, of fabricating "needs" in people? Needs they had never had until exposed to mass-market advertising specifically designed to promote them?

My father begged to differ. He enjoyed the money and power his profession conferred. But he never seemed to be having much fun. Looking back, a big part of the problem was all that constant travel. He and Mom would take off for months at a time, scouring the globe to build Grey into one of the world's first truly international ad agencies. It was an exciting lifestyle, the envy of many, but the toll all this travel took on us all was immense. It created vast reservoirs of stress and anxiety. Even back then, decades before I first heard the term, his work/life balance struck me as hopelessly out of whack. In my mind, the money his work brought in would always remain associated with tension, frustration, and agony.

Witnessing the personal price my father paid for his prosperity made me consider my own future. I wondered what might constitute meaningful success. At that point in my life, I had only two things to compare: school and surfing. And neither one made a consequential difference in the world. Surfing was fun. School was not. What, I wondered, would working most be like? I had my suspicions; and as soon as I was able, I put them to the test.

Fertilized by the deepening guilt of my privileged life, the seeds were planted that would grow to consume me. From my perspective, the central question was not so much whether the dominant social paradigms should be attacked, but how to fuse that interest in creating revolutionary change with the desire to build an alternative. This would require creating a new type of organization. A business motivated by good intentions for the world. Perhaps the discomfort wasn't about the money but about making it do something that everybody could believe in rather than feel guilty about. Maybe it was about trying to find a better way to do business, one that generated a fairer, more just outcome, rather than richer "haves" and poorer "have-nots." Here lie the roots that many years later grew into the movement that spawned socially responsible business.

At the age of fourteen, in partnership with Peter, I founded my first business: the Westhampton Window Washing Company. We discovered that people would pay good money to have their windows washed. These were, after all, houses facing the ocean, and oftentimes, the only viable cleaning strategy was steel wool and elbow grease. We could do a house in a day and charge $100 to $200 cash for the job. Even today that would be a lot of money for a teenager.

Running a service agency required us to bone up on our interpersonal skills, which meant charming moms into paying top dollar for an extravagance performed by two kids too young to shave. It wasn't the most glorious job, but it had its perks, which, for me, included the weekly trips Peter and I took down into the gritty whirlwind of Canal Street on Manhattan's Lower East Side where we haggled with wholesalers for cleaning supplies, a business skill that would prove eminently useful.

Yet years later, the biggest reward of washing all those windows was how it taught me to become comfortable asking people for money, something too many entrepreneurs struggle with. It's a major stumbling block as most people have never had to raise funds before, and the mere idea leaves them dry heaving. I've long had an issue with shyness and can relate. But at fourteen I was conquering my bashful nature, going door-to-door with my hand outstretched and gaining vital confidence that has served me well ever since.

Peter and I knew we must be doing something right. Despite my burgeoning anti-capitalist inclinations, I enjoyed running my own business and earning my own money. I was following my father's commandment to make it on my own, and the most satisfying part was how it felt so different from school, where I was working for other people— my parents, my teachers, and all the other external authority figures. But now I was working for me, and I was doing it my way. It was surfing with squeegees and spray bottles.

But life is not as simple as a dirty window. Somewhere along the way, my innocent adolescent rebellion became a full-fledged identity crisis. With no idea who I really was or what I wanted to become, home had become less supportive. My parents weren't getting along, and our domestic atmosphere grew increasingly tense. As my parents prepped for yet another long trip, I elected to move out of the house and board at Riverdale rather than commute. Only for the escape it afforded.

For a while, I was relatively free of family stress and living in a place with great friends and lots of pot—an important rite of passage for the 1960s. But things at home became even rockier. Everyone was unhappy for one reason or another—my brother's antics had finally landed him in a psychiatric clinic, my father's stress prompted a heart attack, my parents' absence continued unabated. The air on Park Avenue was heavy with the kind of tension that weighs down the body even as it wears down the soul.

As I approached my sophomore year, keeping more daylight between me and the Upper East Side remained a good idea. This time I went north to seek respite—at the Putney School.

Founded in 1935 by avowed communist Carmelita Hinton, the Putney School is all kinds of classic Vermont—from its decidedly alternative attitude to its bucolic setting off a dirt road at the top of a perfect hill. Filled with mostly affluent kids like me—Senator sons and Hollywood daughters, offspring of industry and Wall Street—the school was built on the idea that students should not be content as parasites but should instead justify themselves as useful contributors to society.

To that end, everybody had to work on the school farm. That meant getting up at four or five in the morning to shovel shit out from underneath the cows, among other chores, all of which invariably involved some kind of arcane tool and an odor to match. For someone who grew up on Park Avenue, this was about as foreign an experience as I had yet had. Literally milking an actual cow? Now that was new.

The highlight of my time at Putney was undoubtedly the Boone's Farm Apple Wine parties. Though I still have no real idea how we so successfully engineered these, over half of the school would regularly sneak out into the woods to smoke dope and drink a wine-like travesty made for people who don't like wine. Those were some raucous nights, and more than once, they left me literally crawling back to the dorm on my hands and knees because walking upright was out of the question. That in and of itself would have been no big deal. But the swamp that sat between the forest and my bed changed the equation dramatically. Drowning turned into a viable possibility several nights. And I wasn't the only one facing marshy doom. Sometimes that wetland was a scene out of a zombie movie, a dark boggy horror filled with slowly moving, vaguely human forms covered in muck, cursing and howling in the night.

The swamp didn't kill me, but eventually the disinterest did. Three months into eleventh grade, I sought out my advisor to vent my frustrations. His advice was equally rebellious. "Why don't you just leave?" he asked. To the undying distress of my parents and the school administration alike, I picked up that suggestion and ran with it as fast as possible.

My parents cajoled the Riverdale administration to let me back in for the remainder of the year. When the term came to a merciful end in June, I stuffed the proceeds from six weeks of window washing into my pocket and headed out to California with a simple plan: Go surfing.

On my drive out west, I picked up Tahoe, a stray dog wandering along a Nevada highway. He was a little worse for wear, but he had a good soul and was fine company. I drove my ancient mustard-colored Volvo station wagon to a dismal place called Thousand Oaks, where I ended up for no reason other than a party I stumbled across that left me too drunk to drive.

I had been randomly invited there by strangers who had taken an instant liking to Tahoe. They had an extra bed and fondness for dogs. As sweet as the dog was, the prospect of spending a night on a real bed with him out in the yard was one I just could not pass up.

The guilt I felt about living back on Park Avenue weighed on me. Maybe the cure was to stay in California. With about ten dollars in my pocket, I left Tahoe and the party house behind and parked in a little corner of paradise directly above a world-famous surfing beach in Isla Vista, picked up my board, and paddled out to sea.

I surfed the days away to my heart's absolute content and spent my nights in the back of my rattle-trap car. It was warm. I was free. I could shower at the beach, and the cops left me alone to live a perfect life. If I needed money (which wasn't often and never much), I washed the windows of Santa Barbara or pulled weeds out of backyards. I was pretty good at being a hippie.

But despite the waves and the weed, the wind in my hair and the wild streak in my heart, Alfred Hollender's eldest son was still somewhat semi-reasonable and quasi-responsible. I enrolled in the senior class of Santa Barbara High School, a transparently desperate bid to persuade my anxious parents that I hadn't gone entirely off the deep end and deserved my hard-won freedom. Incredibly, I persuaded a University of California student I met at a party to pose as my legal guardian. With forged paperwork in tow, she took me to the school office and enrolled me in the twelfth grade.

It worked out better than expected. The school days weren't terrible, and when the last bell rang, there was still room in the day for a few hours of ocean time before I'd return to my car for a feast of white bread and an evening of homework by flashlight.

As winter approached, I spent my nights filling out college applications by candlelight. It was all very romantic, and it was certainly a sign of the times when a recruiter from Oregon's progressive Reed College practically admitted me on the spot when he learned how I'd written my admissions essay in a seaside parking lot scrunched down in the progressively tattered back seat of my increasingly battered home on wheels.

Eventually I saved up enough money to move out of my car and into a house occupied by a bunch of UC Santa Barbara kids. Yet despite all the sudden roommates, I was still living a pretty solitary life, feeling desperately isolated and surprisingly depressed. The turmoil I fled in New York had been supplanted by the turbulence that accompanies being alone and rootless. Compounding it all were my problems with shyness. A stranger in a strange land, with no ties, a lonely existence despite the appearance of community.

For the first time, I realized that the happy surface of my life—the freedom, the surfing, the West Coast weed, and the California sun—was just a veneer, and it was thinning fast. Sitting just below the waterline, treacherous shoals of depression were waiting. It was my first encounter with the disease, and all the hippie romanticizing in the world couldn't slow it down. I was running as fast as I could from myself, from my family, from their money and the status quo it bought. And I was about out of road.

I tried to tough it out, but six months into my senior year, I took a deep breath and drove back to New York to complete the final three months of high school at Manhattan's Baldwin School, where my father was president of the board. Not only did he pull the strings necessary to enroll an itinerant wanderer for a mere three months of final prep school education, he was also the signatory on the diploma I received.

That semi-miraculous graduation was followed by my oddest summer yet.

I found an alarmingly disgusting studio apartment on Greenwich Street in the West Village with an entire ecosystem of insects as roommates. It was a place so foul and forsaken, I'd keep my eyes closed when turning on the lights to avoid the sight of a thousand terrors scurrying back behind the cabinets in the sudden glare. These days, that apartment is likely a private million-dollar paradise, but in 1973 it was about as low as low-rent could go in deeply disturbing ways.

My father, the same man who insisted that nothing in life was more important than making it on one's own, got me a job—in advertising, of course. My daily destination was no longer the beach, but an advertising firm called Tele-Rep. My task was to analyze TV ratings and their demographics to find the data necessary to sell advertising for the networks. I spent my days studying the Nielsen numbers, looking for bumps in the viewing habits of women 25–49 and surges in men 18–24 that would tell the soap sellers and car makers where to aim their dollars.

At the same time, my brother was getting into increasingly problematic troubles with drugs and other addictions, from gambling and alcohol to prostitutes and theft. He'd been tossed out of a mental health facility and seemed hellbent on wreaking the kind of unique havoc of which only victims of addiction are capable. In an attempt to (again) cure him of his ills, the entire family enrolled at an institute called AREBA, where a form of primal therapy found the whole Hollender family punching pillows and screaming, "I'm good enough!" Sessions involved yelling into the void with all the oxygen we could inhale before revealing intimate truths that should have never seen the light of day.

One of my assignments in the program was to break free of my profound shyness by going out to pick up women. We would literally go in groups, as if we were on some lust-centric field trip, and descend en masse into a local watering hole. Peter, being the attractive, charismatic soul he was, had his pick of the crowd and no problem checking the box for these particular assignments. For me, anything beyond awkward small talk was an impossible task. Peter would lend a hand by introducing himself only to women who conveniently had a friend for me, but even that didn't usually help.

However, the answer to whatever questions my own issues posed lay not in anonymous sex or broken vocal cords. It was waiting in college. And I was ready to get out of New York and go.

In life, we're faced with many choices. Even those born to rich and famous parents make choices that can derail their lives. Sadly, my brother Peter consistently made poor choices that perpetuated destructive cycles, and his life eventually ended by his own hand. Meanwhile, I was lucky enough to make choices that moved me forward, even in failure. Knowing the degree to which I'm able to influence my destiny helped guide me to a path that was both deeply fulfilling and one I could feel proud of.

CHAPTER THREE

Learning Experiences

In January of 1974, after a long, stupefying season of advertising demographic hell, I drove north to Amherst, Massachusetts, and entered Hampshire College.

Based on the recruiter's enthusiasm for my back-seat candlelight essay, I had applied to exactly one college: Reed College in Portland, Oregon. My mother, who possessed at least a modicum of the foresight I lacked, had suggested Hampshire as a backup in case I ended up on the East Coast instead.

It was one of her enlightened moves, and to this day, I've no idea why she offered up Hampshire and not a more traditional local option like New York University or Columbia. My guess is she didn't know that much about Hampshire because the school had less than a decade under its belt when I arrived. She must have thought it was a nice New England college whose unorthodox approach would appeal to me.

Whatever her reasoning, her wisdom was solid. Hampshire was

as progressive as institutions of higher learning are likely to ever get, though I didn't realize this back then. However, I felt confined by the institution's innate insulation from the rest of civilization rather quickly. In the end, the college was a largely closed culture whose horizons largely ended at the campus gates. Beyond them, human civilization was quite unaffected by any extraordinary revelations I was experiencing, and I wanted to have an impact beyond a paper landing in my professor's mailbox.

Like many people in that era, I was searching for something but didn't know where to look. What was the point of life? What was my purpose? It was a big messed-up world, and I wanted a role in making it better. Was a bachelor's degree in mass communications from Hampshire College the best way to make that happen? The deeper I delved into my so-called college career, the more uncertain I grew.

After three semesters, I decided to quit Hampshire and head to Ithaca College in London. In an attempt to give formal education one last chance, I enrolled in a media program that involved some hands-on experience with British communications.

I arrived alone, which wasn't my best idea ever. I found a boarding-house in Bolton Gardens with a room that was little more than four narrow walls between which a twin bed had been awkwardly squeezed. In the building were twelve rooms and two small bathrooms shared by the dozen-plus tenants, a motley assortment of immigrants who often queued up impatiently for a coveted flush or a weekly (and badly needed) scrub. Inside my room were two coin-operated boxes, one for a little thankful heat via a Victorian-esque gas fireplace, the other for a few meager watts of electricity. Dump in some coins and you got a bit of both. Forget to trade in some pound notes for a pocketful of silver, and you were in for a cold, dark night.

After completing one semester, I quit the Ithaca College program and took a public relations job at W.H. Allen Publishing—a job that again I acquired with a little help from my dad. For several months, I worked as an author escort for writers running around London giving interviews and signing books. In between, I ate liquid lunches in the pub downstairs and spent most of my afternoons in an unproductive stupor punctuated by great rounds of Xeroxing.

My journal from this era is a deeply disturbing read. Its pages are stained by tears, and the words reflect what was undoubtedly the darkest period of my life. I felt I had nothing to live for, no purpose or possibility, and depression came roaring back with a vengeance. I spent the bulk of my free time staring at the claustrophobic walls in my tiny room, writing long, weepy letters.

For the first time in my life, I seriously contemplated suicide, but the source of my existential angst wasn't so much the circumstances as it was my ongoing quandary about the point of it all. Like the coins that disappeared into the heat and electric meters, my attempts to locate personal meaning yielded nothing substantial. All I could do was keep shoving metaphorical pennies into the slot and hope for the best.

At the same time, I read the works of Scottish psychologist R.D. Laing, founder of the Philadelphia Association, an experimental psychiatric community where I found a therapist. With his guidance, I embarked on what was thankfully my first partially successful treatment for depression, mapping out my own inner landscape with greater clarity and genuine understanding. In the absolute nick of time, I was rescued from despair and a little thing called hope crept back into my life.

On the spur of the moment, I decided to take this renewed interest in life on a trip to see a former girlfriend in Toronto. I put my wallet in my pocket and caught a cab to the airport. Arriving at Logan Airport with neither luggage nor return ticket, I set off every security red flag in the book and was promptly treated to a luxurious airport strip search. Missing my flight to Canada, I spent the night on an equally comfortable concourse chair, but eventually I made it there.

Glad to be back in the Americas, my mental state had improved and things were looking up—and life was looking more purposeful, too. During my first few weeks in Toronto, two quite amazing events transpired that helped shape my future.

The first was meeting Marshall McLuhan, a Canadian philosopher whose work is among the cornerstones of media theory. He was in the process of writing a seminal book entitled *City as Classroom*, which dovetailed nicely with my evolving thinking about education. McLuhan's work had always inspired me, shaping my own revolutionary and reactionary approach to the world, so one afternoon I showed up at his class and asked if I could sit in. He couldn't have been more accommodating.

The second momentous happenstance saw me falling under the spell of Ivan Illich, an Austrian Roman Catholic priest. A theologian, philosopher, and social critic, his 1971 book, *Deschooling Society*, envisioned a continuing education program of practical skills taught by practitioners rather than professional teachers. "Deschooling" was a concept I could get behind, and quite a revolutionary idea in 1976. Having "de-schooled" quite successfully myself, I was inspired by Illich's idea that the problem wasn't the teaching or the learning itself, but rather the way both happened.

Illich believed that, in the modern world, education needed to shake off the shackles of institutional convention and remake itself in a more enlightened image that emphasized self-direction. He proposed that education should rely more on social networks than institutions and occur in less rigid, more personal settings spread out across a lifetime rather than just a few choice years of one's youth. By democratizing education, he proposed we could restore its potential to change lives and improve society. If we could "dis-establish" formal schools, we'd go a long way toward de-institutionalizing society, too, making it more responsive to human needs and desires.

Illich believed ordinary people possessed enormous reservoirs of knowledge. Given the right environment and encouragement, they could then exchange knowledge in a reciprocal system of barter and benefit, with little or no money ever changing hands.

"This should be the education system of the future," I thought. And thus was planted the seed for the Skills Exchange of Toronto, the business I founded in Canada.

The ultimate irony of the Skills Exchange of Toronto was that it required no real skills to start. I had no business plan, no teaching contacts, nor any Canadian business connections. My experience of running a business was a trunkful of Windex and a couple of industrial squeegees.

What I did have was a three-thousand-dollar loan from my parents and a cocksure attitude that I could—and more importantly should—turn Ivan Illich's philosophies into a viable educational option for the good people of Toronto. After all, the idea wasn't exactly rocket science: Find people with valuable knowledge and connect them with people who want to learn. Aside from a few solvable logistical issues, it seemed like a pretty simple concept whose execution was eminently possible.

Help was found in a handful of new acquaintances. I met Buzz Burza at a party, and he wanted in immediately. Roger Hollander (different spelling, no relation) was an avowed Marxist with unflagging enthusiasm for anything that put the power in the people's hands. And with him came a French woman named Patricia Olivier-Martin, who was looking for her next passion project. Loving the idea was the only qualification I required.

Based out of the rented ground floor of a house on Brunswick Avenue just north of the University of Toronto, we started with a series of classified ads in local newspapers looking for teachers. In August of 1977, the results of that search appeared in a thin newsprint circular that materialized in the free literature racks of local shops. The Skills Exchange of Toronto had arrived on the scene with forty-six courses lasting anywhere from a single evening session to a month of classes, each for the bargain price of around twenty-five Canadian dollars.

"The Skills Exchange is a learning community without classroom walls," I told a reporter for the local *Free Press* shortly after our launch in August of 1977. "The photographer's darkroom, the carpenter's workbench, the poet's living room, the potter's studio, a courthouse, the backstage of a theater, the kitchen of a fine restaurant, a tearoom, a laboratory, a chess tournament . . ."

The possible "classrooms" were endless. Suffice it to say, we were officially in business. And better yet, we were an immediate hit.

There was something almost magical about it all. We'd gathered a group of people with knowledge and talents to offer, people who had no background or training in education. They put their unique and sometimes slightly oddball offerings down on paper that we dropped in every store that would let us, and suddenly the mail filled with checks and the phone started ringing off the hook.

Today, we take the idea of continuing adult education for granted. You'll find programs in virtually every American city, some offered by actual colleges and schools, others as part of programs like the Skills Exchange. But in the 1970s, the concept was new and surprising. Our organization and its format, as well as the actual subjects we taught, represented a new species of learning that had never been seen in the wild before. We struck an eager public nerve that, in hindsight, was ripe for the striking. And it was bigger than I'd thought it would be.

The classes themselves didn't necessarily suggest the level of success we'd so quickly achieved. Our first catalog was an almost hyperactive hodgepodge of courses. There were practical sessions such as "House Renovation," "Health Food for Fun," and "Radio, Phone, and Hi-Fi Repair" alongside more creative subjects like "Introduction to Bottle Neck Guitar" and "Want to Be a Comedian?" To this we added a fair amount of intellectual esoterica—classes like "An Introduction to Marxism" taught by our own Roger Hollander, who promised that "In part, the purpose of this course is to shatter smug illusions."

My own skill seemed to be having a good sense of what would sell, and I slid into the role of an academic director, inventing new subjects and finding teachers to teach them. I built on the success of our initial courses with more classes just like them, everything from "Self-Defense for Women" to "Creative Horsemanship."

We were a shoestring operation, and with no personal computing in 1977, everything was horrifyingly manual. No software to organize mailing lists. No hard drives to store records. No websites for online registration, nor digital payment platforms to ease the way. Absolutely everything was on paper, including the endless piles of personal checks streaming through the door. Our fanciest piece of equipment was a clunky fax machine we used to send the teachers their student lists.

I spent at least one night a month in the basement of an Asian gentleman who owned a (very) primitive printing business. It was dark, dingy, and loud, the sort of scene that could have easily opened a Stephen King novel. I sat in a sea of freshly minted Skills Exchange catalogs, the rich perfume of petrochemical inks scenting the damp cellar air with piquant notes of solvent and synthetic dye, inspecting the latest edition for hopelessly smeared type and photos turned into Rorschach tests.

Looking back, there wasn't much logic to what we did on any given day (or night). We were just veering wildly from one situation to another with no time to really think about anything we were doing, let alone whether or not it was worth doing. There was just an overwhelming whirlwind of tasks that needed to get done yesterday. As is the case with most startups, you just went where the gears of the machine were screaming loudest. And we had a lot of gears.

Still, eventually we each settled somewhat naturally into our respective roles and together kept the whole thing running. I was usually so busy developing classes and building teacher relationships that there wasn't much time for me to do anything else.

Roger helped run the rest of the operation while Buzz handled catalog distribution, delivering 100,000 copies of our foldout each month to seemingly every retail outlet in the metro area. Patricia handled registrations, cashing the checks, keeping track of the sign-ups, and generally keeping it all from flying apart.

For a while, everything flowed into place. Yes, I was working from 7:30 a.m. to midnight every day, seven days a week—my first full-blown encounter with the workaholism that would mark most of my professional life. But it was a true labor of love born of the purest possible passion, so I had no sense of work/life imbalance. I was literally manifesting my beliefs about improving the world into a concrete effort. I didn't have a job. I had a mission. And it was moving.

We were in the press on a regular basis. "Is Trading Knowledge from Mundane to Arcane an Idea Whose Time Has Come?" asked the headline in the *Toronto Globe and Mail*. We even attracted the attention of none other than media maestro Marshall McLuhan, who called me to ask if his book had been my inspiration. Maybe he was a little disconcerted by the splash we were making. He had recently co-authored *City as Classroom*, and here was this upstart East Coast college dropout who had actually figured out how to do exactly that. When I respectfully credited Illich as my entrepreneurial beacon, he took it in stride.

We were operating on the edge of the known business universe. Illich may not have been a Marxist, but Roger was, and under his rabidly committed guidance, the Skills Exchange had been formed as an egalitarian non-profit collective with no "owners," per se. The basic foundational concepts were to run the business on consensus and split the tuition 50/50 with teachers. At the end of every year, we'd take whatever money was left over and put it into a primitive profit-sharing plan.

My father thought I was crazy. "What kind of idiot are you to work so hard for a non-profit in which you have no real ownership?" he wanted to know. "Why are you breaking your back to teach chess and carpentry when you'll never be able to sell the company?"

"Because it's the right thing to do for society," I answered.

Needless to say, that didn't satisfy the adman in him.

As our program listings expanded, so did the energy we were putting into maintaining what was quickly becoming an overly cozy workers' paradise. We were a true "hippie operation" in every sense—good and bad—and as a result, discussions about process and perspective were endless. Even with only four of us, working through the group's issues and emotions took so much time and energy that often there wasn't much left for the concrete concerns upon which the organization's fate truly rested.

As the business exploded, the demands placed on us became increasingly urgent. During our first year alone, the Skills Exchange offered 1,000 courses and found 12,000 students to take them. There was a lot to do, and the whole "check-in" process we had to go through every day felt more and more like a waste of time we absolutely did not have.

As a direct result of all the navel-gazing, entropy set in, a slow and steady sense of decay characterized by a steady stream of arguments and infighting. The energy expended to maintain our little cooperative community was going from a snowball to an avalanche.

The unfolding soap opera went into its third act when Roger and Patricia began a relationship. What little functioning our tiny organization had cobbled together seemed to fall into disarray somewhere between those sheets. Patricia quit in the inevitable heartbreak, and I completely lost my taste for taking the collective approach to business management. I reasserted myself as leader of the Skills Exchange, and Roger couldn't dissent because his standing had been so tainted by a lack of sexual restraint. He left soon after.

The lessons learned from the Skills Exchange were many and would follow me to Seventh Generation later on. The management by consensus process turned out to be too cumbersome. A more traditional structure at an earlier time in our development would have been preferable. That doesn't mean that input and involvement from employees should have been abandoned. Rather, it provides valuable and essential advice and should be a part of all management structures. But a fully democratic process of decision-making was untenable.

Our very loose business purpose, while critical, didn't provide enough direction to make good decisions. For instance, a course's popularity alone was a poor way to guide our decisions and created confusion about what we stood for. Clear and measurable goals and impact are necessary ingredients for successful social entrepreneurs.

Also, inadequate working capital can't be replaced by twelve-hour days, seven days a week. Burnout is sure to follow.

The whole experience also supported my belief that experience is not always a prerequisite for success. With no college degree, never having taken a course on finance, management, or leadership, I still managed to launch and run a small but successful business. In many respects, not having spent four years in college and two more getting an MBA provided me with a six-year head start relative to entrepreneurs who begin their journey after business school.

After Roger's departure, the organization was getting back on track and was no longer an experiment in Marxist ideals. Most of our classes were popular. Registrations were strong. And the press attention we were gaining was off the charts, from articles in the local *Globe and Mail* and *Toronto Star* to overseas publications like the *London Free Press*. We didn't even need to advertise. We were lodged firmly in the public eye, which was great.

Until it wasn't.

One April day in 1978, I was sitting in the office nursing a badly strained back when two Royal Canadian Mounted Police officers showed themselves in.

"Are you Jeffrey Hollender?" one asked.

"Yes," I said.

"We have a warrant for your arrest."

CHAPTER FOUR

Class Act

Say what? Completely blindsided, I was thrown in the back of their car (somewhat disappointed they had not arrived on horseback) and was hauled off to face charges. I soon learned the charges stemmed from my application for Canadian working papers—specifically, my failure to follow up on the rejection.

At the time, the Canadian government was cracking down on illegal immigration. Parliament had recently passed a new law, and the government was eager to make an example out of a few high-profile scofflaws. Having spent the last year bathing in Toronto's media spotlight, an American flouting legal working requirements on Canada's sovereign soil made me an ideal target. The fix was in. And I was suddenly in handcuffs.

To say it was surreal would be an exercise in extreme understatement. As I was being hauled off to jail, I kept arguing with the police, who had their orders from above and could not have cared less about my protestations:

"Look at all the jobs I'm creating for people! This is good for the economy. Why would you let a lack of working papers stop someone from doing this? This is just a simple bureaucratic snafu!"

"Nope," came their reply. "You've got to have papers. And you, Mr. Hollender, do not."

The headline in the *Toronto Sun* said it all: "His Success Was Illegal."

"The whole thing has taken off," I proudly informed the reporter, before going on to confess that I was "dismayed" by these recent developments. "If they deport me, they jeopardize the whole operation," I said. "I can't understand why they would throw all these people out of work when unemployment is so high."

The argument made immeasurable sense. I was hardly a villain. I was helping people learn new skills while advancing the fortunes of local teachers and others via a non-profit organization that had everyone's best interests in mind. I wasn't slinking around the back alleys of Toronto selling heroin to school kids behind a dumpster. I was a job creator boosting the economy in a new and inventive way. These were my sins?

Apparently, they were. In the words of an assistant to Immigration Minister Bob Cullen, "It's just not in the national interest to have him. It seems he's deliberately set out to break the law."[1]

Not true, but it didn't matter. It seemed the law had already won before I could fight back. If there was any good news, it was that we had a teacher on our roster who taught immigration law. He was my one call from the slammer, and he told me not to worry. This was not an offense they could hold me for. He'd get me out.

The next day he did. A hearing was scheduled, and its eventual verdict (a foregone conclusion) was deportation. The *Toronto Star* headline ran: "He Taught 8000; Canada Ousts Him."[2]

Oddly, there was nothing in the order about not coming back. I literally crossed the border into the United States, then promptly turned right around and re-entered the nation that had just given me the unceremonious boot.

However, I was not up for flaunting the legal decision and did not go back to work. The damage had been done, and I'd had my fill of Toronto, of non-profit work, and everything else. With generous assistance provided by Canadian immigration authorities, I abandoned the Skills Exchange. I couldn't stay in Canada, and I didn't own the business. After all, it was a non-profit collective, run by a board of directors.

With me opting out, one of our teachers offered to take over, a much more traditional manager who kept the idea itself going, minus the original Marxist flavoring. The Skills Exchange kept going for over a decade, during which it lost its edge and then its novelty, becoming a much more traditional adult education program.

Instead, I went to Martha's Vineyard for a badly needed vacation after almost two years of eighty-hour work weeks. As summer drew to a close, I decided to visit my cousin at his ginseng farm outside Plainfield, Vermont.

That fall, my cousin was going through a break-up. He'd separated from his wife (again) and I could relate. Departing Toronto had also meant exiting my own long-term relationship, and I, too, was a bit battle-scarred. We were two bruised and confused comrades, perfect company for each other.

My depression returned tanned, rested, and ready to rock. If I'd learned one thing in Toronto, it was that work was a great balm for my state of mind. At the Skills Exchange, I had plenty to do, which had held depression at bay, if not subdued it entirely. Now, it was just me and Steven and a couple of horses lost in the deep white vacancy of a Vermont winter, where the hours bled together in a haze of wood and other kinds of smoke.

In a helpful way, our days were meditative. There was unquestionable magic out in the forest, where a world made of sky and snow did strange things to light and sound. The world was monochrome and still, emptied by wind and cleansed by cold into the purest form of its own self, and there was healing to be had in that austerity. Life was simple and uncluttered, reduced to the task in front of your face.

Leave it to the isolated depths of a Vermont winter to clear the mind and refocus one's intentions. Clarity emerged. Building the Skills Exchange from nothing taught me I could do it again. I knew what it would take, but this time I would do it right. This time I would do it in New York.

With some trepidation and nowhere else to go, I decided to head back into the belly of the psychic beast, back to New York City with its equal measures of promise and peril. Call it a change of heart. Though I'd built the beginning of a solid entrepreneurial foundation for myself, I was in my roaring twenties, and my appetite for more was a powerful influence. It was January 1979 and high time to declare the '60s dead and the "me decade" ascendant. I was eager to make my mark—and finally make some money—in the Big City. After all, being a hippie was turning out to be the best qualification for becoming a yuppie.

New York, that scene of parental crime and adolescent misdemeanors, may have held a cache of personal baggage, but it was also filled with friends and familiarity. At the same time, my father's influence was finally breaking through. With the implosion of the Skills Exchange, I could see his point that it was idiotic doing all this non-profit stuff instead of applying my talents to making serious money the old-fashioned way.

While the Skills Exchange had been a positive experience, the collective nature of its management structure simply had not worked. Were I to do it all over again—which was the plan—I would do it without endless hours of negotiating every last scrap of organizational minutiae. I would play first chair. Mine would be both the first and the last word. Full stop.

I traded the woods of Vermont for a Greenwich Village apartment on East 12th Street, and a flannel shirt and worn jeans for a decidedly bourgeois suit and tie. A dress code fit to steer my keen competitive instinct straight onto the fast lane.

There was another side to the story, though. Work was an escape. In those early years, its primary purpose was not so much to maintain financial solvency but to stave off the lonely feelings of hopelessness. To be consumed by work meant not being consumed by despair. As a fortuitous side effect, this strategy dovetailed nicely with my father's fundamental lesson that obsession with work was good. If you weren't working your ass off, you weren't really working. Of course, this is a generational myth we're better off without, but in 1979, running on overtime was working for me, so I ran with it.

Armed with fancy threads and a new attitude, I quickly raised $60,000, mostly from my parents' friends, and rented a loft-like office space on East 11th Street in Greenwich Village, set on bringing the Skills Exchange of Toronto to New York City.

Well, sort of.

I knew Manhattan was very different from Toronto, and if I was going to grow the business as fast as possible, I'd have to do things differently than in Canada. Content, as always, would be king, so differentiating our subject matter was crucial. Practical courses like "Introduction to Marxism" and "Furniture Refinishing" wouldn't cut it. Those topics may have been somewhat unique in Toronto, but in New York, they would elicit only yawns.

My close friend Josh Sapan was a cable programing impresario who later went on to head the AMC television network. He introduced me to a brilliant woman named Mary Daly (not the feminist writer), who had a preternatural ability to think up course ideas unlike anything else. With her insight, we dreamed up classes whose topical insanity was equaled only by their sheer chutzpah. Our initial catalogs were filled with courses like "How to Lose Your Brooklyn Accent" and "The Art of Flirting." Meanwhile, I exploited every personal connection I had to find teachers. Josh taught a class in his office on cable television, a high school friend's father, John Rand, handled the session on advertising copywriting, and so on.

In September of 1979, the New York Network for Learning made its debut with sixty classes and a print run of 100,000 catalogs that appeared without warning in apartment building lobbies and free literature racks across Manhattan. With the help of the amazing public relations firm I'd hired, we immediately discovered our courses were the stuff of media coverage dreams, and we got noticed almost instantly.

But there was a hitch. Many of the classes were so outrageous, we didn't expect anyone to actually take them. They were only there for the free advertising they provided, a hook to draw attention to our catalog and lure students for somewhat more traditional offerings like "How to Start Your Own Bookstore" and "Japanese Cooking." In many cases, these more unorthodox subjects existed in name only. We'd whipped up a quick course description, but that was it—often there was no classroom, no syllabus, no instructor. Yet to both our delight and dismay, people signed up for these oddball sessions in droves. It was a good problem to have, but it left us scrambling to find someone to actually teach them.

In January of 1980, *The New York Times* published a substantial story about us in a piece that focused on "The Business of

Broadcasting," one of our more "traditional" course concepts. This was just the beginning of the paper's fortunate obsession with the Network for Learning. A second, much longer piece in the *Times* greeted the roll-out of two of our most popular offerings: "How to Meet Men," taught by a data processor who used the pseudonym Mara Lynn Shaw, and "How to Meet Women," a session with notorious pick-up artist Eric Weber, author of the dubious tome *How to Pick Up Women*. By the end of the year, yet another *NYT* piece characterized me as "a bold, 25-year-old entrepreneur who's doing just fine in his role as a one-man seismograph recording the vogues and channeling the eruptions on this trendy Richter scale into quickie night courses."[3]

We were enjoying the fruits of willfully frivolous courses like "Wrinkles, Wrinkles, Wrinkles," which we billed as a "one-night face lift." That one garnered us national coverage in *Time* magazine, which cheekily suggested that our "phenomenal success (was) due, in large measure, to Hollender's shrewd ability to live off the fad of the land."[4]

Classes like "Learn to Make Sushi" and "How to Get Pregnant After 30" (complete with a catalog cover illustration of a sperm assaulting an egg) were hitting bullseye after bullseye with the in-crowd, and the attention had legs. The Network for Learning grossed $1.5 million in its first year, an impressively hefty sum considering that the fees for our courses averaged $35. For every $10,000 to $20,000 we spent on advertising, we were generating somewhere around $100,000 in tuition. (At one point, that ROI hit the quarter million-dollar mark!) It was almost like we had permission to print money. Our initial course load rose to 200 offerings, and our student count increased from 400 to an incredible 60,000 students per year.

This was a brand of success totally different from the Skills Exchange. From a values perspective, our courses were dismally bereft of moral standing, but I didn't see the problem at the time. I had no qualms about any of our content and said so when faced with rare challenges by reporters. Nothing was broken, so I sure wasn't going to mess with success by trying to fix it.

After our debut, we quickly outgrew our dinky little office on East 11th. We leased a gigantic new space in Midtown but only after leveraging all my powers of persuasion on the octogenarian landlord. He couldn't quite see the wisdom in renting to a twenty-five-year-old and begged me to reconsider, presumably to bypass the trouble of turning me down.

"You don't want to sign this lease," he said. "It's a huge financial obligation. You don't need to be on 32nd Street."

Oh, but my ego did. And just like that, I had my office fantasies fulfilled by a well-windowed wonderland with a private balcony and a room just on the other side packed with a hundred people opening envelopes and cashing checks.

The Network for Learning continued to grow, along with the kinds of complications I could dream about at the comparatively sedate Skills Exchange. Soon, we started hosting classes with 400 to 500 people in them, crowds so large we needed auditoriums. Desperate for cheap space, I even made a deal with the principal of my final high school (the Baldwin School) to use the building at night.

There were teachers to be coddled—and students, too. One morning, I was called to the scene of a class and found an angry crowd milling around a locked door. The teacher hadn't shown, and after a bunch of frantic calls that went nowhere, I had to cancel the class. To cushion the blow and spare myself a PR crisis, I took everyone out to breakfast. At another no-show, I paid for everyone's cab ride home. With thousands of students taking hundreds of classes every month, you never knew when the phone would ring and send the day spiraling down the nearest drain.

Then came our *pièce de résistance.*

"How to Marry Money" was a one-night stand taught by Joanna Steichen, the forty-eight-year-old widow of famed photographer Edward Steichen. Joanna had married her late husband when he was half a century her senior. It was the apotheosis of the Network for Learning zeitgeist and our defining contribution to the great font of human knowledge. The class was an instant sensation.

Joanna, if you'll forgive the phrase, was a consummate character and real hoot. As she blithely informed the *Wall Street Journal,* "If you are a successful person in life, blessed with options and self-esteem, there is no reason to pick someone poor."[5] Large swaths of the public apparently agreed. The class immediately became our biggest best-seller ever. Offered on a regular basis, it routinely packed huge rooms with hundreds of people.

Though it was the class that put us on the adult education map for good, "How to Marry Money" was also the first to show the cracks in our model.

At one of the class's earliest sessions, I sat in the audience as Joanna broke the ice with some typical performative small talk. When she asked the class why they'd chosen to come, a woman stood up and said, "You know, I've got two boys and they're not as motivated as I would like them to be. I'm worried and figure if I can teach them how to marry a rich woman, that'll be a good thing for them."

Then a man stood up right after her and said, "Well, I'm here because I have two daughters, and I want to teach them how to stay away from your sons."

He had a point. But at the time, I didn't see it. I thought the whole exchange was amusing and simply further proof of the topic's genius.

The suggestion that we might be contributing to cultural decay bounced right off me.

A few years later, alongside other rising stars in my generation like Christie Brinkley, Joan Jett, and one "Steven Jobs," I was featured in a book by New York writer Ralph Gardner, Jr. called *Young, Gifted, and Rich*. Its title served as a reasonable bumper sticker for my state of mind at the time. The Network's success and notoriety were pure sugar for my ego. I was eating it up and ever hungry for more, high on fame and money that seemed unlimited. The idea that "How to Marry Money," or any other class for that matter, was anything but an object of purest pride didn't register. I was a clear believer that no publicity is bad publicity, so I rushed ahead eagerly.

Television seemed to prove me right. As a result of all the attention "How to Marry Money" garnered, I was invited to appear on both the *Today* show and the *Phil Donahue Show*, where I sat alongside Joanna in one of daytime television's most notable studios at the time. The *Today* spot was uneventful, and everyone had a good insular chuckle. But at the *Donahue Show* . . . things took a dark turn.

The difference, of course, was that the *Today* show was broadcast from a closed set while *Donahue* was taped in front of a live studio audience whose members were actively encouraged by their frenetic host to take the microphone and speak their mind. When we sat down to face the crowd at the *Donahue Show*, it was packed to the gills with Midwestern housewives—and they were not happy.

"I can't believe you're teaching these values," was the general angry refrain. "What a terrible thing to do! You should be ashamed of yourselves. Making money off of such a shallow idea. How dare you!"

The outrage was as universal as it was vehement. Everyone went to town on Joanna and me, and we could only sit in shock on the hot seat as we were heckled as low-down, mercenary, reprehensible, money-grubbing yuppie scum in front of literally millions of Americans.

I was caught completely off guard by the response. And I was ashamed because now I could see their point. I had been dancing on top of this table I'd built, oblivious and carefree, but that surface had a dark underside I just hadn't seen. Confronted with this new and disturbingly different perspective, I sat there blinking under studio lights that grew warmer by the moment, stuck in front of rolling video tape recording every nervous twitch.

Oh my God, I thought. *What am I doing?*

Out of the blue, I realized the entire business was built on taking advantage of people's insecurities. I was making money off of whatever everyone feared and hated about themselves. It was a terrible day and the first sign that I was headed in the wrong direction. I couldn't wrap my head around it, partly because I had been so swollen with pride. After the purity of the Skills Exchange experience, the idea that I would operate counter to the public good was utterly alien to me.

Walking off the set, I confronted an unexpected personal reckoning. What had my life become? Was this really who I was? Had I totally sold out? It seemed like I had, and, worse, there didn't really seem to be any way back from it. The damage had been done.

Sure, you could (and we did) apply a linguistic veneer of respectability to the business and label it "the democratization of culture." But in those few moments of honest clarity, I knew it should be called "selling out." And just as bad, catering to society's lowest common denominator.

Unfortunately, my moment of truth was just that: momentary. I swallowed my dismal and conflicted introspection and got back to work. In some ways, I had no choice. We had over 100 employees now, a staff of teachers, thousands of students, and even a new outlet in Houston started as a first step toward building a national franchise model. The thing was a juggernaut, and I had investors counting on me to steer it to profitability. Success, wealth, and fame made it easy to look the other way.

When it came, redemption would come in failure and a teachable moment whose ultimate lesson was that learning from one's mistakes is not exactly all it's cracked up to be. The truth was that the Network for Learning had fallen prey to that common commercial condition known as overweening pride and excessive optimism.

We were akin to the surfer who's discovered a sweet spot where the winds and waves are just perfect. Month after month, we were out there beyond the breakers all by ourselves, tearing up the surf. Then word got out, and the crowds showed up. Suddenly we were no longer alone on the sea of success. We were dodging unwanted interlopers, loose boards flying everywhere.

I don't know what we were thinking, but we never considered the possibility of someday losing the exclusivity that was bringing the reporters and paying the bills. But competition arrived—and they were better financed. The New School and Parsons School of Design got into the short evening course game, and so did PACE and New York University. The fiercest of our competitors was the Learning Annex, founded by William Zanker (the same Bill Zanker of Donald Trump's meme coin fame). He came out of nowhere and immediately started taking for-profit adult education to an entirely new level— commercially if not intellectually.

Zanker was so intent on mimicking our meteoric success that he copied not just our courses but their actual descriptions in our catalog—right down to the grammatical errors we'd made, duplicated without apparent shame. We immediately sued and won the lawsuit just about as quickly. Still, the damage had been done. We were a little too successful for our own good and now the endless publicity was bleeding us, not feeding us, as a world of imitators lined up to meet demand. In a couple of years, the *Sunday Times* came stuffed not only with our catalog insert but a bunch of others, too, and we watched our registrations plummet as the trend proliferated.

In only two years, we'd gone from zero to $2 million in registrations, but we were spending even more, and with registrations falling off a cliff, we were rapidly going broke. We paid fairly lavish salaries by the startup standards of the time. The offices were way too big, as was the half-million-dollar debt I was holding. Something had to give.

On a single terrible day, I let go virtually the entire staff, which left me feeling like a complete and permanent failure. Just one employee remained, a young guy named Andre Cartier, and that was only because he refused to leave. "I don't care if you can't pay me," he said. "I'm not going anywhere."

By late 1982, I was forced to give up my suite of offices in midtown and to run the business out of my apartment. The Network for Learning wasn't on life support as the *Post* suggested. In reality, it was even worse than that. I'd pulled the plug and killed the whole thing virtually overnight. This was easier than it should have been. Since we were operating on a monthly catalog cycle, all I had to do was not print the next edition. No catalog, no classes.

Looking back, I seemed to have the ability to anticipate what people wanted before they knew they wanted it. That prescience allowed me to position my effort to meet the demand well before the rest of the world. I was always a little bit ahead of the curve. But the curve is a dangerous place. It can be a boon or bane. Get too far out ahead of it and you'll miss it entirely.

It's a lot like surfing—if you're way out beyond the break, you won't catch the wave. You want the sweet spot. You have to find that edge and stay right on it. Where the knack came from—who knows. But somehow, I could spot the wave, and so far it had served me well.

I had also discovered, albeit the hard way, that no matter how bad things look, no matter how grim the bottom line, if you put your head down and work hard, you can find a way out of even the most impossible situations.

As was the case at the Skills Exchange, the journey at Network for Learning also generated a host of other valuable lessons. First among them was to never underestimate the threat of competition. I was so enamored with my own success that I never considered the risks posed by potential competitors. Nothing we had done was patentable or could be trademarked.

We had a single marketing strategy, which was easy to duplicate. There was nothing so unique about the classes that couldn't be recreated by someone else, which happened quite quickly. Plus, our competitors were better resourced than I was.

I built my overhead of fixed expenses way too high, much too quickly.

As great as the media coverage was, the press always wants a new story and they grew tired of giving us so much coverage. The problem with meteoric success is that meteors burn up on their way down.

CHAPTER FIVE

Books on Tape

Just like that, I'd gone from golden boy to tin man, and my head was spinning. I had no idea how to reverse direction and extricate myself from the mess Network for Learning had become without destroying my life and my reputation. Bankruptcy seemed like the best (and indeed only) option. I went to see my lawyer, an ancient pipe-smoking crustacean of an attorney named Asher Lance, to get the wrecking ball rolling—and me out from under it.

Asher's office had recently caught fire, and he sat before me in the charred ruins, feeding its sooty miasma with the tobacco smoke curling up from his pipe as he stroked his graying beard and patiently doled out perhaps some of the best advice I've ever gotten:

"Don't do it."

He continued: "No matter what else you do in your life, never file for bankruptcy. It'll ruin your credibility. You've got to spend whatever it takes and do everything you can to get out from under that debt. Find a way to pay this money back. Find a way. Make it work. And it might not take nearly the time you think it will either."

He talked about character, integrity, and the value of one's good name—and I listened. Thankfully, I was able to listen to good advice, even if I didn't want to hear it. I also learned that it's critical to know how much you don't know and to always be open to learning. That ability alone enabled me to start businesses I knew nothing about. Find people smarter than you who can teach you what you don't already know.

"You've still got the courses-on-tape thing, right?" Asher asked. "Make it work."

He was talking about a recent deal Network for Learning had made with Waldenbooks, then the second-largest bookstore chain in the country, to turn some of our courses into "books-on-tape" audio cassettes. The president of the company, Harry Hoffman, was a great believer in our ideas, and he'd given us a five-thousand-dollar advance for each of ten titles that were sold under the imprint "Listen & Learn."

Harry wasn't interested in our more notorious offerings. He didn't want "How to Marry Money." He wanted classes like "How to Invest in Real Estate" and "How to Stop Smoking" whose advice was more practical wisdom than trendy infotainment. I took the money but didn't buy the idea. And I thought Asher was crazy. There was no way I was going to make this tiny little side business work hard enough to pay back all the money Network for Learning had burned through in its short but glittering life. It had flash-in-the-pan written all over it. But when we received our second order from Walden, I started to suspect we were on to something.

That something led me to taking our small but early success and running with it to bookstores everywhere. The Walden account was a great start; but I now wanted to get these cassettes in front of as many people as I possibly could. However, that idea wasn't going to put a smile on Harry's face as he had assumed we were exclusive to Walden. After an incredibly difficult meeting where I broke this awkward news to Harry and his people, we were ready to take on the rest of the bookstore industry.

In the early days of the new business, I'd brought my brother Peter on board to manage the classes-on-tape project, a circumstance born as much of brotherly love than anything else. I probably could have handled the new business on my own, but Peter was struggling and needed something solid to grab on to. Though he'd experienced a slight renaissance as a semi-successful commodities trader dealing palladium on Wall Street, he remained an addict. Snorting coke in the company bathroom took its inevitable toll. He made some trades he shouldn't have made and lost enough money to get fired.

If he worked with me, I figured I'd be right there to harness his immense positive traits while mitigating his negative impulses. The hope was that Network for Learning might serve as a stabilizing influence and give him something to do besides drugs and alcohol. And for the most part, it did. Peter took the work seriously, and thanks to his efforts, I quickly changed my mind about this "minor" sideline.

The "Listen & Learn" cassettes were selling briskly. There was clearly an untapped market for audio presentations. Why not put some actual books on those cassettes as well? It was—no pun intended—a novel idea.

Books-on-tape did not exist in the early 1980s, and no one in the publishing industry thought they needed to. Given the roaring success that audiobooks ultimately became, this lack of interest was astonishing in hindsight, but it provided us the one thing we needed: super low-cost content. We quickly discovered that because publishing executives thought audiobooks were essentially worthless, we could get the rights to best-sellers for virtually nothing.

Peter was brilliant at convincing authors and agents to make deals with us. We sought and bought whatever we thought would sell and ended up with hundreds upon hundreds of titles—from *Portnoy's Complaint* by Philip Roth and *In Search of Excellence* by Tom Peters, to *Curious George* and modern American classics like *Truly Tasteless Jokes* and *Lewd Limericks*. At one point, we owned the rights to half the titles on *The New York Times* non-fiction best-seller list.

With rights costs so low, our portfolio continued to grow by cheap leaps and budget-conscious bounds. We even plundered the public domain for kids' books like *Peter Rabbit* and *Alice in Wonderland*. In London, we met with the BBC and walked out of the room with the audiobook rights to the *Goon Show* and *Monty Python*, T.S. Eliot reading his own poetry, and countless other broadcasts from fifty years of British radio programming.

In just a few years, Peter and I managed to somewhat inadvertently assemble one of the world's largest portfolios of audio rights. We had a volatile relationship characterized by epic fights in front of the entire office followed by doors slammed so hard you'd think they were going to fly off their hinges. But Peter was so charming and gifted at sweet-talking literary agents, the fights scarcely mattered.

Once again, I was riding another wave and back in the money. Our royalty payments were low. Recording sessions were cheap, staffed with NPR editors looking for some extra dough. The cassettes themselves were easy to manufacture, and once we had the templates, the packaging took care of itself. We had just a dozen employees—a far cry from the Network for Learning's peak—therefore, not much overhead. We were off to the races.

Though we had tons of product and had developed all kinds of point-of-sale displays and materials, we couldn't afford the necessary sales force to get our cassettes into thousands of independent bookstores. It was the classic startup conundrum: not enough money to afford the things we needed to earn enough money to afford the things we needed. Yes, our audiobooks sold well when they were available, but our market penetration was minimal.

What I did have, however, were connections at Warner Bros thanks to a failed video experiment and the fact that my father's ex-partner, Herb Seigel, sat on the Warner board of directors. Warner also happened to have a books division with an army of salespeople going from bookstore to bookstore.

I approached the company with a distribution proposal. It seemed like a no-brainer—they already had people pounding the pavement schmoozing up bookstore managers from coast to coast. We'd just piggyback onto their existing infrastructure, and Warner would earn what was essentially free money doing what they were already doing anyway. What's not to love? In my view it was an offer they simply could not refuse.

But Warner did refuse. They had absolutely zero interest in being our distributor. Instead, they had a better idea. They wanted to buy our business outright. Warner Bros had crunched our numbers and saw the value hiding inside an audiobook business ready to boom. At least several millions' worth of value to be precise, which is what they offered me.

To Warner, it was a pittance, an amount I suspect was less than their romaine lettuce budget for the company's cafeterias. But for us, it was an absolutely huge return, and more importantly, it was exactly the kind of money I needed to pay back my investors and get out from under the crushing weight of the Network for Learning's rubble. God bless Asher Lance. Turned out he knew what he was talking about: Find a way. Make it work. And it might not take nearly the time you think it will either.

A few months later, we assembled in a Warner Bros board room and checks were passed around the table. My Network for Learning investors could not have been happier. Thanks to Warner, they made a healthy 1,000 percent return on their original investment while I made enough to pay off all the company's debts and, at the age of just twenty-nine, sock away my first million. It was a great moment, but the money wasn't really the reason.

That day, my father was there, and not only had I successfully managed to enrich his friends, but one of the checks had his name on it. Along with the check came a huge turning point in our relationship.

He'd always told me there was trouble waiting for me up ahead. "You're going to go for job interviews," he said, "and they're going to ask you where you got your degree, and you're going to have to tell them you don't have one. You'll embarrass yourself right out of the job."

My retort was always the same: "I don't plan on ever going to a job interview."

I believed I would always be able to employ myself.

As my father sat there holding his check, I think he believed that for the first time. The proof was in his hands, and he finally was able to accept that I could find success without taking the traditional path. It was a day of redemption for both of us. I had made it in his eyes, and he was truly proud—a fact which made me proud, too. His hippie, Marxist, college dropout son had at long last proven his worth, and that was worth more than any check anyone could ever cut.

One of my dad's close friends, Mark Finkle, put it more bluntly when he called to congratulate me. "Do you know what that money is called, Jeffrey?" he asked.

I had no idea.

"It's called 'fuck-you money,'" he said. "For the rest of your life, if you're ever forced to do something you really don't want to do, you can now answer 'fuck-you.'"

Other relationships were developing as well. A few years earlier, an old girlfriend, Cynthia Pitts, had moved to New York with her fiancé, a fellow Hampshire alum named Chris Purvis, and we were getting reacquainted in the big city. At some point, Cynthia invited me to attend the birthday party of Chris's close friend—Sheila Barcohana. Sheila was a Persian Jew who'd also attended Hampshire in the years following my own brief sojourn there.

At the time, I was in full-blown outrage mode over the whole William Zanker debacle. The guy had been blatantly ripping us off, which was front of mind to the exclusion of all else—even the beautiful Persian woman sitting next to me. I could not refrain from letting everyone know how I felt about this charlatan Zanker's attempt to steal my business.

Sheila was quick to chime in. "Before you go any further," she said, "I want you to know that I just broke up with him."

I'm sorry—what now?

Indeed. In a strange twist of adult learning fate, Sheila had recently dated Zanker. Thankfully, she'd broken it off, which left us free to go on an uneventful date or two. That's what we did, but the relationship didn't go anywhere. I was young and foolish, somewhat rich and semi-famous, and a little too full of myself.

My mistake.

A couple of years later, I was eating at Spring Street Natural Foods in SoHo with my therapist when Sheila and a gaggle of girlfriends showed up a few tables away. As Sheila tells it, she recognized me and told her girlfriends the story of our failed attempt at dating. They thought I was cute. Sheila thought I was gay because I hadn't pursued her in the first place.

I saw her and realized I'd blown it the first time. When we said hello, I invited her to join me at a gigantic anti-nuke rally being held in Central Park the next day, and this time things were decidedly different. I fell for her instantly, and within days found myself miserable whenever we weren't in the same room. Within weeks, I was pleading with her to move into my 12th Street apartment. Unfortunately, her parents had just bought a co-op for her and her sister, and we both knew it would be awfully tough to explain why Sheila wasn't living there. So we compromised, and she spent half the week with me and the other half with her sister.

Sheila's influence was seismic. She taught me that not all was fate, and life was hardly without options, both physical and emotional. I could make choices not only about where I wanted to be and what I wanted to be doing, but also about how I felt about it all. I could choose happiness. Yes, there was a light side and a dark side to most situations—good and bad, pros and cons—but how one chooses to see things makes all the difference in terms of where you land. In many ways, I'd waited my whole life for someone to teach me this, and Sheila was proving adept at providing me with fresh perspective.

The need for unconditional love is universal, but I'd never received much and hadn't really returned any either. My father's love was always very conditional. My mother, on the other hand, was mostly consumed with my brother, and I was largely an afterthought. Sheila filled this void in my soul, and it was a huge turning point in my life. Suddenly, I had unconditional love—and it was transformational.

Sheila and I were married in 1984, and I've never looked back.

Getting married was the best and smartest decision I ever made, and it brought me the family I'd never had. The Hollender clan had been a tiny one.

But now I had the Barcohanas and what seemed like hundreds of relatives. In many ways, Sheila's parents—whom I adored—treated me better than my own had. They were so pleased and excited that she'd met me, a son of Park Avenue with his own successful business and his picture in *The New York Times*.

At the time, however, my reality was a lot less financed than I made it look. The Network was on the skids. The audiobook thing had yet to pay off. And I was still stuck in the middle, juggling creditors and calamity alike. Happily, just a few months after we wed, I sold the books-on-tape business to Warner Bros.

That deal came with a major string attached: me. Not to put too fine a point to it, but Warner Bros said, "We're buying your business and you're part of it." So it was that I officially became the head of their new audio publishing division, the youngest president in the company in charge of its smallest unit with a five-year contract and all the perks.

At first, it looked like fun—a great shot of adrenaline coupled with relief from business ownership. I had a fancy company car, all I could eat in the executive dining room, and even free haircuts in the corporate salon. I went to the editorial meetings at Warner Books and had an unlimited expense account from which I extracted an ungodly amount of cash to take people out to eat. It was an entertaining place to work, and I didn't even have to go to Midtown to do it—because I was living in the Village and preferred to stay downtown, Warner had even let me rent my own office at Houston and Broadway.

In many ways, I couldn't have been better off. I had enormous respect for my new boss, Bill Sarnoff, who was the first real boss I had ever had. Bill and I shared a common bond. He, too, had run a window washing business as a kid and purchased his supplies at the very same soap shop on Canal Street that Peter and I had frequented. We worked well together and made a good team, but almost as soon as I started, that five-year deal felt like a prison sentence. Barely settled into my new office, I was already marking off the days in chalk on my metaphorical cell wall.

My restlessness was hardly a secret. Bill knew I was dying to get out from under the arrangement if only because I wasn't shy about airing my feelings. He kept offering me more and more time off, hoping that I'd get my head clear and return refreshed and ready to jump back on the velvet corporate couch. But instead, those blissful vacations only solidified my intention to depart the Warner Bros fold as soon as possible. The biggest issue was that while I had made quite a career leap, I was still promoting "How to Marry Money" and all the rest. But now the karma was even worse because these weren't just courses anymore. They were books on tape, their presence cemented in the world. And my feet remained trapped in that concrete.

I was still a workaholic, to the point my new wife joked I must have a second family somewhere. But our love made me realize I no longer needed work as an emotional distraction. At the same time, I finally had a little money in the bank and no real need to immediately return to the grindstone to earn more. Most importantly, my forays into the murky waters of adult continuing education had given me a measure of confidence for navigating an often capricious business world. I was lucky to have followed both Asher Lance's and Sheila's advice. I also realized more clearly than ever before the value and wisdom that a seasoned advisor can bring even to the most challenging of times.

Though it was enough to give me mental and spiritual whiplash, I was able to engage in the luxury of introspection for the first time in a long while. Despite the trappings of success that again surrounded me, I was wandering aimlessly through my own winter of discontent. Yes, the audiobooks thing had taken off (who knew?) and we'd begun publishing worthy literature and poetry that helped take the sting out of our shallower titles, but it simply wasn't what I wanted to do. I didn't want to be in publishing. It was just a hole I'd accidentally fallen into, and I had to dig myself out.

I kept thinking back on the Skills Exchange and couldn't dodge the distinct feeling that I had been on the right track back in Toronto. I had better values and a stronger ethical compass. My instincts about how to live life had been right, but somewhere along the way, they'd gotten buried by more pressing concerns. I knew I had to reclaim those values, and I knew I couldn't do so at Warner Bros.

Our parting came at the two-year mark, and it was amicable. Generously, they let me out of my contract, and I left to explore how I could make the world a better place.

And ironically, I started with a book.

CHAPTER SIX

Just What the Doctor Mail-Ordered

How to Make the World a Better Place: A Guide for Doing Good wasn't so much a book as it was my attempt to figure out what it was that I wanted to do with the rest of my life. The book was also a quest masquerading as a publishing venture, a search of the soul with a table of contents.

Restless from my time at Warner Bros and still reeling from the psychic bruises left behind by the Network for Learning, I decided that writing a book about all the ways one could have a positive impact would be the best way to discover the impact I could have myself.

For me, the book was also a personal act of redemption.

The effort was in no small part informed by my developing interest in environmental economics and what came to be known as full-cost accounting in subsequent years. Simply put, this more honest form of financial management attempts to remedy what is perhaps the most egregious sin of our modern economic system, namely that corporations don't account for the larger societal costs they cause, like pollution and the natural resources they consume or destroy. Instead, they leave these very real expenses off their balance sheets, absent from ledgers, and out of their budgets. They leave it to others—governments and the public—to pay the price.

You can see the problem in places like the fossil fuel industry, where oil and coal companies neither acknowledge nor pay for the asthma, cancer, and climate problems directly caused by the use of their products—not to mention the lasting ecological harm done by extracting and processing the raw materials needed. Instead, that burden is shifted entirely onto the backs of taxpayers and consumers, who are left to grapple with the industry's vast consequences for human health and the Earth itself.

Other consequences abound as well: If these costs had to actually be paid by the companies that are profiting so handsomely from the burdens they create, fossil fuel energy prices would skyrocket, and you can bet the world would very quickly seek cleaner and greener sources that didn't come with such insane price tags.

This far more accurate accounting system was championed by Herman Daly, who was best known for his time as a senior economist at the World Bank from 1988 to 1994. In 1996, Daly was honored with the Right Livelihood Award for "defining a path of ecological economics that integrates the key elements of ethics, quality of life, environment and community."[1] A well-deserved accolade given how Daly's framework would shape almost everything I did for the next three decades.

How to Make the World a Better Place was an attempt to find a viable workaround to the problems that traditional economics had created.

I was fascinated by an idea put forth by R. Buckminster Fuller who believed that if one could change the minds of just 5 percent of the populace, one could effectively change the way society operates. That seemed doable—and a book seemed like a good way to start.

With that belief front-of-mind, I decamped to the New York Public Library on 42nd Street in January of 1987 to do my homework. In the days before search engines, the library's vast collection of periodicals was an unrivaled treasure trove of research, and the generous tables in its reading rooms let me spread everything out and dive in.

I explored the emerging world of socially conscious activism, from human rights to ways to lessen waste and increase sustainability. I studied new ideas like ethical investing and responsible travel, and I tracked down companies and organizations that were doing good:

Save the whales.

Plant some trees.

Bike to work.

Buy fair trade.

Day after day, I took notes on it all, and over the course of the next nine months, I wrote out the book longhand on tablets of yellow legal paper. Keep in mind these were also the days when desktop computers required a second mortgage and laptops were a sci-fi dream!

By the time autumn arrived, I had a book that I felt was worth something and had identified that value in a subtitle: "117 ways you can make a difference." Within this menu of possible actions and options, I believed the book was a practical way for me (and readers) to contribute to Fuller's 5 percent tipping point.

I made a deal with one of the legal secretaries at my wife's law office to type the whole manuscript into a word processing document. (They actually had one of those aforementioned big-budget desktop computers!) Then I took the completed manuscript to Richard Pine, an agent I found through my contacts at Warner, and he sold it rather quickly to William Morrow & Company.

While the book didn't move nearly enough copies to change the world completely, it did surprisingly well. Sales were north of 120,000, and somewhat paradoxically, it also made my bank account a better place, too. More importantly, the book restored a little of the self-worth I'd lost peddling schemes to "marry money" and "lose one's native accent."

The results of my research were encouraging. I was heartened to find so many remarkably effective and relatively easy ways in which one could actually make a meaningful contribution to a more enlightened and equitable civilization.

For example, something as simple as moving your money from a commercial bank to a local credit union, where you were actually part owner and your savings would be invested in your local community, could have lasting ramifications. Indeed, most of the strategies I uncovered remain viable, and I still promote them today. What the book did not do was convince me that the world's definition of professional success could be compatible with how I defined success. But it did set me on the path to that destination.

During my time at the library, I'd discovered a tiny mail order company called Renew America that sold oddball environmentally focused products like water-conserving faucet aerators and toilet dams. I thought the products were great and that the catalog itself was a kindred spirit to my book—full of relatively simple yet empowering ways to make a difference in the state of the world that one might not have otherwise considered. I was so enamored of the company that I devoted an entire chapter of my book to its unique products, which were as obscure as they were thought-provoking. The business and all it stood for struck me as an idea whose time had come.

Unfortunately, it hadn't.

During the book's fact-checking phase, I learned that the Renew America mail order catalog had all but shut down. In the era before environmentalism went mainstream, they hadn't been able to make a successful go of their unorthodox merchandising proposition. In a last-ditch effort to save the catalog, they had offered it to the person who had been handling their fulfillment operations—an entrepreneur named Alan Newman who was based in Burlington, Vermont.

In 1983, Alan had helped launch a fulfillment services company for small progressive-minded catalogs that couldn't afford to set up their own operations. He christened the new business Niche Marketing.

Meanwhile, Renew America was actually the fundraising arm of a DC-based non-profit organization of the same name, which served as a clearinghouse for environmental solutions. But sales were dismal when there were any at all. The products were motley at best, and the catalog itself was an ugly, impenetrable mess.

About a year after Renew America signed on with Niche, Alan's pity grew so great that he sent them a note outlining ways to improve and survive. This was a fatal mistake. Renew America was so thrilled by his suggestions, they made one to Alan in return: Why don't you buy the catalog? He immediately rejected the idea. He had no cash for the purchase, and he certainly didn't have the resources on hand to grow the business.

Renew America, however, felt otherwise. They continued to plead with Alan to buy the operation to keep the mission alive. Finally, they gave up, but not in the way Alan had hoped. They simply called one day and said, "Okay. That's it. We're done. You can have it for free. Either we ship everything to you to do whatever you want with it, or we're tossing the entire operation into the nearest recycling bin."

It turned out to be an offer Alan couldn't refuse. Now he had a problem on his hands, and it was a big one. The transfer took place in early summer giving him only six weeks to make the vital August mailing season for holiday sales, which he suddenly had an unexpectedly vested interest in boosting as much as humanly possible. In the mail order business, that's the equivalent of playing an entire 162-game season of baseball in a single month, a herculean task by industry measures. Alan had his work cut out for him, and he knew it.

For my part, I didn't know any of this when I called the Renew America office to fact-check my book. They simply told me the catalog was underwater, that they'd given it away to this guy in Vermont, and that I shouldn't hold my breath. The nation, it seemed, did not share my eager fondness for low-flow toilets and dryer vent covers. A great concept built on solid solutions to some vexing problems was headed for history's slag heap.

On a whim, I called Alan and introduced myself.

"I love the catalog," I told him. "I'm sort of heartbroken that Renew America has walked away from it, but I think it's great that you're trying to keep it alive. Is there anything I can do to help? I have some connections. Maybe I could raise some money."

Alan barely had time to say "not right now." He was in the thick of that first harrowing catalog cycle and asked me to call back in early January 1989 once the holidays were in the rearview mirror.

I went back to the fact-checking, and Alan went back to bailing as fast as he could.

With no time for new photography, he shrunk the catalog down to digest size to make the pictures appear bigger and made a shaky revenue-sharing deal with a local printing company. He cranked out a quick batch of slapdash benefit-oriented copy that focused on educating consumers about the importance of saving water and energy. Importantly, the new copy emphasized the money you could also conserve in the process.

It worked. The rejiggered catalog was a shocking success that generated a relatively significant number of orders. When I called back in the new year, hope was rekindled, and Alan was game to take the catalog to the next level. Oddly, unbeknownst to either of us, we had a mutual friend named Artemis "Timmy" Jakowski, who had made an investment in Niche Marketing. He organized a meeting out in the mountains of Warren, Vermont.

One frigid January day in 1989, Alan and I sat down together for the first time. He was nothing like the businesspeople I'd been surrounded by for the last handful of years. He was pure Vermont—laid back and loose, a little eccentric, incredibly smart, with a very 1960s attitude that appealed to my ancestral hippie nature. I liked him right away.

It was clear he knew a lot about the catalog business, which was an alien industry to me. At the same time, by his own admission, he had no idea how to write a business plan or raise serious money. As different as we were at that point in our lives, we were both immediately respectful of the individual contributions we'd brought to the table. But on that winter's day, we were also trying to suss each other out to see if there was any potential in a partnership.

We started with me writing a business plan designed to help raise a couple of hundred thousand to keep the catalog temporarily afloat. With Alan working on the next catalog, I laid out what we needed money for and just how much we needed. As the plan slowly materialized on paper, the total rose higher and higher. When it hit $800,000, I asked for a timeout.

I called Alan and said, "We're going to need some serious money, and I'm raising most of it from family and friends. I'm putting a lot on the line, so if I'm going to stick my neck this far out with all my Network for Learning investors, I really need a larger stake. We need to be equal partners in this."

Alan agreed, and we came to an easy revision of our initial arrangement. I'd write the business plan, raise the cash, manage the finances, and deal with the merchandising and product selection. He'd run the marketing and fulfillment operations. I'd commute between Vermont and New York because that's where the money was. We'd both own an equal 23 percent of the new company, no other shareholder would have more than 3 percent, and together we'd see if we could get it off the ground without belly-flopping into oblivion.

I didn't know it yet, but this would turn out to be the best deal of my life. But at the time, I was elated for many other reasons. I was captivated by the idea that every product we sold helped someone do something good for the environment. The more product we moved, the more people we helped, and the bigger our positive impact. At the same time, the more stuff we sold, the bigger the business itself would grow, including its impact.

Since then, I've seen how businesses make their most meaningful positive contributions when they mitigate their own internal negative effects and figure out how to turn their operations into a force for good, rather than settle to operate in a way that's less bad. At the time, the basic structure of the company's very existence seemed like a nearly perfect solution. It was a dizzying positive feedback loop in which environmental success begat economic growth and vice versa, giving both investors and the planet increasingly larger returns. For me, the most compelling notion was its limitless potential.

To my own surprise, I was all-in as an environmental mail order catalog cofounder. The creation of *How to Make the World a Better Place* was rooted in an environmental economics perspective, but the research I had done for the book had drawn me more and more to issues of social justice and human rights. Not to say I didn't care about the planet. Far from it.

But for whatever reason, on a gut level, I discovered that the ignition switch for my own passions was more directly connected to the human sphere than the environment. If the act of writing the book was really a journey of self-discovery in disguise, I hadn't expected to land on social concerns as a professional target.

The problem was that I wanted to start a new business but, at the time, didn't really see any options for combining my sudden interest in human rights with that desire in any legitimate, non-exploitative, for-profit way. I was looking to start a company that paid dividends to its shareholders, not a non-profit organization. As is sometimes the case in life, interest and opportunity weren't aligning, and a new path was needed. In the Renew America catalog, the universe had suddenly presented a solid—if unanticipated—alternative possibility that held significant appeal.

As an entrepreneur, you must always stay open to the possibility that the journey you're on may not lead directly to your hoped-for destination. While the purpose of a business evolves over time, you do need to be careful about the risks of compromising your values when moving in a new direction. I was pleasantly surprised to discover that the evolution of purpose toward becoming an "environmentalist" still represented the use of business as a means for doing good. That, as I discovered over time, was the essence of both my purpose and passion.

CHAPTER SEVEN

What's in a Name?

In the first few months of the catalog's new life, few things were certain. But one thing that was most certainly clear was how we needed a better business name—badly. A new brand was required, one that would capture the spirit of the new company's mission to make the planet a better place for the next generation.

In the summer of 1988, as Alan was struggling to save Renew America, he put the question to the staff of his fulfillment company in the form of a contest: "What should we call this new catalog?"

Denise Dunbar, an employee of Indigenous American descent, suggested "Seventh Generation," a name based on the *Gayaneshakgowa* of the *Hau de no sau nee*, an oral document also known as "the Great Law of Peace of the Six Nations Iroquois Confederacy."

Created sometime between the twelfth and fifteenth centuries, Gayaneshakgowa emerged after many years of constant fighting among the Cayuga, Mohawk, Onondaga, Oneida, and Seneca peoples, warfare that had taken a vast toll. Recognizing the unsustainable nature of the situation, the great leader Deganawideh—along with Hiawatha, an accomplished orator—embarked upon a mission to heal the divisions between the tribes. After years of travel and negotiation, they at last forged an alliance among the Iroquois nations, which together became known as the *Hau de no sau nee*, a name that translates as "We are of the extended lodge." To govern this new union, Deganawideh's far-reaching vision of a sustainable future was transformed into Gayaneshakgowa, or the Great Law of Peace, an oral set of operating principles that revitalized the tribes by emphasizing equality, consent of the governed, and peace among all peoples.

Since Deganawideh's time, Gayaneshakgowa has been passed down orally from generation to generation. Today, many centuries later, this Great Law of Peace still resonates powerfully, and the Iroquois nation continues to adhere to its tenets. For the staff, the idea was a perfect choice, one that aptly embodied the new catalog's philosophy that the ecosystems we depend upon for life are delicate places entrusted to our care temporarily, and that our lives can send repercussions rippling across future generations.

This historic keystone of Earth's oldest living participatory democracy, the alliance of First Nations that call New York State their ancestral home, provided not only counsel to its people but much of the inspiration for the founding document of the country that displaced them, the Constitution of the United States. The Great Law of Peace spells out exactly that "in our every deliberation, we must consider the impact of our decisions on the next seven generations."

It's an eloquent idea, one that speaks of peace and harmony, but the wisdom it reflects was obtained at tremendous cost.

Had the naming contest been held in more recent years, the "Seventh

Generation" suggestion might have been debated with today's awareness of the problem of cultural appropriation. It is, after all, a Native American notion being used to promote a for-profit company started (mostly) by white people.

Crucially, though, it was a Native American who offered the idea, and I know for a fact that the name was chosen with great respect and has always been used with reverence. There was no subterfuge involved. Rather than stealing the words and claiming them as its own, the company has been open about the history of its name and the intentions behind it—both ancient and modern. Most importantly, the use of the name supports a mission and a vision that are themselves extensions of Gayaneshakgowa. Seventh Generation's ideals hew to the Great Law's essential principles and deliver their largely forgotten wisdom to the modern world where it can again become a driving influence. Today I see this name as I always have: a respectful homage and indebted tribute that embodies shared beliefs and the earnest passion to express and defend them.

This, however, is not to say that many, many others have not expended an incredible amount of energy trying to get us to change it. For years, marketers and consultants have implored successive generations of management teams to switch to a name that more clearly and obviously describes what the company sells. Designers have begged us to adopt a name that's shorter and easier to squeeze onto product labels and ad space. Over the course of more than thirty years, the company has received a lot of alternative suggestions, and every one has been politely rebuffed.

The Seventh Generation name, while complex and challenging (like much else about the company!), has a beautifully rich heritage and a deeply resonant meaning. Its bedrock idea takes the aspirations of employees, their hopes for the Earth, and their desires for our collective future, and bakes them right into the top line of the company's conversation with consumers. I don't think a better name exists.

Yet my emerging focus on social justice meant that I set myself on this unexpected new path with a handicap. While I certainly had some sense of environmental awareness, I quickly found out that I was essentially an eco-novice. I had a lot to learn about issues of sustainability and their solutions, and that was a fascinating process for me, one I completely credit my Seventh Generation adventure with providing.

Suddenly I was smack in the middle of America's rapidly growing environmental discussion, shepherding a new company that sought to add its voice to the conversation, and I was surrounded by experts, from Alan himself to our company board of advisors, which included luminaries like Indigenous rights activist Winona LaDuke, Greenpeace Executive Director Peter Bahouth, and Amory Lovins, founder of the Rocky Mountain Institute.

But first things first. There was a catalog to produce, and now I, too, had a lot riding on making it work.

Alan had based Niche Marketing out of a small industrial building located on an anonymous side street, directly across the road from the regional state prison.* For someone accustomed to Manhattan offices with vast skyscraper views, private hair salons, and executive dining rooms, South Burlington, Vermont, was about as unglamorous a reversal as you could ever hope to engineer. I'd gone from president of audio publishing at Warner Books to cofounder and CEO at Seventh Generation, now in charge of a massive staff consisting of myself and

---

* Niche Marketing was ultimately shut down as the complete focus became transforming Renew America into the new entity, Seventh Generation.

a woman named Gail Lacey, who was married to future Ben & Jerry's CEO Chuck Lacey.

Gail and I were based in a temporary trailer plunked down into the parking lot outside the building and which I can tell you with great certainty was one of the worst places to spend a Vermont winter. Though we ran extension cords out from the office and through the windows to run space heaters, it was still an ice cube on the best of days. Yet I absolutely did not care. I was far too excited by the company, its mission, and its products. My comfort was an easy trade for me to make.

I commuted from New York every week and lived out of a somewhat incongruous Austrian-themed motel close enough to walk to and from the office, such as it was. Every day, I'd trundle the few blocks to my frozen trailer and plunge into a world of mail-order madness that was all-consuming.

Ours was a tiny operation of just a dozen or so people with everything right there—customer service, warehousing, fulfillment, the whole nine yards. We were surrounded by shelves filled with faucet aerators and racks crowded with cases of recycled fiber toilet paper. As business operations go, it was more than a little ramshackle and always somewhat disheveled, held together by piano wire, duct tape, and the sheer force of belief that somehow we could make it all work.

It was a chaotic place in a frenzied time. Everyone was working overtime to get our new company off the ground. We deployed new strategies on an almost weekly basis, ad hoc systems that used logbooks and color-coded forms to try and keep track of who did what for whom.

Increasing sales meant a growing staff, and by summer we were bursting at the unsustainable seams. Product samples and customer service call records mingled with dot-matrix sales reports and piles of outgoing packages on every available surface. Noisy printers clicked and clacked over the din of incoming telephone orders and conversations happening in every corner.

As warm weather set in, the building became infested with so many flies, we made a box of fly strips available for people to hang when they couldn't take it anymore. With so many of us working in the same space, it was becoming impossible to think, let alone work.

Nerves were fraying by the end of summer.

According to the minutes from our August 30 staff meeting, "There was a great deal of discussion about the atmosphere in the office. Could it be that there were just too many of us in such a small place? Or could it be that there are things to be said that are not getting vented at the meetings and just lingering around in our atmosphere?"

Alan was worried. He knew the pitfalls that came when a business expanded too rapidly for its own good, and he knew we were on the cusp of falling into that same trap. "People lose the ability to do it all and do it all well," he said. "But they become afraid to admit that they're making mistakes, and that fear becomes a serious barrier to communication and progress. We needed to foster an environment where everyone felt free to identify problems without worrying about the consequences."

This was a solid insight. Creating a corporate culture that respected its employees' humanity and supported honesty and openness through the practice of compassion and empathy was not only the right thing to do, it was a management approach that yielded concrete dividends. If we succeeded in making people feel happy, trusted, and empowered, secure and valued, they would go the extra mile.

We built our company out of these ideals, and there in South Burlington, we laid the foundations.

We started with the weekly all-employee summit where anyone was free to speak about anything on their minds. We began opening each of these meetings with the "$5 mistake," a weekly contest that voted on voluntary self-confessions of the prior week's biggest errors and awarded the victor who'd done the most damage a crisp five-dollar bill. It was a friendly and often funny way to acknowledge that nobody was perfect and create an atmosphere of trust and safety. Everyone was eligible—I won my own fair share. In later years, it became the "$5 bad thing" and was supplemented with the "$5 good thing," which rewarded the week's top genius move as well.

Every morning, the entire company would gather at the mail table, a giant surface on which the day's incoming mail orders would be opened and sorted. This got the mail processed, but much more importantly, it was a great team-building ritual to start each day. We laughed and cried over that mail. We learned each other's stories and discussed our greatest hopes and deepest fears. We celebrated personal milestones and individual victories, and we marked life's darker moments, too. It helped make us not just better co-workers but friends as well, and that helped everything when push came to shove.

The company parties did, too, and there were a lot of those. There were free lunches with neighboring businesses and beach outings on Lake Champlain. Company retreats and team-building days. Summer celebrations and holiday affairs. Solstices were official company holidays and there was no occasion too small to warrant a beer or two. Over time, the company became a remarkably tight-knit group, one that worked together, played together, and often even lived together. I'm convinced that's one of the main reasons Seventh Generation was able to ultimately survive.

At first, I was clearly the odd man out in this cast of tie-dyed-in-the-wool, Birkenstock-bearing Vermonters, who were about as anti-corporate as it comes. I came to work each day in a coat and tie, the strange new "money guy" from New York. But beneath the tweed, a hippie heart was still beating, and it didn't take me long to embrace their remarkable spirit. The vibe was contagious and there was a lot of fun waiting when you caught it.

Good thing, too, because our challenges were not for the faint-hearted. For instance, we were spending much more on customer acquisition than what customers were spending on our products. Essentially, every time we secured a new customer we lost money, and even a business school novice can tell you that's not a winning strategy. The idea was short-term pain for long-term gain. Our bedrock hope was that, over time, repeat purchases from these new buyers would make us profitable. An expensive proposition familiar to many businesses.

Like most of the mail order industry, Seventh Generation mailed a ton of catalogs at a fairly high cost, yet something like 99 percent of these so-called prospects didn't make a purchase—a dismal response rate. We were going for lifetime value, but that payoff was years in the future. In the meantime, we had to stay alive to get there. And the numbers showed that was no mean feat.

Produced in the summer of 1988 for the holiday season, the first catalog had generated $100,000 in sales. While not exactly a gold rush, the amount was a vast improvement from what Renew America had brought in. Impending doom had at least been staved off temporarily off thanks to Alan's mail-order acumen. Now we had to build on that foundation.

In our second year, we rented the mailing lists of every environmental organization, hoping the addresses belonged to concerned, environmentally aware consumers. We mailed hundreds of thousands of digest-sized catalogs, each filled with a slew of oddball offerings.

One of the weirdest was basically a brick that you put in your toilet tank to reduce the water used for each flush. Another was our infamous recycled paper bath tissue, which was brown and scratchy and made using the toilet in your home like visiting the bathroom at a third-rate gas station.

We built on that second catalog with a third one mailed for the 1989 holiday season. Together, the two sales cycles generated a stunning 1,000 percent sales increase and one million dollars in sales, leaving us all grinning ear to ear. After all, growth is like cocaine for entrepreneurs, and we had just inhaled an enormous line. Suddenly, the future went from murky to clear, and the horizon seemed boundless.

Our joy was tempered by the stark reality of our cash flow. A million bucks in sudden sales helps keep the lights on, but it came with equally outsized expenses, and we were still hemorrhaging money wildly. My second search for financing took on new urgency, but happily, I now had a hint of a track record to run on. A ten-fold increase in sales caught people's attention and would help secure the cash we'd need.

I worked the phones to set up lunch dates with prospective investors out of a spare office at Sheila's law firm. We marketed the company as a self-described socially responsible business. For this second capital raise, we felt it was critical to more clearly state our purpose and hope to run our business as responsively as possible. We needed investors to know that we were after more than money.

A decade or more before such ideas became common, our prospectus was a self-portrait that many saw as uncomfortably quirky if not downright incomprehensible. "Responsible corporate citizenry? What the hell is that?" went the typical refrain—and I could see the point. In 1990, business and social responsibility were words that had never appeared together in the same sentence, let alone in a business plan.

Plus, I had to sell the company's unusual ecological and equity propositions, a set of eyebrow-raising priorities that were alien to the bedrock capitalist idea of profit at all costs. To be fair, these were somewhat new ideas to me, too.

But overall, Seventh Generation was a return to original form for me. I was more comfortable with a freewheeling and egalitarian approach to business, and Seventh Generation was showing me it didn't have to get crazy (like at the Skills Exchange). There was a hybrid model where not all decisions were consensus but where transparency and fairness played central roles. We were pioneering a critical compromise that thirty years later came to ultimate fruition with the phenomenon now called "stakeholder capitalism."

But in the late 1980s, we were largely figuring out social responsibility by ourselves. We were vaguely aware of a few other companies attempting to do something similar—Ben & Jerry's being the most prominent and certainly the most local. Fortunately, we soon discovered the Social Venture Network, which had been formed to share similar ideas and inspiration, and we signed on as a member. Started by philanthropist and venture investor Josh Mailman and Calvert Funds founder Wayne Silby, the Social Venture Network was a sort of hippie country club. Back in the early 1990s, SVN (as it became known) was the center of the universe when it came to the art and science of creating responsible businesses.

Almost immediately, we became acquainted with people and companies like Anita Roddick and the Body Shop, and Gary Hirshberg and Stonyfield Farm. Something new was bubbling up in these ex-hippie brains, and we'd been part of it all along. Now our secret was out in the open, and we didn't feel like we were nurturing it alone.

Joining SVN was a relief. We suddenly realized others were rowing the same "socially responsible" boat. Together, we were stronger and could more easily push what were then pioneering values out into the world, where they would be more readily accepted. This would help me with raising money, too. Now I had examples of the company we wanted to become when I met investors and shared our somewhat unorthodox business plan.

It was a delicate balancing act. We didn't want to push the idea of social responsibility too far—certainly not at the expense of the quest for profitability. We had to be different, but not so different that we turned investors off. We walked a tightrope through a whirlwind of odd-couple dog-and-pony shows starring me in my suit and crewcut, and occasionally Alan in his sandals and scraggly beard, but we never failed to raise the cash we needed.

Indeed, we quickly raised the initial $850,000 we needed to get the company through to 1990, mostly from my old investors in the Network for Learning who had seen returns of almost 1,000 percent from its sale to Warner. My pitch was pretty simple: "Why not take some of that money I made you in the Warner deal, reinvest it in my new business, and we'll do it all over again?"

Yet while the fundraising was successful, my attempt to have a prosperous personal life was less so. With the business growing as fast as it was, I was working 24/7, which fed into my historic obsession with workaholism. On the other hand, however, was a wife and two kids for whom that really wasn't working. The back and forth between New York and Vermont had taken its inevitable toll and had become too much for all of us. The ties that bind were fraying—and my nerves were, too.

After a conversation with Alan, we agreed to open a New York office with a handful of staffers to help me find products and raise cash closer to my own center. I found a place just down the block from the Empire State Building at 5th Avenue and 36th Street, brought on our first CFO—a wonderful man named Hank Clark—and engineered our first brush with celebrity by hiring Fabian Cousteau, son of the famed marine biologist. It was an arrangement that was better for the business and created far less stress for me, better suited to my lifestyle.

Also, this move was strategic because the clock was ticking. I didn't have any time to waste commuting. We'd spent that first $850,000 almost immediately, and before you could say "the check's in the mail," I was back out on the street looking for another round of financing thanks to projections that showed us needing another one million fast.

Starting a mail order company is terrible from a cash-flow perspective. You need wads of money up front to purchase inventory, print catalogs, and get them into America's mailboxes, and it's all spent well in advance of getting any actual cash back.

Case in point: Our recycled paper bath tissue and paper towels. Somewhat shockingly, they were early best-sellers, especially around the holidays, where they became inexplicably popular gift items. I suspect their environmental appeal combined with their uniquely utilitarian necessity made them a novelty that could not be refused, a product that was part-joke, part-serious, and an all-American original no matter how you looked at it. Yet getting it into our warehouse was no simple task.

At the time, you'd only find recycled household paper products in the world's worst restroom, off-color and off-putting, a stiff and unyielding sort of proto-toilet tissue or sand-paper towel. But we knew this stuff was as raw as it looked and that meant it was just what we wanted. All we had to do was find out who made it.

We tracked down the mill in Appleton, Wisconsin, and asked about the manufacturing process. When they confirmed it used 100 percent unbleached, post-consumer recycled fiber, we said, "Fantastic, we're in. That's exactly what we want to sell."

They thought we were worse than crazy. The product's recycled content had long been a mark of shame—something they actually hid from buyers, believing that if the truth ever got out, sales would tank. Suddenly, here was this dinky company from Vermont ready to print the horrifyingly naked truth in big bold type on every label and aggressively promote it as a feature, not a bug. And therein lay the fundamental problem—we were a dinky company looking to sell a dinky volume that was virtually insignificant to a manufacturer accustomed to selling product by the tractor trailer load. All we needed was a minivan's worth, and we had to pony up for more than 100,000 rolls and print a couple of million labels, most of which would spend eons sitting in a warehouse waiting for demand to materialize. Both we and the mill had to make an investment we hoped would eventually pay off—and we tied up a lot of money doing it.

Beyond paper products, there was other merchandising to think about as well. Though "green products" as a category would explode in popularity in the decades to come, they were as scarce as organic free-range hen's teeth in the late 1980s. In that prehistoric, pre-internet era, it took immense legwork to find even a single item for the catalog. Despite attending natural product trade shows nationwide, Alan and I would frequently return to Vermont empty-handed.

Fortunately, Europe was a lot further along the sustainability curve. We were overjoyed to discover their green marketplace moving in many different directions America had yet to consider. We had much better luck finding suitable ideas at European "eco-organic" trade shows, and after hours, we'd haunt local natural food, grocery, and drug stores looking for anything that might have a legitimate environmental angle. We found our cleaners in these shops and our feminine care products, too. I remember excitedly stumbling across a package of brown unbleached diapers in a shop in Amsterdam and feeling like I'd won the lottery. Such victories were rare, but when we had them, they were sweet.

However unlikely, our home turf in Vermont also happily turned out to be a hotbed for emerging green products. With its deep-rooted environmental ethos and agrarian heritage, the appropriately named Green Mountain State had long been a place that thought differently. It hosted a populace that had banned billboards, refused big highway projects, and enacted historic land use laws. When the late '60s sent a wandering stream of back-to-the-land hippies its way, Vermont leaned all the way into its nascent progressivism and never looked back.

Now some twenty years after that migration, the influx of earnest idealists had begun to bear real entrepreneurial fruit. We found an organic baby food supplier in a local company called Earth's Best. Chelsea Green Publishing in Sharon, Vermont, helped us fill a page with DIY environmental titles, and a local startup called Autumn Harp, creators of "unpetroleum jelly," provided a slew of natural skin care products.

Items like these helped us distinguish ourselves and elevate the catalog from the dull depths of its Renew America days. Our far-ranging creative merchandising strategy was increasing our sales, and I saw it as solid proof of concept—and when the product's environmental value was clear and legitimate, consumers were willing to pay a higher price, too.

We could make Seventh Generation work, and as 1989 drew to a close, with the year's final catalog mailed, orders flying out the door, and fresh financing flowing in, we finally felt that survival just might be assured. We could stop and take a breath, a quick one to be sure, but a well-deserved pause, nonetheless.

It would be the last one we'd get for a very long while, for unbeknownst to us, a great consumer wave was forming on the horizon, and it was barreling straight for us. In just a few short months, this convulsion would generate a perfect marketing storm, and our little mail-order-company-that-could would find itself facing the eye wall as a life-changing event rearranged the Earth under our feet, sweeping us into a new and unexpected future. Earth Day's twentieth birthday was coming in April 1990, and we had absolutely no clue how it would change everything.

CHAPTER EIGHT

Unearthly Results

1989's holiday break was short-lived. I had just enough time to sip a little New Year's champagne and sweep the confetti from the floor before I found myself back on Farrell Street juggling a few too many mail order balls and desperately trying not to drop any of the ones that mattered. There was money to be made and, with our first round of financing nearly complete, money to spend. The goal now was to get it all done without premature hair loss.

Despite the stresses, everyone was nevertheless elated and filled with a brand of optimism that acted as pure operational jet fuel. Our little environmental catalog had produced an astonishing and wholly unanticipated 400 percent increase in sales from August through the holidays, a jump far above and beyond our predictions. We realized that we had unwittingly tapped into something much, much bigger than we could have ever imagined. We were a bona fide hit, which made for some serious system strain from back-order headaches to staffing shortages, but these were good problems to have! And we tackled them with exuberance.

First up was a fresh spring/summer catalog to get to the printers, and even under the best of circumstances, that was always a gargantuan task. There was merchandising to finalize and purchase orders to place, photos to take and copy to write, layouts to create and mailing lists to sort. For an operation still running largely on a shoestring budget and perennially overworked pants, that to-do list represented no small challenge.

In the fall of 1989, Alan and I realized that sales had finally outpaced our tiny facility's ability to keep up. Too much product and too many people in a ridiculously undersized space. But with the financing about to come in, the real estate hunt was on. In an anonymous industrial park in Colchester—a barely-there town just north of Burlington—we found exactly what we were looking for: an absolutely gigantic space that would allow us to consolidate all our operations under one roof with room to grow.

Still, the location was . . . well, let's just say "not ideal." Out front, just beyond the parking lot, sat Interstate 89. Behind it lay a medical waste incinerator. To the right, there was a diesel truck repair shop. On the left, they were breaking ground for a new Costco, the nation's temple of overconsumption. We shared a wall with the pasta sauce company next door and a border with the local Vermont National Guard training camp. If you had intentionally designed the worst location for a company like ours, you could not have done better.

What the building did have going for it was abundant space, it was ready to occupy, and the rent was right. That was enough. We didn't have much time to waste looking for perfect. We bought a whole bunch of used office cubicles, leased a copy machine and some other equipment, and moved everything over during a raging snowstorm.

Our emerging company traditions came with us. There was still a mail table at which everyone would gather to open the day's orders. The company parties, official and otherwise, never stopped. And staff meetings continued to reward weekly heroics and the latest foolishness alike, which served to reinforce a culture of never making the same mistake twice even as it honored staff honesty. It was just one of the many unorthodox trappings of Seventh Generation's "corporate" life, and others were soon added as part of our change of address.

A ping-pong table was installed in the warehouse for quick games between orders. We let dogs roam freely* and put chalkboards in the bathrooms, where people could confidentially voice thoughts and opinions they weren't yet comfortable airing in the open. There were endless company picnics and pizza lunches, donation drives, and new product shows. We established a series of "Work Area Culture Meetings," and held contests to name the various parts of our offices. When we moved in, a ritual ceremony inaugurated the new space with sage smoke—and other kinds, too.

One of the few spaces with four walls and its own door was outfitted with a plush sofa and declared the official company nap room. Another became one of the first company-sponsored lactation rooms in the country. The employee lounge was populated with bean bag chairs kept in a giant pile, and no matter how busy we were, Alan insisted we gather there for weekly "check-ins" when every employee was invited to report on new projects, problems, or just about anything else. The idea was to create a culture of absolute honesty in which employees were unhampered by fear.

This model of openness and transparency was reinforced at regular "staff retreats," where everyone was encouraged to air their thoughts and speak their peace. At a business built on a freewheeling 1960s

---

* Eventually, the office collectively decided to allow just one dog—a perennially ravenous chocolate lab named Virginia that was owned by our copywriter, Linda Catling, and Bob Johnson, our warehouse lead. Virginia was a sweet creature with a penchant for snatching unguarded lunches from desks and escaping to Costco, where the hot dog vendors stuffed her so full of treats that she'd lie in a stuporous processed meat coma for the rest of the day.

ethos, these gatherings, whether held at a corporate conference center or the office, were as wild as you might imagine they'd be. Beer was the beverage of choice, and it combined with copious amounts of cannabis to fuel some truly memorable events that shall go unrecorded in order to protect the not-so-innocent.

Alan was clearly the driver of the culture that attracted our growing team, and though it looked ad hoc—an accidental hippie den spontaneously sprouted from Vermont's fertile bohemian soil—much of what we did was quite intentional. We had to protect that spirit, the Seventh Generation zeitgeist that not only made the madness tolerable but also alchemized it into gold. A staff that operated like a band of brothers and sisters was fast becoming an essential part of what made us go, and we took pains to create an ecosystem where that spirit could thrive.

With the company sprouting new departments, Alan also knew he had to encourage people to operate independently. He understood how we needed an environment where people were unafraid to make mistakes and empowered to work unilaterally. We were all human, all bound to screw up sooner or later. But with the right culture, we could own these lessons proudly and make sure they didn't chip away at the individual can-do confidence a growing company requires.

For my part, I loved what was happening. Mostly. It was new and inventive. Fun, too. And by all appearances, it was working. Admittedly, I was still more comfortable in a jacket and tie, but I was also learning a tremendous amount about how to build a company culture that was aligned with its business values, which was a lesson worth leaning into with enthusiasm. So while I took no small amount of heat from investors for the nap room ("Aren't these people supposed to be working?"), I never considered saying no. As unorthodox as things like a nap room were, they promoted magnificent staff cohesion, and they made great media fodder, too.

Still, there were places where I had to draw the line. For example, Alan wanted to also replace the tables and chairs in the central conference room with bean bags, but I pointed out this was impractical. We had a company to run. There were documents to spread out, products to examine, and notes to take, so the furniture stayed.

In hindsight, we were pioneering the idea of Culture as Brand. At the time, we were simply noticing how a progressive work environment created all kinds of positive outcomes, and it wasn't all internal. We were establishing a deep sense of authenticity that made us stand out from the corporate pack, a benefit that became increasingly important in the face of rising competition. As press coverage grew, we saw that the draw wasn't so much that we sold green products, but that we were a green company. This made the difference between interest and inattention.

Throughout the years to come, our authenticity would be a distinction I'd watch countless other environmental products companies fail to make. Those omissions created no shortage of fallout and would later be known as "greenwashing." In an educated landscape of passionate consumers—i.e., your target market—it became crucial for companies to embody the spirit of their offerings and the people they served. Anything less was fatal.

Nevertheless, we didn't go completely off the corporate culture deep end. At one point, after the advent of the internet, we considered installing video cameras in the office so customers could watch us work. Fortunately, we rejected the idea in the end as too voyeuristic and Big Brother-y for our tastes. Had we done this, it would have become an example of taking things too far and harming your original intent in the process.

For the most part, however, our culture, while conceptually intentional, was ultimately formed by serendipity. We established a basic free-spirited environment, which gave us ample room to experiment. Some ideas stuck. Some didn't. In the end, this organic evolution helped us become the company we became quite authentically. Whatever we did, it had to be deeply aligned with our true nature. Establishing that sense of outward earnestness generated myriad rewards with the media and our stakeholders. Even our warts became an essential part of this self-portrait.

As we settled into our new digs in the late winter of 1990, that clearly meant addressing Earth Day.

We knew two things . . .

The first was that Earth Day 1989—while hardly front-page news—had been a big moment for the company but had caught us unprepared. With so many fundamental projects airborne at once, including our fundraising frenzy, we had been deep into triage mode and only the greatest challenges received real focus. It was survival mode as standard operating procedure. Earth Day buzzed in like a small fly to be swatted away so we could focus on all the alligators growling outside the door.

Looking back, this was a glaring mistake, especially from the perspective of the culture we were building. Honestly, what were we thinking? It was as if we sold heart-shaped trinkets and had not only failed to leverage Valentine's Day to our marketing advantage but had failed to even notice. Yet despite that fairly incomprehensible oversight, we'd garnered some badly needed attention on Earth Day that had juiced our sales. Not stratospherically, but there were enough Earth Day dollars to notice.

The second thing we knew was that Earth Day 1990 was the twentieth anniversary, which was likely to be front-page news. Putting two and two together, we understood that we were just a few weeks away from an outsized opportunity and no excuses this time.

We had at least enough awareness to put "Earth Day Starter Kits" on prime page-2 real estate in the fall/winter 1989 catalog, which generated close to $70,000 in sales by March, along with a promised $10,000 donation to Earth Day's organizers. But in early February, the phone started ringing with Earth Day inquiries—people wanting products, asking questions, looking for help. Many callers wanted to know what we were doing to celebrate—and we kept telling them we had no idea. Amusingly, according to my notes from the time, Alan and I told everyone to stop admitting we were clueless. That's the problem with being a company that was maybe a little too honest for its own good.

With the event rapidly approaching, I found help in an old friend, David Levine, who had started a non-profit in Manhattan called the Learning Alliance. They combined the Toronto Skills Exchange model with an activist agenda, creating an educational program filled with environmental and social justice topics. David was going to have a table at the big Earth Day Eco Fair in New York City, and I convinced him to share his spot with Seventh Generation in exchange for a donation. It wasn't perhaps the best way to make a splash, but it was a lot of fun.

Back in Vermont, however, all hell had broken loose. Overnight, the environment had become topic number one on the street and in the press, and media inquiries were off the charts. Suddenly, there was a new Seventh Generation mention in the media virtually every day, and most of these included our new 800 number. The attention made sense. We were, after all, the ideal story—a tiny, wildly idiosyncratic company in super-green Vermont run by a crew of dedicated eco-oddballs. Hollywood couldn't have created a better subject for a nation of reporters hunting desperately for something uniquely "green" to cover.

Also, the January publication of *How to Make the World a Better Place* had acted like a booster rocket on all this exposure. After all, writing the book had started me down this road, so the timing was pitch perfect. The book came out just ahead of the twentieth anniversary of Earth Day, which supplied all the newsworthy relevance and marketing synchronicity a writer could ever want. By the time Earth Day arrived, the book was well on the way to selling 120,000 copies and had begun popping up on best-seller lists. I did a book tour in maybe a dozen big cities, and each appearance generated local press coverage, all of which brought Seventh Generation a tremendous dose of attention.

Despite the reality that I'd written the book before saying two words to Alan, the lines between the book and the company were blurred in the public's mind, which only helped elevate the company. We weren't just a catalog hawking products—we were actively making the world a better place. As far as the media was concerned, the book was a Seventh Generation tie-in. As the author—and therefore "spokesperson" for the book—it put the spotlight on me as a de facto company figurehead, which generated some tension between Alan and me back at the office. But we both knew the book was working overtime for the company's bottom line, and it was largely pointless to disabuse people of the notion that the book and business were related.

In the beginning, we had a PR firm helping us fill the hearts and minds of America's journalists with ecologically pure visions of tie-dyed warehouse workers shipping enormous boxes of recycled paper toilet tissue all over the Earth. But soon enough, we didn't really need any extra PR. Even without an article in *The New York Times* or the *Wall Street Journal*, there were days when the phones were buzzing like Geiger counters at Chernobyl. Our fledgling customer service department was completely blindsided by a phone bank glowing so fiercely with the unexpected eruption of incoming calls that it practically burst into flames. In a matter of months, over 400,000 people dialed in to request the catalog, an unfathomable volume of phone traffic. Without warning, we'd set the mail-order world on fire.

Though we probably should have seen it coming, it was a stunning turn of events. In a single year, the catalog had gone from hospice to superhero. And the whiplash reversal of fortune left everyone gasping for air and giddy as hell. Yet as exciting as it was, unexpected success brought unanticipated problems. The biggest problem was immediately apparent: We did not have remotely enough string bags.

In a red-hot instant, these odd little reusable shopping bags had bizarrely become our biggest seller. Literally made from cotton string woven into a loose mesh bag, they resembled giant hair nets with handles. They were added almost as an afterthought because we felt they were the kind of alternative we should offer. We sold them for about four dollars each, so they weren't a big money-maker, but what they lacked in their margins, they were quickly making up for with volume. For unbeknownst to us, our odd little *objets d'environment* had become a sustainable novelty. They were the new poster child for the evils of disposability and waste. Their uniqueness and utility had transformed them into a badge of eco-honor, proudly borne by card-carrying, eco-warrior shoppers from coast to coast.

The bags were selling faster than we could buy them. A lot faster. And the backorders were piling up into a mountain of woe. We couldn't get anywhere near the quantity that we needed. Our rudimentary computerized order system was only allotted five digits for total system backorder quantities at any one given time, which was wholly logical—not even a catalog company run by circus chimps would ever have more than 99,999 items on backorder. It had just never happened in the history of mail order. Until somebody decided to sell reusable shopping bags during the twentieth anniversary of Earth Day. Now all bets were off.

When we entered in the 100,000th backordered string bag, our entire system crashed in an apocalyptic Y2K-like scenario. The software simply had no way to handle the extra digit and experienced a meltdown that lasted until we could get the base code rewritten.

In an attempt to resolve the crisis, Alan and I made an emergency trip to the French company that made the string bags. We found the factory owners as surprised as we were by the bags' popularity, which was utterly incomprehensible to them. Though once a consumer mainstay, by 1990 the "French farmers' market bags" were a dying anachronism, and the factory had long ago reduced their output. Now suddenly there were these two crazy Americans asking for jaw-dropping quantities in record time.

Despite all the apparent absurdity, the factory said it would ramp up production for us. Yet while their hearts were in the right place, we found their assurances lacking. Promised deliveries kept failing to materialize, and with every new delay, we had to turn around and tell our customers the wait for their coveted string bags was not over. Today we'd do that in a nanosecond via automated email, but in 1990, every time the factory missed a date, we had to send every customer an individual notice via snail mail—postcards that had to be printed, addressed, and stamped at the going rate of 15¢ a pop. It was horrifyingly time-consuming and costly. As spring faded to summer, there were days when backorder notices were about all we did.

At one point, we projected that we were looking at a year and a half backlog. And the weird thing was, no one was canceling. For the most part, everyone was willing to wait eighteen months to get their precious string bags, which was nothing short of incredible. These odd little bags had an almost supernatural allure, and people were okay with what was an unquestionably ridiculous delivery date.

In a certain sense, this commitment to our product was pretty maddening—if people would cancel their orders, they would cancel our supply problem, and we could all move on. Yet on the other (much happier) hand, this commitment to green products and environmental ideals would be the force that eventually carried the company to success.

Faced with this cataclysm in supply and demand, we started looking for other sources. We found 10,000 in Greece, but we'd made the mistake of including string bags in our Earth Day Starter Kits, and with those proving popular as well, these were spoken for before the ink on the contract had dried. In Korea, we discovered another supplier, but they would only sell us 40,000 at a time. It was better than nothing, but hardly enough to resolve the issue.

A few months into the crisis, our French friends came through with a huge delivery, but in what was the coup de grâce of the entire affair, they screwed up the shipping paperwork. When the boxes arrived at the border, they were held up by customs, and what happened next was a cruel exclamation point in the form of $120,000 in fines and penalties. We'd filled the orders at last, but we'd lost our shirts doing so. For us, the string bags had held only misery and mayhem, and we responded in typical Seventh Generation style—with a huge party to celebrate filling the final backorder at which every employee got their own set of dreaded bags.

Yet the string bags were just the tip of the out-of-stock iceberg. In general, back orders were becoming a huge problem, all arising from our unexpectedly meteoric rise.

Now that we knew what we were doing, we could make logical assumptions about our growth curve. To that end, we had projected a relatively modest $1.6 million in income for 1990, an amount that represented a reasonable rate of expansion. But Earth Day's twentieth anniversary had blown that estimate to absolute smithereens.

Admittedly, there are worse problems to have—and in later years we'd have them! But at the time, the unforeseen explosion in attention and unprecedented demand had completely wrecked our inventory management, which in turn transformed our cash flow into one of those grab-all-you-can game show tubes filled with a tornado of dollar bills. It's one thing to have to print more catalogs in response to rising demand. Predicting how much inventory to carry during a "tornado" period is much more difficult. It exacerbates what is perhaps the industry's biggest financial challenge: You have to have a huge inventory in your warehouse before you mail a single catalog, which eats up capital long before it turns into sales. If you're successful, you start to build both credit and cash reserves to float subsequent catalog stocking cycles without squeezing cash flow too hard—but we weren't there yet in 1990.

That took money—which remained in short supply—and significant lead time, a luxury we absolutely did not have. You couldn't just dial a number, order a thousand cases of toilet paper on Monday, and then stroll down to the loading dock to take them off the truck on Thursday. The lengthy procurement process demanded that we plan our purchasing quantities carefully. But with the business literally growing by daily leaps and bounds, we had no idea what those quantities should be. There was just no predicting where all this was headed and when it might abate. All we knew was we were running out of stock far more often than we should have been—and clueless about how much to reorder.

Thanks to Earth Day, every number we looked at was roughly ten times what we'd thought it would be. In the case of something like string bag sales, maybe a hundred times greater. By mid-June, we were mailing hundreds of thousands of catalogs to entire new categories of prospective customers each month. Out in our new warehouse, we were shipping 1,700 orders every single day and well on our way to busting even our most wildly optimistic projections wide open with an eye-popping 700 percent increase in annual sales. You read that right—the $1 million in sales we did in 1989 was headed to $8 million in 1990.

Despite all those orders and all that energy, it wasn't yet paying off. Our elation was limitless, but we were spending $1.15 for each dollar we brought in and still tracking our bottom line in red ink. We were simply mailing too many catalogs that weren't as productive as they needed to be.

It was an ironic clue that things were not at all sustainable at the company that claimed sustainability for its own. But these signals are hard to read against all the noise of a growing startup, where it's expected to spend more than you make for a good while. I saw only good news in the numbers. Yes, they were written in red, but they kept getting bigger. Earth Day 1990 had turned every man, woman, and child into a fanatical environmentalist, and we were the environ-mental company. Eventually, we'd cross the threshold of profitability.

But as is often the case with new companies, the faster we grew, the more cash we needed. Though it had barely cooled in our bank account, we were burning through the $850,000 I'd raised at warp speed. That spring, I crunched the numbers, and they crunched right back. At our present rate of spending, we had about twelve weeks of cash left. I'd barely caught my breath from our first private placement, and now I was facing the gauntlet again.

We had just three months to raise another round of financing. Three months or we were toast. I split the difference—six weeks to prepare the prospectus and six weeks to find the money. Fortunately, in the wake of Earth Day, Seventh Generation was now an easy sell. This time around, people were begging me to take their money more than me begging them.[*]

While we thought we knew what we were doing some of the time, our explosive growth covered up new challenges that weren't yet visible to us. First, never underestimate the impact of luck. And while you want to make the most of luck while it's available, never assume it will last forever.

---

[*] A friend of my father's named Arthur Gray (no relation to Grey Advertising) made my task even simpler. My father had once bailed Arthur out of some financial trouble, and he'd become a close family friend and a second father who was eager to help. He was well-connected and able to make a literal wealth of productive introductions to his friends and associates. As a reward for all his assistance, we'd given him a seat on our board of directors. But Arthur was a staunch Republican and therefore, an awkward fit—the square ultra-conservative peg in a company of round, ultra-liberal holes. Arthur believed in me and in clean water and air, but his ecological buck stopped there. He didn't think climate change was real, nor did he buy much of what Seventh Generation was selling, whether product or philosophy. We often had to avoid discussing most environmental issues at board meetings, a problematic circumstance for a company based on them!

CHAPTER NINE

Looking Ahead

Based on our early success, Alan now wanted to grow the business in a new direction. Our mail order business was doing so well, why not open some stores and establish a brick-and-mortar presence, too? He was confident it would be a relatively easy win.

I wasn't as confident—and nervous about the distraction. We were already drowning in to-do lists a mile long and overwhelmed by a deluge of incoming orders that showed no signs of letting up. In our telephone sales department, we were losing some 350 calls a day—people who just didn't have the time or patience to wait ten minutes on hold to order (heaven help us) a half-dozen string bags. I was already feeling terrible that we couldn't service all the people who were calling us, and that was before even considering all the sales we were potentially losing. Pouring hours and energy into a project that was tangential at best didn't seem to be the most effective use of our extremely limited resources. But ours was a partnership of equals. If a store was something Alan wanted to try, I was willing to let him try it, even if I thought it was a bit of a non-starter.

We worked with a company friend named John Quinney to explore Seventh Generation's retail possibilities. In the end, no matter how hard John tried, even with a store on the busiest street in the grooviest city in the hippie-est state east of the Mississippi, the Seventh Generation store simply could not gain the necessary traction. Seventh Generation as a retail giant was a future that was simply not meant to be,* though we blew no shortage of money trying to make it a reality.

But what did the future hold? What was waiting up ahead? More importantly, what could we do to stay on top of the world?

One idea evolved into what we called the Seventh Generation Board of Advisors. Alan and I reached out to the people we saw as the top environmental luminaries of the moment, and managed to cajole most of them into becoming part of our own private "think tank." We'd scored some heavy hitters: Alan Gussow, chairman of Friends of the Earth; Earth Day founder Denis Hayes; Amory Lovins, the CEO of the Rocky Mountain Institute; Alice Tepper Marlin, the executive director of the Council on Economic Priorities; Sandra Postel, a vice president at the Worldwatch Institute; Greenpeace executive director Peter Bahouth; and Native American activist Winona LaDuke.

The idea was to get together once a year so we could pick their brains about emerging environmental problems, and by extension, what products we should be developing to solve those problems. Designing a business to address environmental issues was a totally new idea, but we really didn't have to twist any arms because our board members thought we were as cool as we thought they were.

In 1990, we had our first meeting of this mutual admiration society at the Rocky Mountain Institute, and it was as exciting and stimulating

---

* Some years later, we tried one more time with a single storefront in California and a merchandising mix that focused on soft goods like linens and clothing. It, too, failed to fly.

as I'd hoped. In just over a year, Seventh Generation had gone from complete obscurity to an entity capable of engineering a summit like this one, made up of some of the greatest minds in the country, engaged in deep conversations about the state of the world.

It was, of course, a highly unusual arrangement at the time—a group of non-profit leaders advising (for free!) a for-profit business. These were not just two spheres that didn't intermingle much—they were traditional adversaries that spent most of their time actively and aggressively fighting each other. This gave Seventh Generation a tremendous amount of credibility and also provided board members with some corporate influence they'd long sought. Everybody won.

Most of my days, however, were not spent in such glorious confines. Most of my days took place in a small warren of unassuming rooms on 38th Street and 5th Avenue in New York City, Seventh Generation's Manhattan office. The place was a far more traditional setting than the one Alan was establishing in Vermont, with actual chairs and genuine tables, offices with doors, none of which were dedicated to naps. There were other differences, too, one of the biggest being that my brother, Peter, had begun working there.

From my perspective, hiring him had been a rescue operation. After working together to build the audiobook business at Warner Bros, we'd again gone our separate ways. Peter had become a commodities trader, specializing in platinum and palladium on Wall Street. With his good looks, keen mind, and charismatic charm, he was a natural salesman, and the rare metals market had turned these traits into a profitable vocation.

Unfortunately, this was happening during the 1980s and Peter being Peter, that equation equaled a whole lot of cocaine. Both his income and his career went straight up his nose, and at the end of that line, Peter was left without much of a future.

I stepped in and offered him a job setting up what we hoped might become a new wholesale division at Seventh Generation. The idea was to put our name on some of the consumer products we offered and experiment with selling them to independent natural food stores.

The idea of wholesaling private-labeled products under the Seventh Generation banner wasn't new. Alan and I had first discussed it in 1989, and went so far as to develop a wholesale catalog. Peter would now start hawking this catalog to independent natural food stores in New York City as a way to dip our toes into the retail waters and gauge the possibilities without too much commitment.

Alan had been uncertain about the concept. But from my perspective, private labeling was simply common sense driven by signals that were clear: The biggest catalog sellers by far were non-durable consumer products—our recycled-fiber tissue products and our household cleaners. The paper products could easily be sold under our own name, which could dramatically expand our market potential while building Seventh Generation into an actual brand, a consumer proposition with far more power than being mere middle-men purveyors of other brands. As I learned over time, the most effective way to create financial value is to build a strong brand. Better yet, a brand that your customers don't just like, but love.

It certainly helped that I was already more comfortable in the wholesale business. Before leaving Warner Bros, I'd run the books-on-tape business for several years, first on my own and then as head of the division, selling those books to bookstores and record stores, dealing with distributors, and figuring out how to merchandise.

Peter's preternatural sales skills were a perfect fit for the role—and he played it well. Years later, we leaned all the way into the wholesaling proposition to become a much different company. Peter laid the foundation for that switch and, more importantly, the corporate survival it enabled. Seventh Generation would not have made it without his work in the early '90s.

Peter joined a staff that was a lot smaller and much more stable than the one in Vermont—a handful of people who helped me with finance and merchandising, the office's two central functions. Yet despite our conventional trappings, the New York staff was not your typical crew of office workers. Underneath our office's regulation appearances was a passion that rivaled the enthusiasm energizing our Colchester co-workers.

But the Colchester headquarters was Alan's realm. New York was mine. We each had our own management styles, cultivating different environments. This was not a bad thing. Good managers understand that to get things done, their expressions of authority must reflect the culture of their employees. Vermont was laid back and mellow, more freestyle and informal. New York City, on the other hand, was the *Hunger Games* with decent pizza. The people there required a somewhat firmer, more traditional structure lest things fall completely apart. Not to say we didn't thoroughly enjoy ourselves in New York. We were a tight-knit team, and had our fun, though it was just a different flavor than Vermont.

Leadership styles, however, were but the tip of the differential iceberg. By late 1990, our Colchester office had swelled to 120 people, and though that was all we could afford to hire, it still wasn't enough. No matter what we did or how hard we worked, we were always behind. Colchester was a hamster wheel. The joy from our sudden Earth Day success was often heavily tempered by intense stress. Compounding the problem was the fact that we'd grown so large so quickly.

Alan and I hadn't planned for any of this. We were the poster children for unexpectedly successful startups. Everything was ad hoc and cobbled together, from job titles to warehouse procedures—from computer systems to marketing programs. We were learning everything on the fly, and at times, the resulting chaos understandably made people unhappy.

The staff was experiencing issues with decision-making and communication. There were complaints about who was responsible for what on which chain of command, grumbling about salaries, and even some resentment toward the New York office, whose purposes weren't always clearly understood or appreciated. And maybe some envy that the New York staff enjoyed an atmosphere that was significantly less of a pressure cooker.

Alan and I knew we had to take action—and fast. Scale can easily become the enemy of community, and ours had grown so large, we were in danger of losing its can-do sense of camaraderie. We realized that we had to find ways to make the Seventh Generation culture work on a much larger scale than we'd anticipated.

Despite the current pressures, we immediately set about creating organizational charts for clear communication. We established a salary structure that laid down concrete expectations. We encouraged people to discuss their concerns openly, including using staff meetings to bring rumor into the light. We even invited input on some of the decisions we were making.

But there were limits, which bumped up against the general sense in the ranks that Seventh Generation was not so much a company as a workers' collective. In some ways, I was back in Toronto where everything was run by committee, and I knew how that had gone. There had to be some guardrails. Alan and I asked people to understand that Seventh Generation was not a democracy. It was a business and the majority couldn't—and shouldn't—rule.

It was a necessary effort, and to a certain extent, there really wasn't any choice. Dealing with staff emotions was not a luxury, but it was also not an obligation we could afford in too large a measure.

In mid-June, I shared the news that the fall/holiday catalog would be at least doubling in size. It would have 125 percent more products, including the addition of recycled-plastic garbage bags, drinking tumblers made from used glass, batteries without heavy metals, organic skin care products, and—for the first time ever—our own private-label Seventh Generation branded products.

The formula was mail order 101: grow your sales by creating bigger catalogs containing additional products and send those catalogs to more people. With our mailing lists bursting with fresh Earth Day inquiries, we had a huge pool of potential new customers. It would have been corporate malfeasance not to expand our merchandising as far and as fast as we could.

Not to say it was easy. The green products marketplace hadn't yet caught up with the year's green exuberance, and there was still a lot of hunting and gathering involved in the process.

Ironically, our most unique products were also our most mundane—day-to-day consumables like laundry detergent, baby food, diapers, and paper towels. Certainly each had some kind of environmental advantage, but at the time, mail order catalogs didn't sell consumables. They sold durable goods. Offering things like toilet paper and dish liquid was an absurd proposition in the industry's eyes. Who in their right mind would buy paper towels through the mail? Nobody! At least, that's what everybody thought.

Our environmental focus, however, set that paradigm on its head. It created the rationale required to push past consumer hesitancy and establish a viable mail order marketplace for common household goods that had been ignored by direct marketers. And it proved to be the key to our success. Because consumable products were consumed. And as soon as they were, we'd get a repeat order. That made our customer base a lot more valuable on an annual spending basis than most catalogs. It was the mail order jackpot, and we'd figured out how to win it.

On November 12, the pinnacle of our success arrived in the form of a perfectly timed spread in one of the most popular magazines of the era, *People Weekly*, a publication sold at virtually every supermarket, drugstore, and newsstand from coast to coast. It was the kind of exposure most entrepreneurs can only dream about—four full pages with pictures and the only photo on the table of contents—a cheerful shot of me pushing Alan in a shopping cart loaded with our own branded products. Our 800 number was in the second paragraph, and our holiday hopes were written in the headline: "When America Thinks Green, Eco-Preneurs Alan Newman and Jeffrey Hollender Think Greenbacks."

We were not disappointed. The publicity we got from the *People* article combined with Earth Day's activist consumer afterglow, a summer of media mentions, and our dramatically expanded catalog blew holiday sales into truly eye-opening territory. We were looking at numbers that were totally outside anything we'd believed possible.

It was exciting. But also scary, stressful, and messy as hell. I was exhausted, Alan was beat, and the entire staff was over the edge. At the same time, we were absolutely elated by our unimaginable success. Just two years ago, Renew America had been on the verge of shutting the catalog down forever. We had all gambled we could save it, and now we had. One fact seemed clear to me: The company's future was going to be absolutely unbelievable.

Turned out I was right—just not in the way I thought.

One unexpected outcome was a lesson from our dreams of retail store expansion: Focus and clear priorities were essential. A lack of focus would burn through more cash and distract us from doing what was most important—such as being able to answer the phone. One of the challenges that all entrepreneurs face is the danger of too many good ideas. Here we were beginning to be the victims of our own success.

Also critical: Plan for the future in a way that ensures you are excellent only with what is most important. Unfortunately, we didn't spend enough time and didn't have the experience to figure out what those things were. We wanted to offer many new products rather than make sure our current products were selling as well as possible. We wanted to save the whole world rather than make it incrementally better than it already was. And those were lessons that would have to come the hard way.

CHAPTER TEN

Life After Death

Propelled to light speed by a very merry season of mass media exposure and a holiday sales forecast that had us over the moon, we entered 1991 intent on harnessing the considerable energy of our meteoric rise and aiming our hopes for the farthest stars. We were the masters of the mail order universe, riding a direct marketing rocket to infinite success, and no force in the cosmos could stop us.

The confidence splashed across our projections like a perfect wave. Based on every trend line we could see from here to the boundless horizon, we foresaw a 300 percent annual growth rate and $20 million-plus in sales for 1991. To prepare for that inevitability, we had laid our money down on eye-popping amounts of fresh inventory and invested in dozens of new employees, doubling our ranks from 60 to 120 souls, each and every one ready to change the world. We ramped up catalog printings, boosted our mailings, and braced for the first storm of the new year.

January was sleepy as shopped-out holiday consumers set their battered wallets aside and hit pause on the impulse to buy. That was fine.

After a year spent trapped in an eternal game of mail order whack-a-mole, it was a welcome breather. There'd be plenty to do and then some in the coming months, and we all knew it. Everyone who'd been along for the previous year's wild ride was happy to rest on our collective laurels for a few weeks.

The break was well deserved. There was just one problem: It didn't end.

February came, and the phones stayed quiet. The mail table, which only a few weeks ago had been buried in an avalanche of order forms and personal checks, sat uncomfortably tidy. You could hear the sound of crickets in the conference rooms and drumming fingers on empty desks, united in a cadence that grew more anxious day by day.

March came in like a lackluster lamb and went out like one, too. Suddenly, inexplicably, we had the first quarter under our belt, and we'd not only missed our targets, we'd missed them by a fairly alarming margin.

"Huh," we said, scratching our heads. "That's . . . weird."

Hindsight is easy, but in the moment, we didn't know what to make of our surprising reversal of fortune. A strange entropy had entered our well-ordered world. And nothing we were seeing made any sense at all.

We'd studied our sales and knew the exact rate at which they'd grown: a stunning 800 percent. And we'd been reasonable in predicting that 800 percent was an utterly unsustainable trajectory. Few businesses can maintain those kinds of stratospheric numbers year on year no matter how good the tail winds.

Still, our response rates strongly suggested we could see 300 percent growth without breaking much of a sweat. In 1990, we'd tested a whole bunch of mailing lists that had done really well, and when we modeled expected sales, we easily reached $20 million or more for the year.

It was a fairly solid methodology—assuming the underlying numbers were at least within spitting distance of reality. Unfortunately, they weren't. Instead, we'd plucked them directly from what turned out to be the worst source imaginable: an exceptionally anomalous year. The twentieth anniversary of Earth Day had triggered a wild universal burst of environmental zeal that had turned everyone into Aldo Leopold and America itself into Conservation Nation.

What we'd failed to understand was that 1990 was all an illusion, a cultural flash in the pan that flamed out nearly as quickly as it had ignited. Now the environment's fifteen minutes of fame were over, along with all the TV shows and articles. The whole crazy ride was unsustainable, but we didn't see that at the time. What we saw were floodgates opened and a great tide of Earth-friendly consumerism released. The world had been permanently changed, or so we thought. It was a heady mix of hubris and chutzpah we'd poured into our crystal ball for 1991. All without considering the possibility of a more rational alternate reality in which the Earth Day blip was just that—a momentary aberration. Nothing more.

There is a Buddhist saying that no snowflake falls in the wrong place, and perhaps this is so. Perhaps the story of Seventh Generation as we know it now is the one that was always meant to be. And who can complain? Today the company is a successful international brand that's making a legitimate difference in the health of its customers and the world they share. Maybe the arc to this place could have gone no other way. Maybe.

But I do wonder sometimes what would have happened had we based our planning on a truer assessment of our operating environment and an understanding that 1990's intoxicating circumstances would not be recurring.

Seen in this light, Earth Day 1990 was more curse than blessing, an artificial trick of the light. We'd been blinded by that light, and now its glow was fading. Hundreds of thousands of hot new catalog requests had gone exactly nowhere, and orders had plummeted from 1,200 a day to barely 100. We had a warehouse overloaded with goods gathering dust.

And it wasn't just Earth Day's false sense of security. An economic recession was dampening consumer enthusiasm. The Gulf War was distracting the nation. Pessimism was the order of the day. None of these factors by themselves would have meant disaster. A recession might lead to a 10 to 20 percent drop-off in sales, not the total reversal we were seeing. The disruption of war was temporary. No matter what, people still needed toilet paper. They just weren't buying it from us anymore, which was a far more fundamental problem.

One of the biggest issues was that our mailing list strategy had about run its course. Over the prior two years, much of our success had come from dropping catalogs in the mailboxes of like-minded donors to environmental organizations. Turning non-profit support into for-profit patronage was an unorthodox approach at the time, but we were an unorthodox company. The approach had paid real dividends, but by 1991 we'd hit the wall on that kind of prospecting.

Every week we were missing our numbers by huge amounts, so we adjusted our expectations by degrees: "Looks like we'll bring in nineteen million, not twenty. Oops, make that seventeen million." And so on. As the weeks passed, we started to think the unthinkable: We might not even match 1990. We simply did not know where the bottom was. We had jumped out of the plane without a parachute, and we had no idea how far we would fall.

Not wanting to panic, we made some minor course corrections, hopeful we could weather the storm without anyone losing their job. We slashed salaries: Alan, myself, and the rest of the upper management team took 50 percent pay cuts so we could keep the rank-and-file pain to a more manageable 10 percent. We did everything possible to cut our costs down to size, at one point even renegotiating the lease on the company copier. Every penny suddenly counted, and in our atmosphere of transparency, everybody knew it. The mood in the office was grim but resolute. We were happy to find that our inclusive company culture was paying off in the form of a staff who very much believed in our mission and had faith that the company would prevail in the end. Nobody jumped ship, which meant a lot to us.

Alan and I were trying like crazy to understand what was happening. Theories ran wild. At one point, we suspected the Postal Service had somehow lost the bulk of our catalogs. But mostly we clung to the notion that this was just a weird hiccup and that we could make up the unexpected shortfall with a solid second half of the year. Our hopes were on a big holiday season, which was where the lion's share of annual sales typically originated anyway. Yet it soon became clear that we were slipping beyond the reach of any holiday rush to save us.

Alan and I were emotional but trying to remain analytical. He spent hours working to optimize sales by fine-tuning our mailings, like mixing a song to find the perfect sound. But nothing worked. Sales stayed stuck in place, stubbornly anemic, and Seventh Generation remained a seven-figure company with eight-figure overhead.

By the end of summer, the situation had turned critical. We were hemorrhaging money with no end in sight. The well was quickly running dry, and fundraising to cover the shortfall was a difficult proposition. Faced with imminent collapse, Alan and I were forced to do the unthinkable and lay off half the staff.

In a small town like Burlington, this was a big deal. We'd made the decision to announce the staff cuts on a Monday versus a Friday so everybody could have one more weekend without the distress of impending unemployment. That Saturday Alan went to a party where half of the guests were on our unfortunate layoff list. In future months, I'd be served at restaurants by ex-seventh genners we'd had to let go. There was just no escaping the pain in a community our size. But after a summer of pinching every last penny, we had no choice but to cut costs drastically. Payroll was the last place to go.

Again, our company culture served us well. We'd tried desperately to spare everyone the worst and everyone knew we had. We could honestly say we'd arrived at the last option. It was this or go under, and the staff understood. No one was blindsided by the layoffs. The phones just weren't ringing, and that was that. There was sadness and disappointment, but not much anger. In some ways, it was a flashback to my Network for Learning Days and that same narrative: We went out of our way to take full responsibility for the mess and blamed only ourselves for having mismanaged the situation.

"We really fucked up," we said. "We did our projections wrong, and we shouldn't have hired as many people as we did. It's not your fault. We just screwed up, and we're sorry."

It was the truth, but having to say it sixty times compounded the pain for Alan and myself. We each reacted in our own ways to the trauma. My own response was to quit using the bathroom at work. That was where the chalkboards were, and in the wake of the staff reduction announcement, they were filled with heartbreak and the occasional bitter invective. It was just too hard to read.

At the end of the layoffs came the two biggest and most unthinkable of all. We furloughed our operations manager, Steve Hood, and our finance wizard, Hank Clark. Indispensable though they were, and as horrifying as that decision was both personally and professionally, we could simply no longer afford their services. Full stop. So Alan and I divvied up their responsibilities and piled them onto our already daunting to-do lists.

A week later, Alan walked into my office and announced out of the clear blue that he needed some time off and intended to take an extended leave of absence.

I was thunderstruck.

As he explained how he needed some time to think things through and regain his bearings, I sat there slack-jawed and bewildered. The last two years had taken their toll, and he wanted a break from the sturm und drang. Alan had shown no signs of flagging will. If he'd left any handwriting on the conference room wall, I hadn't seen it. We were all going through the wringer at the time. Everybody was under maximum stress, but I had no idea he was feeling so burned out that walking away had become not just a viable possibility but the only one left.

In shock, I was unable to do much more than stammer out a few non-committal words of tentative hesitation. For me, such a course simply was not an option. I had Alfred Hollender's admonition burned into my brain: You never give up. No matter what. Fight to the bitter end, and go down with the ship if that's what it takes. But never, ever throw in the towel and go home. Whispering right behind him was Asher Lance, whose advice to avoid bankruptcy at all costs was suddenly looming larger than ever. There were other pressures as well. I had taken a lot of money from a lot of people, many of them close friends and family, and I had an obligation to honor that generosity and fight to keep the dream alive despite the odds.

And I still very much believed in that dream. Despite our travails, I never really seriously entertained the possibility that we'd go belly up. For one thing, such thoughts just aren't very helpful. For another, there's always a way out. We just hadn't found it yet.

Now Alan was sitting across from me telling me he didn't have it in him to keep looking.

My shock turned to dismay, and dismay turned to anger. I felt utterly betrayed, and a cold fury welled up inside me. Over the course of the last few years, Alan had become one of my closest friends. We traveled together. We worked together. We played together. Now suddenly he was abandoning me, and I couldn't wrap my head around the idea. It was like an ill-conceived prank, but there wasn't any "gotcha!" coming.

When he said, "I need to do it for my health," I got it. To a point. Everybody's health was suffering under the strain of such a stressful time, but that's sometimes unfortunately the way it works in business, where the rewards can be great but the stakes are always high. But the captain doesn't get to take a seat in the lifeboat when the company is sinking. That's not how it works. We'd just let sixty people go and there were sixty people left looking to us to save their livelihoods—not to mention our customers, investors, vendors, and all the rest.

Alan was tossing all that aside. In my view, he'd violated a sacred oath, which inflicted a fatal wound on our relationship. The one person who was supposed to be steering through the storm with me just bailed as the ship hit the shoals. I could no longer depend on him, and there was no coming back from it.

There didn't seem to be much to say. If there was, I didn't know how to say it. I only knew there wasn't much to be gained by fighting him on it. So in the end, I agreed, and after a few conversations about logistics and messaging, a six-month sabbatical was hastily arranged. We drew up a skeletal letter of agreement with some bare-boned terms, including re-hiring Steve Hood, who thankfully hadn't yet found another job. Then Alan walked out the door.

The staff was nearly as surprised as I was, and our board of directors was fairly apoplectic. Arthur Gray was adamant that Alan not be permitted to return, and led the board in that direction. "You don't get to just go off on a holiday when the house is on fire," he said. As we headed into the now doubly important holiday sales season, our weekly numbers remained weak, and Alan's departure was fanning the flames of distress.

With Alan removed from the picture, I moved into the Hampton Inn around the corner from the office and spent my weeks living out of a suitcase* while trying to keep the company afloat. I don't really know what Alan did. If we talked during his leave, it wasn't much at all. Though we communicated formally in writing a few times, I have no recollection of even a single personal conversation, and that was a difficult change to accept after having been so close.

It was a painful divorce. Any time a close relationship falls apart there's nothing to feel good about, and in this case the problems were magnified by the haste with which everything had gone down. I was flabbergasted by Alan's proclamation but distracted by all the responsibility I had to the company in its hour of greatest need. The result was some pretty poor planning. We didn't put anything in writing to govern his eventual return. Alan and I were left instead with very different experiences and divergent points of view about what the outcome of his sabbatical would be.

---

* The inn eventually assigned me a permanent room to keep my stuff in, even when I went home to New York on weekends. It was virtually my Burlington studio apartment until we permanently relocated to Vermont.

In mid-March of 1992, Alan got back in touch.

"Dear Jeff," he began, "This letter is to formally let you and the board know that my leave-of-absence is about to end and I am ready to rejoin Seventh Generation. As we discussed both prior to my leave and since the leave began, we need to discuss what role I will play with Seventh Generation from this point forward. For discussion, I offer the following thoughts . . ."

What came next was a quick outline for resuming normal operations with both of us in command. But there was also uncertainty.

"I am unclear about the process," Alan wrote. "Your letter of February 4th, 1992, states that the board will meet to discuss what, if any, opportunities exist for my return. My leave ends on March 15th and the next board meeting is in April. Does this mean I have another unrequested, unpaid month of leave or will a decision be made before that meeting? By whom? How?"

In my mind, Alan's time was over. All that was left was to make it official. Still, I must have had some final shred of hope. In a last-ditch effort to see if we could overcome the violation of trust and find a way to salvage things, I insisted we go to couples counseling and hash things out with an arbiter. But we were both locked too deeply into our individual perspectives. Alan insisted he always intended to come back. I insisted he gave up that right when he left. There was nothing the poor therapist could do. Neither of us was willing to accept that the other had some valid issues worth discussing, and we gave up after a scant handful of unproductive sessions.

I can't speak to what Alan was feeling. Perhaps he, too, felt a sense of betrayal when confronted with my refusal to allow his return. What I know is that, for me, the profound personal and professional disappointment was too great to overcome. In no uncertain terms, he had left me holding a really ugly bag, and in the situation's wake, I had reorganized the business and taught myself to wrangle the mailing lists and plumb the mysteries of marketing.

Financially, things had stabilized at last. 1991's total sales had ended up about where 1990's had landed—and we were back on more solid footing. There were reasons to be hopeful again, and Alan hadn't had much to do with any of it. "I don't really need this guy anymore," I thought. "And he's forced me to this conclusion."

I sent Alan what amounted to a "Dear John" letter, informing him that the company was severing its relationship with him, and on April 17, 1992, he officially resigned. It was a sadly bitter end to a great friendship and a wonderful business partnership, one that pains me to this day.

Over the years, the hot white glare of my anger has faded and allowed a more positive light into my memories. I learned a lot from Alan. He's incredibly talented and highly capable, a guy who had many skills that I didn't have, especially at the time. In some ways, many of the things I tried to do at Seventh Generation were either learned from or inspired by his example and wisdom. He later founded the Magic Hat Brewing Company with brewmaster and ex-Seventh Generation warehouse manager Bob Johnson, where he has shown a masterful ability to create an incredible culture and a lasting community. Had we remained close and continued to share the helm, who can say what might have happened. But we parted acrimoniously and have remained at arm's length to this day.

Shortly after Alan left, my brother, Peter, also departed from the company, and in some ways that blow was even bigger. It wasn't just the loss of one confidant and co-conspirator on top of the loss of another. Peter was also single-handedly running the company's brand-new wholesale program, which was a basket we had loaded with a lot of our eggs during the company's sales crisis of 1991.

In Peter's hands, the wholesaling experiment had proved quite successful. He was a gifted salesman, charming and confident, and he effortlessly stoked store manager interest in our tiny little product line. When those managers gave our products a shot, sales were typically good and the store usually ordered more. Slowly, we were building a minor retail presence in Manhattan, but throughout the 1990's sales explosion, wholesale remained the ugly stepchild.

Now that the mail order operation was on life support, it was time to look at the resuscitation options. Wholesaling was the best bet I had. If we could take the success we'd found in New York City national, we just might survive the scary tailspin we were trapped in. I had no intention of abandoning the catalog at the time, but having a Plan B is always a good idea. Even better if it had potential to turn into Plan A. So with Peter's help, I started mapping that plan out.

First, we had to expand beyond paper products. Needing just two basic essential attributes (recycled fiber and chlorine-free production), these were the low-hanging fruit. All you had to do was buy in bulk and put your own label on the package. Simple.

Cleaners, on the other hand, were something else entirely. They were more complicated to engineer and were manufactured in a complex and arcane world of bizarro chemicals and incomprehensible formulas—some of which worked better than others and most of which were entirely (and often dangerously) synthetic in origin, something our products by definition absolutely could not be. Add to this an industry with zero interest in healthy alternatives, and it proved to be quite a puzzle.

We made many calls, held many meetings, and endured much laughter. Then, across the river from Manhattan in Kearny, New Jersey, Jeff Phillips, our supply chain and product development guru, found the Stanson Corporation. A small family-run chemical company, Stanson specialized in manufacturing private-label cleaning products, and they had a family of formulas they sold to anyone looking to create an in-house brand. The company was not only open to working with us, they had even developed a few "green" formulas they were willing to let us use. The formulas weren't perfect, but with the help of Martin Wolf, an independent chemist we hired, we managed to tweak them into an acceptable state.

Our goal was to be 90 percent as effective as the leading brand, a very high benchmark that in those early years we repeatedly failed to meet.[*] The lack of interest in sustainability in cleaning product science meant we had to compromise on our selection of ingredients. Finding a non-petroleum-based surfactant, for example, proved impossible in those first few years, and we would have to wait for science to catch up.

Once again, we found ourselves in the role of pioneers trying to be green in an industry that not only didn't care about being green, but didn't even really understand what that meant or, worse, why it was needed. There was neither demand for nontoxic cleaners nor awareness of their importance, and no one was working to develop alternative sustainable ingredients and formulas. We were largely on our own in a strange new materials wilderness, and we could not have navigated a path through it without Stanson's help. They were an invaluable partner in those early private-label years, and I'm grateful we found them.

Fortunately, our third branded product category was easier to bring to market. During our forays to Europe, Alan and I had discovered something called "green cotton," a basic, light-beige cotton fabric that had the singular advantage of not being chlorine-bleached, a feature that dovetailed nicely with our paper products and their bleach-free

---

[*] For years, I joked in presentations that our customers were so dedicated to our brand and its ideals that they were "willing to spend twice as much to get things half as clean."

focus. All we had to do was find a manufacturer that would skip the bleaching process to produce bolts of unbleached fabric we could then fashion into t-shirts and towels and all the rest.

Now that we had the products, we needed to lean the company in this new private-label, wholesale direction and, hopefully, restore some fiscal equilibrium. As Peter took them out into the world, they were generating sales that, despite my confidence in the idea, were still pretty amazing. I had been cautiously optimistic about what we were cooking, but until it comes out of the oven, you just don't know whether you're half-baked or not. Happily, our products sold well just about everywhere we put them, and in the depths of our post-Earth Day malaise, we birthed a strategy to put them everywhere.

Everything was gelling nicely. Until Peter told me he was leaving.

I completely flipped out over his decision. On the one hand, I understood—working for your older brother isn't necessarily the greatest career move in the world, and he had a new business opportunity that looked like a winner.

On the other hand, he was our entire wholesale department at that point, and we were pinning a great deal of our future on growing that business. There were also personal matters to consider. Peter's predilections were well known, and thanks to his role at the company, I was able to help keep them in check. This would be much harder if he went elsewhere, and everything was already hard enough. Yet there wasn't much I could do. Peter left, and I was left holding yet another bag, not entirely sure what to do with it.

Defying our fiscal instability, we hired a replacement, Michael Brown, a sales executive from Campbell's Soup, to help us shepherd this new wholesale division forward. We also lucked out and landed a distributor, which suddenly allowed us a reach far beyond Manhattan and potentially beyond natural food stores, too. The economics weren't great—selling direct through the catalog offered better margins than a pricing model where a distributor took upwards of 30 percent off the top and the retailer commanded an additional markup of 40 to 50 percent. But we also knew that the way we would be valued by professional investors was as a multiple of our sales, profits be damned. So wholesale was an investment in a brighter future, though painful at the time, and we made that investment enthusiastically.

By the end of the Q2 of 1992, our situation had become much less perilous. Alan's departure and the associated trauma were receding, as was the pain of our recent downsizing. Our sales forecasts were once again relatively accurate, and finally we had a company that was appropriately sized for the predicted order volume. Staff morale rose again, and our collective mission to change the world was once more active within the company zeitgeist—even as it remained quite unusual in the world we wanted to change. Things stopped looking so disturbingly bleak and daylight crept back in.

I was even positive about the catalog again, which was itself a remarkable turnaround. For one, I had cracked the circulation code—when done right, we could mail half as many catalogs and still generate about the same amount of revenue. This change alone saved us a ton of money.

An even bigger change involved the catalog itself. One of its major ongoing problems was a lack of repeat orders. This suggested a merchandising issue: We were failing to offer products with the necessary appeal. At the same time, we'd run out of non-profit mailing lists and were now prospecting lists from companies like L.L.Bean and Williams-Sonoma. These had a potentially much different customer profile, which suggested we should shake up our product mix.

This seemed like sound strategy. Diversifying the kinds of goods we sold would bring different categories of customers on board and help us sell more items to more people. Slowly, we added soft goods and lifestyle items to the catalog. We still sold light bulbs and faucet aerators, but now they sat alongside natural fiber blankets and sustainable household décor, which we hoped would attract customers who weren't even environmentalists. We were now targeting prospects who were into a broader "natural and healthy" lifestyle. It was a shift that would predict the emergent LOHAS[*] movement a few years later, but at the time, we were just trying to boost sales through a more universal appeal.

All in all, it worked, and 1992 was turning out to be a much better year than 1991. At least, until I made one of the biggest mistakes of my business career.

---

[*] LOHAS = Lifestyles of Health and Sustainability

CHAPTER ELEVEN

Public Affairs & Private Travails

The year of Seventh Generation's revival was also a presidential election year that found Bill Clinton running against George H.W. Bush. After the hell of the Reagan years and a terrible and terrifying Gulf War, my profoundly progressive soul had had about all it could take. I was terrified what would happen to the country if Clinton and Gore were not elected. And I thought the company should put its money where its mouth was and use this pivotal election to do something positive to help.

My thinking was fairly simple. Companies give money to politicians all the time, yet consumers know nothing about most of those donation dollars. When someone buys a bottle of Tide detergent, they don't realize that Procter & Gamble has earmarked some of their profits to support candidates and organizations that are promoting the company's interests at the expense of the community's wellbeing. The product may be getting your clothes clean, but behind the scenes, it's making an ugly, dirty mess of everything we hold dear. Consumers unwittingly support this awful carnage every time they support the company.

The whole point of Seventh Generation was to subvert that paradigm by being a fully transparent business that openly parlayed its own consumer loyalty into support for the common good rather than private greed. What better way to trumpet those values than by putting them front and center on the cover of our fall catalog and encouraging our customers to vote in alignment with our shared commitment to the environment?

So we hired an artist and created a catalog cover featuring an exceptionally unflattering cartoon of Bush hugging the Earth. Behind him, a gaggle of Republican cohorts wore buttons professing their love for the environment while simultaneously spraying pesticides, dancing on oil barrels, approving clear-cutting projects, and denying the ozone hole.

Atop it all, we ran a quote from Al Gore, "It's time for them to go," and inside the front cover, we put a cherry on top with an impassioned essay asking people to "Vote for the Earth!" In a way, it was a big political coming out party for us. It seemed like a great idea at the time.

It wasn't.

We later calculated that we lost about half a million dollars in sales from people we'd pissed off with our political stance. They either didn't like us supporting Democrats or they didn't want the company that sells them toilet paper to tell them how to vote. We thought we had made a careful case for why it was important for us as a business to take a political stand and that our focus on an environmentally driven agenda made our foray into electoral waters more than acceptable.

Not only was the fallout wholly unanticipated—I had thought people would be cheering us on—but that turned out to be a big miscalculation in an era where socially responsible businesses had yet to flex any political muscle. Interestingly, that changed dramatically over time, before the big chill of Trump's second term. But people just didn't know what to make of such a proclamation at the time. Again, we were pioneers, and sometimes the first boots on the trail are the ones that get bit by the rattlesnake. This one stung like hell.[*]

Though Seventh Generation was still standing in an upright position again, after our brief entry into politics, that was really all it was doing. We were leaner and far more appropriately sized for a company with our sales volume and armed with a much more realistic set of projections. Our self-inflicted operational wounds had healed over, but we were still operating at a loss week over week, though the red in the margins was perhaps a lighter shade than before.

---

[*] That election season, President Clinton visited Burlington, and I had the chance for a photo op. He told me he'd had our controversial catalog cover blown up into a poster hanging in his campaign plane. It made me feel a bit better. At least someone had gotten something positive out of it!

On the plus side, our wholesale trials had been a modest success and that was clearly one direction to follow ASAP. Also, our efforts to mellow out the catalog's hardcore environmental bent and broaden its appeal were also showing signs of working. To prosper, we needed to lean into these two strategies with everything we had.

Unfortunately, we didn't have enough money to continue down this path. Simply maintaining the status quo was costing us too much money, and financing new growth was a practical impossibility. Equally unfortunate was the fact I had run out of family members, friends, associates, doctors, dentists, and mailmen I could convince to invest in the company. Fellow board members like Arthur Gray had, too. The well had finally run dry, and we were left with few options, none of which were appealing.

One was venture capital. At trade shows and conferences, we were occasionally approached by speculators offering us good money, but it came with strings attached and a whole new level of risk. We'd have to trade a chunk of ownership and put strangers on the board who no doubt wouldn't be as interested in our mission as they were in pulling the company in a purely capitalist direction, no matter what the social and ethical costs. I had nightmarish visions of hideously off-brand products being forced into the catalog just to make a quick buck and a devastated company culture forced to turn its cherished nap room into more space for the finance group, enlarged to watch over the new investors' money.

In discussing these offers with the board, it was clear that it would be preferable to have several thousand little investors rather than one big investor. This option would have its own issues, but ultimately our judgment was that it was by far the lesser of two evils. Small investors weren't as sophisticated or as demanding as venture fund operators, and the individual investments themselves were so relatively slight that no single investor would be able to exert influence on the direction of the business. There were philosophical considerations as well: With small investors, our social aspirations would hopefully be better understood, and we'd be able to keep our focus on our so-called dual bottom line, which placed an equal priority on profits and public good.

Our best option was to turn to the stock market with an offering that would transform us into a tiny public company. We'd take advantage of a boom market for initial public offerings (IPO) that seemed to fund any business that had the remotest chance of success. With the money we'd raise, we could get serious about our wholesale business and pursue an intentional full-throttle repositioning of our catalog.

Having made the decision to pursue an IPO, my exhausted Rolodex was again drafted into action. I started the process by asking a friend, David Nussbaum, to recommend an underwriter for the IPO, and he referred me to a small New York firm he had just started with some friends called GKN Securities. They agreed to not only shepherd us onto the NASDAQ stock market but to also provide us with a bridge loan to keep the company running until our stock hit the streets.

Suddenly, I found myself with two full-time jobs: One was running Seventh Generation. The other was working on its IPO. The result was an average workweek of 100 hours and sometimes more. The work soon felt like an endless tag-team colonoscopy performed by GKN and the Securities and Exchange Commission (SEC), which both sent lawyers and accountants to set up shop somewhere deep in our corporate bowels where they poked and prodded parts of the company I didn't even know we had.

For its part, the underwriter, GKN, just couldn't wrap its collective head around our company. For example, they did not like how we had an employee representative on the board of directors and were insisting we eliminate the position. Like diva cups and recycled toilet tissue, the idea was just a little too weird for their taste.

Even my hair became a subject of debate. "It's way too long," they said. "Hack it down to conservative length and you'll add a dollar to the stock price," they claimed, thus causing me to draw a very clear line in the Wall Street sand. I was willing to cut a lot of things in the name of financing, but my hair wasn't one of them.

Hair styles, however, were the least of our problems. There was also the SEC to contend with, and they didn't like anything we did. "Please clarify and explain . . . Recalculate and rewrite . . . " the SEC demanded over and over with letters that critiqued our documents. It was a complicated, convoluted nightmare.

Eventually—finally—and a little unbelievably, the work paid off. On November 29, 1993, we published our tortured prospectus (printed on recycled paper, of course) and sold 1.2 million shares of common stock for $5.00 apiece to the general public. It was an exciting day and at the end of it, we were sitting on a boatload of cash, with smiles all around.

In many ways we were lucky. In the modern stock market, no company as small as Seventh Generation (and doing as badly as we were at the time) would be able to pull off a stock sale. For one thing, the SEC has clamped down on our kind of deal. Regulators' instincts are not misplaced. As we found out the hard way, it's not easy being a public company. Life at a privately held business means you can do almost anything you want within a basic legal (and hopefully moral) framework. Meanwhile, being publicly traded means crazy reporting requirements, complicated accounting rules, and literally hundreds of regulations that have to be followed chapter and verse. It's a brave new world. And an expensive one, too. We weren't fully prepared for going public, making us a risky bet.

On the positive side of the ledger, after commissions and fees, legal and accounting expenses, and bridge loan repayment, we'd netted $5 million. The sale was considered a complete success, and everybody made money almost immediately as our stock price rose north of $7.00 from the initial $5.00 offering price.

Sadly, we were also just grist for the Wall Street mill. With most of our shares held by a relatively limited set of investors, we really didn't have much of a public market presence per se, and when those investors sold the stock to take a quick profit, our stock price plateaued before eventually dwindling away in obscurity. Regardless, several days after the IPO, $5 million dropped into our bank account, and we finally had the cash needed to take Seventh Generation to the next level.

First up was our retail experiment, which had shown impressive potential. But as the "ugly stepchild" of the business, it had always been stuck in a corner and largely ignored while the catalog sat at the dining room table, noisily gobbling up almost everything we had. Nevertheless, by the end of 1993, we had developed twenty-seven branded SKUs,* a mix of household cleaners, paper products, and simple "green cotton" staples like t-shirts and towels. We had plenty of products to sell, but we hadn't been able to sell them beyond the Northeast simply because we couldn't afford the sales reps.

Yet in New England we were doing pretty well. We got our first big break from Tim Sperry, the buyer for a Boston-based chain of natural food stores called Bread & Circus. Tim believed in our brand and was incredibly supportive. Our run of good luck had continued in late 1992

---

* SKU stands for "stock keeping unit," a unique number used by everybody in the product's life cycle, from the manufacturer to the distributor to the retailer, for tracking inventory and sales.

when Bread & Circus was purchased by Whole Foods, a deal that had the side effect of dramatically boosting our presence in the region. In spring of 1993, Whole Foods bought Mrs. Gooch's, a Southern California chain, and we piggy-backed that sale to expand to the West Coast.

Now we had visibility in big stores on both coasts, and a reliable track record to build upon as measured by retail's key metric: net sales generated per square foot of the shelf space. We were a solid success by that measure, and we could use that story to pry our way onto more shelves in new stores and chains.

Meanwhile, we had plans to develop additional products like diapers and feminine care, which would push us into new categories. Only the money had been missing, and at last, this final impediment was no longer a problem. We could build both a sales staff and our product line to fully leverage the luck we'd had so far.

One of the first moves we made with the IPO cash was to hire Jeff Phillips to be our sourcing czar. Jeff came to us from Webster Industries, the Massachusetts manufacturer that was providing our recycled-plastic trash bags, and he was charged with developing new products and evolving the ones we had.

He had his work cut out for him. In addition to cajoling manufacturers who still didn't really understand "green" products into working without their usual toxic stock ingredients and unsustainable production methods, Jeff was also responsible for overcoming the performance issues that came with that largely unexplored industrial territory.

Our goal was still to be 90 percent as good as the leading brand in any product category, and we were constantly testing our products to understand how far we were from that benchmark. The answer was usually "pretty far." Initial iterations of Seventh Generation laundry detergent, for example, were frequently defeated by ink, wine, and oil stains because we refused to use petroleum-based surfactants and insisted on vegetable-based ingredients instead, which were largely brave new chemistry at the time. Our company chemist, Martin Wolf, has long since cracked this natural molecular code, but during that early era, our nontoxic formulas simply weren't up to the task for a modern household. Seventh Generation automatic dishwasher detergent was another case in point. Though we'd acquiesced on using a petroleum-based surfactant in this case because the alternatives simply didn't work at all, we refused to use phosphates or chlorine. The result was an uneven product that often left an ugly haze on glassware, making it look a thousand years old.

Product packaging was yet another nightmare—our use of recycled content in our 32-ounce bottles created weaker plastic prone to developing big unsightly dimples that made our stuff look like factory seconds. Meanwhile, our dishwashing powder boxes had another issue entirely—to maintain easy recyclability, we didn't coat their boxboard interiors with plastic. Moisture was prone to getting inside, and whenever it did, the product itself clumped into massive chunks of sustainable concrete that required a series of earnest hammer blows to regain usability.

There was a constant tension between our environmental standards and our need for ingredients that actually worked, and resolving it was all about the art of the trade-off. Were we willing to shave off a few measures of efficacy for the sake of protecting waterways from an ingredient with known aquatic toxicity? Should we sacrifice 100 percent biodegradability for a cleaner that met consumer expectations? What "bad" ingredients involved which compromises, and were those compromises greater than or less than any a customer might make when they used our products at home?

These were the questions we were always asking. The challenge was to push the ecological envelope while pushing performance—or at least, not pushing consumers into the arms of our mainstream competitors, thus proving their point that green products don't work as well as conventional ones.* The problem was that most—if not all—of the chemicals and formulas offering better cleaning ability were verboten from a sustainability standpoint. The big guys didn't have any qualms deploying these more effective solutions, but our entire brand proposition was based on the fact that we wouldn't.

It was often frustrating work, and Jeff and I got to know each other maybe a little too well as we traveled from manufacturer to manufacturer, trying to resolve formula issues, production problems, and other flies in our natural, nontoxic ointment. The routine was always the same. We'd fly to some distant airport, rent a car, and Jeff would promptly get us lost. Eventually, we'd find a map or get directions and make our way to some bizarre industrial hellscape, where we'd don hair nets and white coats and walk into a maze of confounding machinery to do battle with the latest complication, or strike another deal.

That travel schedule plus my regular long-distance commute between Manhattan and Vermont was all getting to be a bit much. I can live out of a suitcase for a good long while, but now I'd had enough. So Sheila and I took a deep breath and decided to give living in Vermont a try. We packed up our Madison Avenue apartment, rented a house down a dirt road in a town well south of Burlington, and moved in.

---

* More was on the line here than just our own brand's reputation. As a pioneer in the emerging "green product" marketplace, we represented the industry itself by default. When our products didn't work, it left a bad impression of the entire natural cleaner proposition. In some ways, this was not a terrible problem to have—it's never bad to have your brand come to mind whenever consumers think of its product category. But we felt a keen responsibility not to let that association tank an entirely new and badly needed consumer product sector before it could even get off the ground.

Shortly thereafter, Vermont experienced one of its most wicked winters in recent memory, a season of record-breaking snowfall that culminated in a category-5 blizzard locals called "the storm of the century," a cataclysm that dumped over two feet of fresh powder onto our unfortunately detached garage.

To say we did not know what we were getting into would be a gross understatement. It was Green Acres on steroids, and a real shock to New Yorkers accustomed to homes that come with a doorman, a superintendent, and a deli on the corner. We battled mice and spiders in equal measure, and other interlopers, too. One night I bundled into a ski coat with the hood zipped over my face in an attempt to catch an errant bat flapping from room to room. In case you're wondering, the old crab netting I'd found in the basement was not the right tool for the task. A 2:00 a.m. call to animal control proved more effective with an amazing skilled bat catcher who showed up an hour later to catch the wayward creature. More than once, it snowed so much I couldn't even shovel my way to the car. We had to learn to stockpile food and keep a supply of candles and flashlight batteries on hand. It was . . . novel.

Sheila was not happy. She'd been a partner at a big law firm, and now she was stuck in the boonies with two new babies and a house that could have starred in an episode of *Mutual of Omaha's Wild Kingdom* on a road that was often impassable while her husband barnstormed the country trying to breathe new life into a wheezing mail order company. We'd agreed to give the experiment in rural living a two-year trial run. Most of the time, the trial was failing miserably.[*]

---

[*] Fortunately, we eventually met some good Vermonters and established the kind of lasting social ties that were worth the price we'd paid. In 2023, we marked our thirtieth year as part-time residents of a state we've come to love for many reasons. We're still not fond of New England winters, but we've found ways to cope.

Though the wholesale program was beginning to take flight, the catalog continued to tread a path of regrettable mediocrity. Things weren't terrible—after a slow first quarter in 1994, sales had stabilized, and though weekly order counts weren't meeting expectations, the average dollar amount per order was beating them, resulting in a welcome uptick in income. By September, we were roughly a quarter of a million dollars ahead of where we had anticipated. That was good, but it wasn't great. We had to supercharge the company's growth to get to profitability. Unless we grew 25 to 30 percent a year, we'd never survive the journey to that place in the sun.

The good news was that I'd identified a way forward. We'd continued experimenting with mailing lists and had found solid results using names from outfits like L.L.Bean and Garnet Hill, which served up a new kind of customer. These fresh buyers had an interest in soft goods like clothing and linens, and other "natural lifestyle" products whose environmental benefits were much more tangential than hardcore items like faucet aerators and rechargeable batteries.

This proved a major turning point. I recognized that people cared most about their own health, and this was a much stronger driver than concern for the larger external world. Yes, people wanted to save trees and keep local rivers clean, but their greater concern was to protect their families' health. They wanted a safer personal environment via bedding made without pesticides or furnishings with chemical-free finishes. That was the sweet spot. I knew aggressively bending the catalog in this lighter green direction risked alienating our existing customer base of dedicated eco-warriors, but survival depended on reaching beyond the hardcore environmentalists.

To get there, we decided to spend a good chunk of our hard-fought public offering treasure on remaking the catalog from top to bottom and supplying every page with a fresh new look and merchandising strategy. We hired a couple of great consultants to help—Wes Devries, an industry expert who helped us drill deep down in our mailing list demographics, and Leila Griffith, a well-known buyer with an eye for the kinds of products we needed. These two combined their talents with Sheila Hollender's brilliant sense of style and got to work.

Once again, the search for decent merchandise was a supreme challenge. Even products with a soft environmental edge were tough to find. We had to stretch our definitions and look for consumer environmental and lifestyle benefits that weren't always as meaningful. For instance, candles poured from beeswax were our new organic petroleum-free mood lighting.

Products like these were the low-hanging fruit. At one point, we were excited to find "laundry disks"—ceramic balls meant to be put in the washing machine with your clothes, ostensibly to pound against the fabric and literally beat out dirt and soils without the use of any detergent whatsoever. The product sounded good in principle, and we sold thousands and thousands of them.

Unfortunately, we belatedly tested their performance and discovered they didn't work at all. It turned out the wash cycle's natural agitation was really doing the heavy lifting. There wasn't any difference between loads cleaned with or without laundry disks, and in a fit of ethical transparency, we offered a refund to anyone who'd bought them.

Naturally dyed clothing was another case of high hopes turning into a tragic low point. We'd found a company pioneering the use of vegetable dyes to create cotton fabrics that came in all kinds of gorgeous hues. We'd excitedly placed a huge order for what we were sure was the next big thing—a personal wardrobe made without the tremendous environmental costs of toxic petrochemical dyes.

A few months later, our warehouse racks were filled with stacks and stacks of neatly folded tee and polo shirts. Shortly thereafter, as the clothing started to ship, we noticed the unthinkable: The colors weren't lightfast. Simply sitting on our shelves for a few weeks, the exposed fold of every shirt had been bleached out by the sun and our warehouse lamps, leaving each one with a weird off-color strip running straight across its chest. Further tests showed that even an afternoon under strong sun would leave them a faded remnant of their formerly vibrant selves. The dyes didn't work, and we were forced to liquidate hundreds of thousands of dollars' worth of stock.

Happily, abject failures like these were outliers. The majority of products we found at least worked as advertised, and some, like organic and green cotton underwear, went on to be real winners.

By the time the repositioning was finished, we had over 33 percent more products packed into our usual forty-eight pages. We focused on tightening our margins to keep everything competitive with mainstream outlets, and lowered the price for our branded products. We changed the paper to a glossy stock, redesigned everything from our covers to our informational sidebars, and in the fall of 1994, sent the new Seventh Generation Catalog out into the world with fingers crossed.

I was happy, believing we had pivoted nicely into a new era that would turn the tide for the catalog. We had received top-drawer advice from the industry's most experienced hands and applied it with considerable care. My only worry was how much we'd had to water down our environmental proposition. Prior to the repositioning there'd always been a big story we could tell about how our products were saving natural resources, preventing pollution, or safer for your health.

For example, our paper products were made from 100 percent post-consumer recycled fiber that was chlorine-free. It conserved forests and didn't pump dioxin-laden effluent into rivers and streams. A recycled glass candle holder isn't really saving the world in the same impactful way. And even if the candle placed inside it is made of beeswax, it's still not the best for indoor air quality. Justifying a good chunk of our new products was a struggle, and aligning our philosophical underpinnings to account for them was a challenge. We were walking a very fine line, and I knew it. My hope was that the payoff would make all the bending and stretching worth the effort.

It didn't.

The repositioned catalog, while not a complete dud, failed to gain much in the way of new and improved traction. Sales remained anemic, and catalog production cycles became a grinding exercise as we searched in futility for the ever-elusive secret sauce. No matter what we tried, nothing worked the way we needed it to.

Looking back, we faced a basic flaw in our overall catalog proposition: It simply didn't reflect how people shop—a hurdle we could never overcome. Consumers were used to specialty retailers—buying their towels from Bed Bath & Beyond and their hardware from Lowe's. Clothing from Kohl's and outdoor gear bought at REI. Our catalog was trying to mix all that (and more) into a single "storefront," and people just didn't know what to make of it. The lesson learned here is that it is downright difficult—if not almost impossible—to change consumer behavior.

After a year of trying the new angle, we somewhat ironically came to the same conclusion as our customers. It was time to move on. Millions of catalogs later, sales were still flat, and the catalog was burning quickly through our IPO funds. Once again, our options were few.

At a board meeting in mid-1995, the subject was finally broached: We should cut our losses by selling the catalog and better focus on our tiny branded wholesale business.

On one hand, the idea was completely unthinkable. We were an $8 million public company talking about shedding $7 million in sales along with what had been our primary identity—a move that would mean virtually starting over as a far smaller operation in a business we'd barely entered. But the board wasn't looking at it that way. At the meeting, we laid everything out, and the future we saw was impossible to argue with: We had two businesses and only enough money to keep one going. As the character Ron Swanson from *Parks and Recreation* would say, "Don't half-ass two things. Whole-ass one thing."

Despite a heavy investment, the catalog was stuck. The wholesale program, though tiny when measured against catalog sales, was robust in returns. Sales were strong, retailers were enthusiastic, and even in the catalog itself, our paper and branded cleaning products were outshining everything. Those few pages of the catalog's forty-eight pages were responsible for 25 percent of the catalog's total sales.

The costs of the two parts of our corporate personality were equally lopsided. The catalog required sixty people, huge quantities of inventory across hundreds of SKUs, and a giant facility to hold it all. Plus, the model was wasteful as hell—mailing a hundred catalogs for every two or three new customers we'd gain. The wholesale program, on the other hand, required none of this overhead. It required a whole lot less space, cash, and complications, and only five people to run the entire show. Simply put, it was more sustainable.

I was forced to confront the hard fact I didn't want to see: The catalog had to go. Despite my emotional attachment to it and to the dozens of great people who worked for it, despite the fact that it had been both our identity and the spiritual core of the company, the situation was undeniable. The catalog was going down, down, down—and taking everything with it. Action was required to save the business, and

I couldn't afford to spend much time ruminating. We had to move quickly, or reality would make our choices for us, and there'd be nothing left to save.

My intense feelings of loss notwithstanding, we put the catalog on the market in the following days and hired an investment banker to shop us around to other catalogers. We didn't think it would be a hard sell. The idea was that if someone already had the infrastructure, they could slip our operation into their existing systems, thereby making the money we couldn't. We looked at the mailing lists we were renting and approached those companies whose own customers had paid off for us, arguing that our catalog was a sure bet for them.

Almost immediately, we discovered our own inconvenient truth: Everyone we talked to thought we were crazy. No current catalogers wanted Seventh Generation, and no one in the industry thought we'd ever find a buyer. They all said we'd be lucky to find someone to take it off our hands for free. Just like that, we'd come full circle back to Renew America and a catalog nobody wanted.

Then one day out of the blue, somebody did.

Jirka Rysavy was a Czech Olympic track and field star who fled his native country's repressive communist government in 1984. Landing in Boulder, Colorado, he leveraged a minimum-wage print shop job into his own recycled paper business before purchasing an ailing office supply store for $100 and the assumption of $15,000 in debts. A decade later, he'd turned that store into Corporate Express, a billion-dollar business that had cornered the enterprise-level office supply market.

But Rysavy wanted to do something more meaningful and more transformational than putting a stapler on every desk. Having heard Seventh Generation was interested in selling the catalog, he knocked on our door. When I opened it, I found myself scratching my head.

Here was this tall, thin, completely bald and bearded guy inquiring about our catalog in a heavily accented English mumble.

The situation was deeply strange, almost like some sort of *Candid Camera* stunt. Rysavy didn't look, talk, or act like anyone we'd been speaking to about a possible sale. With a background in industrial-scale office supplies and a house in the Rocky Mountain foothills that supposedly had no running water or electricity, he was a thoroughly unlikely suitor.

But he checked out. He had the money, and ample desire—bored and frustrated over the emptiness of his present corporate pursuits. As it had once been for me years earlier, Seventh Generation was exactly the sort of mission he was looking for, and we had a shared spiritual desire to make a positive impact in the world.

There were no negotiations. Rysavy hadn't exactly triggered a bidding war. His was the only offer we'd received in months of increasingly hopeless searching, and it was essentially a "take it or leave it" proposition. We took it, but not just because we had to. The terms were so much better than we had any right to expect that the whole thing seemed positively miraculous.

To this day, I have no idea what Rysavy's calculus was, but the deal was that he would buy the catalog for $2 million (a price far above and beyond what others predicted), and, incredibly, he would pay us $100,000 a year to license the Seventh Generation brand name we were retaining. He'd take the whole staff as part of the bargain, which would keep my co-workers out of the unemployment line, and on top of all that, he'd purchase and resell our own branded products. It was an offer no rational person could refuse.

There was just one problem. Rysavy was hugely worried about word getting out that the CEO of Corporate Express was monkeying around with some hippie-fringe mail order closeout, a revelation he feared might tank the company's stock price. We couldn't breathe a word of the impending sale to anyone, not even our own staff. When he came to Vermont to inspect the company and tour its operations, he arrived after almost everyone had gone home for the day, wearing a clumsy disguise that made him look even weirder than usual. He was accompanied by his business partner, a short, stocky, and prototypically Slavic man named Pavel Bouska. Together with Bouska's bleach-blonde wife, they were a completely unlikely trio of alien tourists who looked and sounded as though they'd gotten lost on the way to the airport after a wild Stowe ski trip. It was difficult to explain to the few employees still in the office at the time just what was going on.

The good news was that they liked what they saw, and we shook hands on a deal. Shortly thereafter, the catalog was officially sold. It was strange to realize that we'd actually shed our very genesis, but not much changed in the sale's immediate aftermath. In those initial months, the change existed almost exclusively on paper. Warehouse operations eventually transitioned to an Ohio facility to address the logistical truth that Vermont was about the worst spot in the country to base a national shipping operation. In January, freed from the need to rent a massive space, we moved what was left to an old woolen mill on the Winooski River just across the Burlington line. Eventually, marketing and customer service functions slowly slipped away to Boulder, leaving just myself and a handful of other people.

Rysavy named his new company Gaiam (an amalgamation of "I am Gaia") and for the next few years, the Seventh Generation catalog continued much as it had with none of our customers necessarily realizing it now had different owners. Over time, it morphed as things like yoga gear and wellness items were added, products which would become

Gaiam's mainstay. A few years after the acquisition, Rysavy and his team realized it was foolish to spend $100K annually to build another company's brand, so they renamed the catalog "Harmony."

The Seventh Generation Catalog era was over but not without teaching us more than what is learned at business school. For starters, stay hyper-focused. Don't try to start a second business on top of a business that is already failing. Don't let the past dictate what you do in the future. It's hard enough to sell consumers a new product that solves problems that they don't even know they have, so forget about trying to change consumer behavior—especially if you are a new, small, and under-resourced company.

But the company was ready to be born again.

CHAPTER TWELVE

The Next Generation

And just like that, things were very, very quiet.

With the catalog sold and the last of its Vermont operations relocated to their new home in the Rocky Mountains, Seventh Generation became a much calmer company. The endless warren of rooms we'd rented no longer held the clamor of dozens of people and the constant creak of ancient wooden floors. Instead, an oddly hollow echo bounced off the old woolen mill's twelve-foot ceilings and lost itself in derelict spaces where loose wires hung down over abandoned desks and a forsaken litter of old phone books, castoff files, and other scattered artifacts of a vanished corporate civilization. It was like a scene out of some strange business-based zombie movie, with the survivors huddled in a corner plotting their next move.

From a staff of sixty, we'd become a virtual startup of five, a number that included me and Anita, my executive assistant-turned-general-office-manager. Jeff Phillips remained to continue working with our manufacturing partners, and Mike Brown was still managing our nascent wholesale program, which now formed the entirety of the company. We'd hired exactly one other person, Tim St. Peter, to work with Mike, and that was it.

It was a surreal moment, and my feelings were completely mixed. On the one hand, it had been very difficult to say goodbye to so many people all at once and face losing the deep sense of community we'd cultivated over the years. Much more than a catalog had gone out the door for good. Though Gaiam had generously offered virtually everyone in the catalog division a job in Colorado, relocation halfway across the country was a viable option for only a scant few. Most of the employees had lost their jobs, which was not a happy event. The disconcerting silence that settled over the office was haunted by the ghosts of these and other memories, which prowled now empty rooms filled with fading shadows of the past.

At the same time, there was also a reinvigorating tide of relief. Seventh Generation was at last resting on some reasonably solid ground, which was an exceptionally welcome change after the last few increasingly desperate years. The nearly fatal expenses of the catalog had been miraculously transformed into a huge new reliable revenue stream, and we'd successfully traded the myriad problems of running a sagging mail order business for the promise of a rapidly expanding wholesale operation. Virtually overnight, we'd become a much more tranquil and focused company. No longer was I running around like crazy to keep everything from collapsing. Now I could be much more deliberate and take the time needed to make decisions without a metaphorical gun to my head. The shift was remarkable.

The change also allowed us to deepen our environmental commitment. Now we had a much smaller portfolio of products, each of which had a much more discernible—and meaningful—set of environmental benefits. We weren't selling t-shirts with endangered species on them anymore. We were selling useful solutions that eliminated toxic chemicals and were legitimately healthier for people and the planet. From the twin perspectives of conscience and transparency, an enormous burden had been lifted. Now everything in our portfolio clearly reflected our company vision and our brand proposition without performing marketing gymnastics.

There were some disadvantages, of course. We were still a public company, and all the bureaucratic headaches born of that position remained. With so few employees, we were all pulling double duty as support staff, answering the phones ourselves, typing our own letters, and making our own airline reservations as we entered a new era of almost continuous travel to court distributors and retailers in distant corners of the country.

The plan was simple: Expand to the West Coast while continuing our steady advances in the East. Then focus on Chicago and the upper Midwest before finally moving into the South. In each area of the country, we needed to find a broker who would help us find a distributor, get into stores, and manage the sales—and that wasn't a relationship you wanted to skimp on. Brokers are a necessary evil unless you're big enough to have your own dedicated sales force. They are expensive and there are only a few good ones in a sea of bad ones. The right broker will supercharge your sales and be worth every penny you spend on them. But choose very carefully. Unlike the catalog days, which were largely reactive, we now had a proactive plan to build these systems on our own terms and at our own speed.

Most importantly, financing was again on our side. In addition to banking the proceeds from the catalog sale, we had a steady stream of wholesale income from Gaiam, which was our largest customer for those first few years. At the same time, both our market share and our sales were growing. In the year after we shed the catalog, revenue was $3.2 million. Three years later, it would stand at $9 million, a 300 percent increase and a dramatic reversal from the days when profitability was an ever-shrinking target. Over the same period, our market share of the overall "green" household products category would expand from almost nothing to an impressive 33 percent. In fact, from 1996 until I finally left the company fourteen years later, we would generate double-digit sales growth every single year.

The key driver continued to be our relationship with Whole Foods. Every time the company opened a new store in a new market, Seventh Generation automatically entered that market, too. Every time Whole Foods bought up a competitor, our products found themselves instantly stocked in yet another chain. It was a prosperous partnership—as they aggressively expanded their empire, we piggy-backed.

And it wasn't just Whole Foods. By the mid-'90s, the entire organic and natural foods industry was taking off for the stratosphere, and it was taking Seventh Generation with it. We were again in the right place at the right time, but unlike the case with the Earth Day 1990 blip, this was not a momentary trick of the consumer light. It was a major long-term trend—rock solid, well-defined, and rapidly growing.

Brands like Cascadian Farm and Nature's Path were rising from local obscurity to the national stage, and consumers were following suit with a growing interest in natural products whose momentum was increasing year over year. The trend was even trickling down to upscale supermarkets, which began to create special natural product sections in their own retail landscapes. As one of the few players in the green household products game—and certainly the only national brand with a full family of products from plastic bags to paper towels to laundry detergent—we were a natural fit (no pun intended). It made a lot of my sales pitches easier to deliver, and without too much trouble, we were able to get our line into chains like Albertsons out west and Star Markets in the Boston area.

As we expanded into more stores and territories, our own internal trend lines became clearer, too. Laundry liquid and bath tissue were our two biggest breadwinners, while products like glass and all-purpose cleaner sat consistently at the bottom of the sales charts. It wasn't a performance issue so much as it was one of simple use patterns—we clean our clothes and visit the powder room a lot more often than we wash our windows and scrub our homes. But the sales disparities between our various products were creating a marketing problem at the retail level, where the dreaded sales-per-foot metric left many stores unhappy about stocking our under-performers. Their preference to offer only our top sellers undercut our attempts to position Seventh Generation as a complete family of household products.

This was one of our key brand propositions: We could help you clean it all safely and more sustainably than the Big Guys—from critical portions of your anatomy to every part of your house. We wanted to reinforce the idea of Seventh Generation as a comprehensive "whole-house" solution. This gave us a lot more exposure in the marketplace because we could put our logo on products all over the place, which helped amortize the costs of building our brand.* That said, the strategy relied on retailers being willing to stock most (if not all) of our products, and it was often a struggle to get them to cooperate, especially in

---

* Another reason was cost—creating a whole new brand for every new product was beyond our means. Money wasn't the primary reason we went with a single corporate brand, but that limitation certainly helped inform our choice.

traditional supermarkets. Still, we never considered walking away from our less successful items.

What we were always considering, however, were ways to expand the cleaning experience of our customers. One obvious way was to increase the size options for our most popular products. We introduced larger boxes of facial tissue and a jumbo bottle of laundry detergent, but we also went smaller, too, with things like baby wipe travel packs, laundry liquid trial-size bottles, and lower-count packages of our paper products that offered a much lower cost than our usual jumbo packs. We also started experimenting with scents by adding a green apple dish liquid to our existing line.

Moves like these helped us gain and maintain market share, but the biggest moves we could make involved developing brand-new products in untapped categories. For every product that succeeded, there were ten that never got off the ground. During the late 1990s, we seriously entertained all kinds of ideas. We thought about making vacuum cleaner bags, non-plastic food wrap, and recycled aluminum foil. We considered air fresheners and disposable cups, sponges and mops, and even furniture and shoe polish. For each of these, we'd identified some kind of technology or material that offered a sustainable difference, and the possibilities were intriguing. In most cases, however, they weren't intriguing enough. But mostly it was a question of return on investment, and in most cases, there wasn't enough ROI to justify the expense of bringing the potential product to market.

Our research on shoe polish, for example, revealed it to be a highly toxic product in a sleepy product category that would never set the retail world on fire. It would have taken us years to develop a safer formula with no guarantee it would ever be a winner. So we scratched it off our list in favor of working on products like an automatic dishwashing detergent gel, a daily-use product category that had greater odds of succeeding. It was a consumer-driven process and provided us with a good lesson: If a product category was huge and growing like gangbusters, that was where we should aim. Better to be a small fish in a big pond than a big fish in a small pond.

In 1997, we introduced the biggest change yet to our product line-up: a new tagline. To my mind, this deceptively simple shift still represents the single most important repositioning Seventh Generation has ever done. Gone was "Products for a Healthy Planet," the line that had graced each product label and catalog cover. In its place was "Safer for You and the Environment," a statement that focused on what's better for you. Our hunch was that the safety of your health and the health of your family was a much stronger selling point than saving the whales.

The switch was not one we made lightly. Taglines are serious business. They are a huge part of a brand's identity, and changes in brand identity can confuse consumers and disrupt the bottom line. A tagline's impact and value also tend to accrue over time, an investment no business wants to casually cast aside in favor of a replacement whose success is far from guaranteed. Change is hard—and for good reason.

In this case, change was also hard for me personally. We'd spent nearly ten years focused on providing products for a healthy planet, and it was difficult to let go of that heritage. Also, it was disheartening to acknowledge that protecting the environment was not a strong enough motivator for most consumers to purchase our products—a more self-centered approach was apparently required.

But the change was also necessary. Consumer research showed our products' health proposition to be a far more powerful draw than any environmental benefits they provided. This is not to say that our customers no longer cared about a healthy planet. They did. But these concerns were secondary to those they had about protecting their health and keeping their homes and families safe. This was the message that was resonating in the marketplace, especially in the natural foods industry.

Increasing consumer sophistication and growing awareness about things like pesticide-free food and chemical exposure-induced cancers had positioned Seventh Generation in the right place at the right time. But as our final analysis literally showed, consumers weren't flocking to our brand for the privilege of keeping Earth's air and water clean. They were using our products primarily because they were better for their own health and safety. Everything else was just a happy side benefit.

The new tagline reflected this essential idea without rejecting our previous call to protect the planet. It contained both our promise and our purpose, and communicated the entire Seventh Generation argument in just six clear and impactful words. I could live with it. The idea of "safer for you" became the context for virtually everything we did from there on out.

There was just one notable fly in the "safer for you" ointment: we had to explain why. Seventh Generation products were indeed safer and healthier to use. They were solving some serious problems, yet these were problems that consumers frequently didn't know existed, despite their growing environmental sophistication. Safer, yes. But safer why? Safer how? What was the story behind the tagline and the various products it supported? These were essential questions our marketing had to answer if we were going to convince consumers to make the switch.

Indoor air quality, for example, was an enormous issue that our products directly and substantially addressed, but most consumers had absolutely no idea it was a problem that they needed to address. They were completely unaware that mainstream, big-brand spray cleaners and scented soaps were also filling the atmosphere inside their homes with often hazardous VOCS. EPA research in the early '90s had shown that the use of such products was the key reason indoor air in the average home was four to five times more polluted than the air just outside its walls. This was a staggering finding.

Our marketing mission became a drive to get the word out so people understood and considered what they put around their bodies. Given the dangers and their consequences, they'd be wise to scrutinize household products the same way they scrutinized food and personal care. This was an innate challenge because the market research showed how people were beginning to understand that they should eat organics to avoid pesticides and maybe choose an aluminum-free deodorant, but they were a long way from realizing that they should use natural cleaners to stay clear of VOCs.

Unlike the case with most consumer product companies, where the concepts behind a given brand are clear, we had a more complicated proposition to explain. Before we could even present the benefits of using our stuff, we first had to explain the problem they addressed, and how we were meeting the challenge. As you can imagine, this makes for a much longer and more complex sales process. Messaging all this was a long, tricky way from ads that could simply say "works harder so you don't have to."

There were two key connections we had to make in consumers' minds. One was between toxic household products and acute and often episodic health problems like asthma and allergies. On this point, the evidence was pretty well-established.

But the connection between the toxic synthetic chemicals in household products and more long-term conditions like cancer, chronic disease, and other ailments was far more challenging to explain. In these cases, cause and effect were separated by what could be years or even decades—thus, scientifically proving the link to consumers in an ad campaign was not easy.

We were engaged in a dual business. One side involved selling unconventional household products. The other needed to educate the public about the dangers of their traditional counterparts, a task that fell very nicely in line with the kind of company we wanted to be. In effect, our marketing efforts became more of a teaching program. We printed rolls of toilet tissue containing "facts about chlorine that will scare the crap out of you" and refrigerator magnets with "five simple steps to a healthy home." I was proud that we were taking such a bold stance about our industry and its products. We were one of the original disruptors, and that disruption brought a badly needed ethical element to the conversation that had been missing.

We were pioneers in other ways, too. As the 1990s drew to a close, we became the first public company in Vermont history to go private.

The impetus was obvious: We were spending hundreds of thousands of dollars on regulatory filings and legal and accounting fees, and we were getting absolutely nothing for it. Our stock was trading at a dreadful 40¢ a share (or thereabouts), yet we calculated the value of the company to be closer to $2 per share. The stock market wasn't giving us any credit for the progress we were making in the wholesale business. Still, it was an uncommon move to put the company into the hands of a much smaller pool of private investors. But it was a move I felt strongly about, since I believed private investors would more readily appreciate what we were doing.

As deals go, this one was relatively simple. First, we found a small handful of private investors willing to purchase our shares at $1.75 each. We used those investment funds to repurchase all the stock in the public market for 76¢ a piece, a price current shareholders were more than happy to receive.

Though it confused the hell out of Vermont state regulators who had never dealt with anything like this before, the process of going private was a quick and uneventful success. My only regret, and one I will forever feel badly about, was all the people who bought our stock at $5 and sold us for 76¢. On the plus side, the private stock was newly valued at $1.75 per share and within five years was worth over $22 per share, which much better reflected the company's impressive growth rates and overall achievements.

Around this same time, we did another private placement that netted an additional $5 million in new funding. But between the process of going private and raising this most recent round of funding, we found that the nature of our investor group had changed dramatically. Thanks to the influence of a board member who had been a friend since grade school, these most recent investors (many of whom would ultimately fire me) were not friends and family, but professional investors with long histories in venture capital, private equity, and hedge fund management. While they were attracted by our mission, what convinced them to invest was our rapid growth and the flashing dollar signs they saw when contemplating an eventual sale of the company.

Still, they would deliver a cash infusion that would give us the breathing room necessary to expand in many areas, from distribution to product development. Also, according to our 1999 business plan, the boost would "provide additional working capital, improve the balance sheet, make acquisitions and build awareness and invest in additional consumer marketing."

In 1999, we also marked Seventh Generation's ten-year anniversary, an event that found us "celebrating ten years of breaking the toxic cycle" with a $10 coupon book and a retailer promotion that rewarded retailer endcap displays with a contest to win a trip to the Galapagos Islands. It was a big milestone—one that I hadn't always been sure we'd ever see. In my mind, it had been a pretty damn painful ten years. While we'd had our brief upsurge in 1990, most of the company's history thus far had been wracked by stubborn money troubles and crisis management that had forced us into a series of last-ditch solutions. There had been a terrible divorce between Alan and myself, and a lot of heartache, and every high had been met by more than a few lows. For the most part, it had not been pretty.

I've come to see that I spent those ten years too obsessed with growth. When we were growing, I felt we were doing great. When we weren't growing, everything sucked. Except that it didn't. Even in the darkest times, even when our bottom line was cratering, we still had our unique culture and the people who created it. We had our mission and our dedication to it. We were aways trying as hard as we could, and we were making a difference—a difference in the way people cared for their homes and families, a difference that demonstrated the kinds of alternative companies that were possible, a difference that illustrated the kinds of values capitalism could embrace. Such things can't be measured strictly by numbers. Their true value is inestimable.

Although it would take a good many years more for me to realize it, this initial era of the company's life taught me that growth is not the end all, be all. Growth is not sacred. It's not even all it's cracked up to be because growth begets its own series of problems—more stuff, more garbage, more waste, and that's never environmentally responsible. Growth is addictive, and given all my experiences with my brother, I should have perhaps been more open to other ways of thinking. But wisdom is a function of time.

I also felt that despite Seventh Generation's new success in the wholesale business, we had yet to successfully tackle the social dimensions of our business. For me, this was a big issue. I wanted to expand our impacts beyond the environmental and into the social realm through things like fair trade products and addressing equity problems in the corporate world. Yet as we entered our second decade, I continued to draw big blanks when it came to expanding this other essential side of our mission.

And I was concerned by the fact that we hadn't yet cracked the code. The notion of what it meant to be a responsible business was starting to mature. We had spent our first ten years defining ourselves through our products, but that was not enough. I wanted Seventh Generation to root itself in a much deeper and wider set of concerns, to become the model for all that responsible business could achieve. I wanted us to define ourselves not by the business we were in but by the way we conducted that business. I wanted us to create a template anyone could use, whether they made natural cleaners or ran an accounting firm. That's a much different kind of work, one more focused on purpose, culture, and systems than products and services.

But we also kept learning how to do the business better and better. We were getting clearer on product positioning, defining tangible consumer benefits, and how to become excellent educators—a skill that was grounded way back at the Skills Exchange. Also, we were learning there were better ways to measure success than just the sales numbers.

This was also the beginning of a new chapter for the company's growth and evolution that took a more systems-based, wholistic view of our responsibility and opportunity to impact the world. This was the mission I saw for the next decade, one that grew to guide me for the rest of my life. And it was time to get moving on it.

CHAPTER THIRTEEN

Bigger & Better

It's hard to say which releases more cortisol: bailing water like crazy to keep a sinking company afloat or rowing like mad to keep a thriving company growing at full speed. Both scenarios will keep you up at night. Both leave you a little crispy around the edges. And each one comes with its own set of paralyzing fears—it's as frightening to think you may be about to hit bottom as it is to realize that riding ever higher only means farther to fall. Still, there was little question which operating conditions were preferable. To paraphrase the old axiom, we were rich and we'd been poor. Rich was better.

Of course, the bigger you grow, the harder it is to keep growing, but I didn't have much time to dwell on that potential pitfall, and at the moment I didn't need to. I had all kinds of accelerants at my disposal to fuel the company's growth.

The first was to take our distribution into new regions of the country, an obvious strategy that was responsible for most of our personnel gains. While Seventh Generation products were readily available now on both coasts, there were still plenty of regions in the middle of the country to tap, and we were busy setting up sales teams, broker deals, and distribution partnerships to get there as quickly as possible.

Other expansions were underway as well. The most important was our push into traditional grocery stores. Big chain grocers had once been impossible territory—but now they were more aware of the need to compete with natural food stores. Stocking our products was a quick and easy way to start. Resistance to our sales calls had been replaced by invitations to talk, and we could not have been happier about our reversal of supermarket fortune. In the early 2000s, the ratio of conventional grocery stores to natural food stores was 10:1, and I knew the ultimate sustainability of the company rested on "mainstreaming" our market position out of that latter niche and onto the much deeper shelves of regular food retailers, where the vast majority of the country shopped.

In addition to seeking more mainstream sales platforms, we also sought more products. As a result, the early 2000s were probably the craziest product development period yet. We were extending product lines, tweaking long-time formulas, and getting into some serious weeds, going so far as to retool the scoop that came with our laundry powder with 100 percent post-consumer recycled plastic. There were all kinds of new SKUs and new problems to match. Our new 150-oz. laundry liquid bottles weren't holding their labels. Our soft-pack baby wipes had mold. Our automatic dishwasher gel was over-sudsing. A constant stream of issues bubbled up and required immediate attention. At the same time, we were continually heading into uncharted territory with the development and launch of whole new families of products, such as our Sensitive Care and Baby Care lines, any one of which could have (and maybe should have) preoccupied us full time.

Much of my CEO time was spent pushing hard for these and other projects, which was making everyone involved at least mildly crazy. Where a company like P&G would spend three years creating and testing a new product, we were going from idea to introduction in three to six months, a blinding speed that didn't leave any room for error. Jeff Phillips was constantly urging me to slow down, but no matter what the product was, I would always insist it needed to be done yesterday. Whether it was out of a fear of returning to the bad old days or that I was high on the drug of growth, my foot was staying on the gas, damn the brakes, and full speed ahead. That was okay when what we were doing was easy. But most of it wasn't.

Our diapers were proof enough. On a trip to Amsterdam, I'd found them in a natural food store—beige-colored disposables made with chlorine-free, unbleached pulp—and I was absolutely ecstatic. Suddenly, I held in my hands the holy grail, a product we'd been trying desperately to develop with zero success. It was a legitimate heaven-sent miracle, and I was experiencing the environmental merchandising equivalent of a religious experience. We were going to sell the absolute hell out of these—immediately.

Others were not as enthusiastic. There were all kinds of doubts when I brought the samples home and plunked them down triumphantly in the conference room.

"It's too complicated," said the product development gang, pointing to currency issues and import challenges. To be fair, they had a point. The manufacturer was in Germany, and we'd never worked with an overseas supplier before.

But that was the least of it. The diapers were also brown and quite significantly so, a fairly radical aesthetic statement that made them a non-starter for our sales and marketing teams.

"We can't sell a diaper that looks like it's already been used," they said.

Meanwhile, I couldn't see any logistical hurdles we couldn't overcome. And that dreaded beige? That was the Big Differentiator, the very thing that declared these diapers were demonstrably unbleached. It was a beauty mark, not a wart.

"There's no way we're not doing this," I asserted.

And we did. The path, as had been warned, was not entirely free of quicksand. When our initial orders were late in arriving, we had to airlift them to the States, which was a bit over the top where both cost and effort were concerned. When that situation stabilized, we started shipping on actual ships, which involved a whole other operational learning curve. There were sizing issues, too—the German system didn't quite line up with the one American mothers and fathers were used to, causing confusion at the retail level. We'd also agreed to pay for our purchases in euros but had failed to understand the intricacies of the currency markets, which screwed us when the dollar weakened. The diapers were great, but that first year, they cost us much more than they should have. It wasn't pretty.

But that shade of brown? Gorgeous! The diapers were a screaming success from day one, and their supposed scandalous appearance had everything to do with it. The thin brown hint of waistband that would appear whenever they'd ride up a little high quickly became a badge of honor for green moms. The product was a major blockbuster, laying the foundation for our appeal to the new mothers, who eventually became Seventh Generation's most important buyer class. All the cool babies had brown diapers. They instantly boosted the company's sales by a full third and became the kind of huge growth driver that is the stuff of CEO dreams. Between 2000 and 2005, the value of our stock shot up five-fold and the bottoms of America's babies had everything to do with it.

Of course not every idea we had was as bright. Seventh Generation light bulbs, for example, didn't exactly light up the marketplace, and were soon pulled from our line-up. The compact fluorescent technology they relied on proved too expensive—the bulbs were a hefty $20 apiece. However, when you factored in their lower power bills and ten-year lifespan, the bulbs were actually a good deal with some great environmental and financial advantages.*

But once again, this story exceeded the limits of consumer attention spans. Despite our best attempts to demonstrate otherwise, all shoppers ever saw was a weird-looking light bulb that cost an arm and a leg. Our efforts to communicate the larger, more relevant messaging about total life cycle savings were not successful, and as a result the product wasn't either.

From my perspective, however, the issue was simpler than that: A given product's story either did or did not resonate with consumers, and the failure to create this sort of emotional connection could be a death knell. Our diapers sold well in no small part because they had a clear and simple story with a strong emotional component: Chlorine-free is safer for your baby. Full stop. Our light bulbs' tale was a lot muddier, and you saw it in the sales results.

There were other complicating factors, too. In addition to a product's overall story, there were stories we wanted to tell about sourcing and process, about the packaging and ingredients used, and often we had to pick and choose which stories to share. All too often, that process was a complete roll of the dice. We never really knew which product story would capture imaginations. Sometimes we'd

---

* The mercury the bulbs held remained a problem, but recycling programs were coming online around the country as compact fluorescent bulbs caught on, so the disposal conundrum wasn't as intractable as it seemed.

strike gold. Sometimes we'd waste a lot of gold chasing marketing that just didn't move the needle.

For example, in the early 2000s, one of our product development wizards, Reed Doyle, discovered a woman who was developing fragrances based on the art of aromatherapy, which sounded like a great idea. Combining nontoxic cleaning products with the healing powers of natural scents was unique and very much on brand, so off we went. We spent months selecting the right essential oil combinations to use, and when it came time to purchase their ingredients, we refused to buy them from big manufacturers. Instead, we sought out farms that would grow, process, and sell oils to us directly. It was by far the more difficult path to take, but it gave the farmers a much better fair-trade type of deal, and provided us with a fantastic product story. Behind every scent, there was a healing factor and at least one farm, which gave us many stories we believed our consumers would be interested in.

They were not. It turned out to be more information than they needed—or wanted. Despite our best efforts to stir up excitement, we got very little mileage out of exploring our fragrances. I was disappointed but not too surprised. We were in the business of storytelling, but it had long since become clear that when it came to explaining both the physical facts and philosophical intent behind our company and its products, there were no guarantees what would strike a customer chord. Every time we thought we knew, a "dud" like our aromatherapy scents would come along to highlight our hubris.

As for the scents themselves, they proved both complicated and expensive to obtain on a regular basis. Given the fact that few seemed to care, we gradually drifted away from our farm-based approach and began sourcing them on the open market, where supplies were more reliable and invited far fewer headaches.

It wasn't like we had nothing else to do. For one thing, we'd outgrown our offices at the Chace woolen mill and found new quarters on the Burlington waterfront. Shortly after the move, we launched a complete brand redesign that introduced new labels, a refreshed logo, a new website, and other graphic elements. Our intent was to both modernize the brand and better reflect its journey to where environmental sustainability intersected with human health and social concerns. We'd learned a lot about our consumers since the shift to wholesale, and we wanted our look and vibe to reflect the hard-won knowledge that ours was a brand most likely to be adopted by LOHAS (Lifestyles of Health and Sustainability) consumers versus mainstream shoppers. Instead of trying to attract everybody, we wanted to refocus the Seventh Generation brand to communicate more effectively with this target audience.

In 2002, all of these efforts—from new products to new packaging—were rewarded with the single most momentous occasion in the company's history. After fourteen straight years of losing money, Seventh Generation finally made some. At long last we had arrived at that glorious place in the corporate sun where black ink outshines the red. In just the last three years, we'd doubled our gross sales to become the leading brand of green household products in the United States. In our native ecosystem of natural food stores, we led every category in which we competed with a 35 percent market share of all cleaning products sold, a 61 percent share of paper products, and 42 percent of the diaper segment. Sales in 2004 were projected to hit $40 million, with growth to $200 million expected by the end of the decade.

Our incredible rise from the near-death depths of catalog bankruptcy to king of the natural products hill had four factors behind it:

First and most importantly, we had been laser-focused on improving product quality. In the beginning, we were essentially putting whatever off-the-rack natural formulas we could find into bottles and hoping for the best. The result was products that didn't always live up to their promises, littering our path with performance issues and consumer complaints. But we had listened to those customers and held strong to our 90-percent-as-good-as-the-leading-brand ideal. We'd concentrated on improving our existing products, and after ten years of hair loss and mad-science experimentation, we had created a full line of household goods that worked just about as well as our conventional competitors.

Second, we'd seriously embraced our role as a storyteller and had leveraged the full potential of the then relatively new internet. We had leaned all the way into digital media—such as it was back then—to communicate our values, explain our products, and brand our company. We were using everything from email newsletters to interactive web pages to foster dialogues with our customers that let us mutually explore each other's worlds.

Lastly, we'd benefited from being in the right place at the right time to ride two conjoined trends all the way to the bank. After more than a few false starts, the LOHAS consumer class had finally arrived on the scene for good, and they were hungry for products that addressed their environmental and personal health concerns. This quest was fueling a huge retailer demand for product, product, and more product, and that need had allowed us to expand our reach by a series of nearly geometric progressions.

There was also a secret fourth ingredient in our secret sauce. And his name was Jeff Phillips. For nearly ten years, Jeff had relentlessly labored to convince me that making money was not an evil thing,*

---

* Somewhere in his attic, Jeff probably still has the copy of an article someone sent to him in which I affirmed my epiphany about how much better life would be once we started making money. He kept it close by during all those unprofitable years and would produce it whenever I'd go off-mission and start throwing grit into the Seventh Generation gears.

all while working overtime to create and source new products and making the refinements that would finally land us on the right side of the profit/loss equation. He had put up with my often crazy demands and dedicated himself to our company at great personal expense. He knew much about the industry that I didn't, and he brought tremendous amounts of acumen and energy to our struggle year in and year out. If we had a hall of fame, he'd get his own wing, because Seventh Generation would never have become profitable without him. As it was, Jeff received something that was symbolically even better. Though company-sponsored massages remained an employee perk, he had forsworn them until we achieved profitability. Now, at last, he allowed himself a well-deserved session on the table.

It was an amazing turning point. I felt liberated in a way like never before. Finally, we were making money and had achieved financial stability. To Jeff's endless frustration, that was something that I'd undervalued for a long time. Now we had a few extra dollars in the bank, and it felt like a new dawn—both for the company and for my approach. Now I realized that profits were something worth trying to engineer, and I had to admit: maybe that quest should be the priority once in a while.

Something else was hiding in those dollars as well. Our profitability gave sudden validity to the environmental product proposition and the entire notion of corporate responsibility itself. It defied the vast multitudes of naysayers who been flatly declaring for years that making money and creating environmental change were mutually exclusive propositions. A business could be a "do gooder" or make lots of money—you couldn't do both. It just wasn't that kind of world. Except now we had. Proving their thinking wrong was deeply satisfying. We also became a wonderful model of a company that set out to change the world while at the same time creating outstanding value for shareholders.

Before this point, all we'd been able to say to critics was that our business model was simply the right thing to do. Now we could also say it's the way to grow faster and make more money. Jobs versus the environment, sustainability versus profitability—these are false choices. You can protect ecology and the economy at the same time. You can be responsible and still reap financial rewards. We'd done it.*

Just as importantly, we'd done it without externalizing too many of our costs and impacts. Unlike so many companies and industries, our business success did not create the negative external conditions that our competitors did. We didn't need to willfully ignore those unhappy effects in order to achieve positive financial results, and I think this aspect of our growth was possibly our greatest achievement of all. At Seventh Generation, making money didn't depend on making a mess for somebody else to clean up. We were focused on solving problems, not creating new ones.

The issue of externalized costs remains one of the biggest problems with conventional economics. Too often, companies' rapacious pursuit of the sacred dollar generates disturbing side effects for which they refuse to take any responsibility lest the costs of doing so eat into their bottom lines. It's much easier and more cost-effective to let governments and citizens deal with whatever social or environmental horrors they've unleashed in the course of doing business "as usual."

Consider, for example, the petrochemical manufacturers that line Louisiana's infamous Cancer Alley. Every day, the processes that produce their profits dump alarming amounts of insanely toxic pollution into the air, soil, and water for hundreds and hundreds of square miles

---

* This refrain would echo through my professional life for the next decade, and was one I proudly touted. Unfortunately, I later discovered that our self-perceived success had its limitations, which strongly suggested that things weren't quite as clear-cut as I'd thought.

in every direction. While anemic regulations attempt to prevent at least some of this chemical carnage, much of it is simply released into the environment, and governments, communities, and citizens are left to deal with the consequences—from increased disease (local cancer rates some fifty times the national average) to wrecked water supplies (levels of benzene, toluene, ethylbenzene, and xylene 2,400 percent higher than EPA "safe" levels). The companies that cause these problems aren't paying those hospital bills or cleaning those wells because that would subtract from their returns. But imagine if they had to. You can bet that pollution would vanish in a heartbeat.[*]

Instead it's just released from all corporate responsibility into the environment. The companies involved save money and boost their profits while the rest of us deal with repairing the ruin. Ecosystems are fouled and employees are left homeless or on food stamps because they're not paid a living wage.

Meanwhile, Seventh Generation was committed to trying to avoid sacrificing the public good to create its own private wealth. Also, our success didn't depend on all the subsidies and tax breaks so many environmentally unsustainable companies and industries receive. In fact, we were profitable despite such factors.

For example, cleaners made from petrochemicals were (and are) typically cheaper than cleaners made with natural ingredients. Yet why is this? Shouldn't products made from simple and relatively unprocessed materials found in nature be less expensive to produce and purchase

---

[*] This is why society absolutely must put a hefty price on carbon emissions and demand that polluters start paying via heavy tax burdens and other intentionally onerous mechanisms. If ruining the atmosphere started costing companies serious money, they'd immediately pull out all the stops to find a cleaner, more sustainable way to do business. The marketplace is capable of policing itself and doing the right thing but typically requires some motivating influence (either pain or profit) whose levels are directly proportional to the amount of common good achieved.

than those made from synthetic substances derived from fossil fuels? Which, by the way, must be located, extracted from the earth, transported, refined, and heavily processed into something new? In most cases, they should be!

Yet they're not, because the fossil fuel industry receives billions of annual dollars in financial aid from the federal government in the form of benefits like exploration and drilling subsidies, tax breaks, and infrastructure assistance. The ingredients in Seventh Generation's household cleaners received none of this absurd largesse. And yet our products made money anyway, and in the process became a model in free market economics our competitors had insisted couldn't really exist.

This was the role Seventh Generation had been designed to play. We were an experiment exploring and demonstrating alternative ways to do business. It's tough to be a pioneer, blazing new trails. Not only in the products you sell but also in the way you do business. It requires a clear sense of purpose, lots of courage, and a commitment to never giving up no matter how hard it gets. Good thing these are all traits that will never go out of style in business and in life.

CHAPTER FOURTEEN

Evolving

An analogy that I've used in the past is that companies can be a bit like onions. As the company grows, more layers develop. Most companies put all the good stuff about themselves on the outer layers where it's easiest to see, hiding the less pleasant aspects deep inside where they hope no one will look. We did the opposite. We put our authentic self—the good, the bad, and the ugly—on the outside. Meanwhile, we left many of our proudest moments deep inside, so that those who were interested in peeling back the layers would discover more and more things to feel good about.

Championed by my wife Sheila, we finally took the long overdue plunge into feminine care in 2004. We did so by purchasing our first external brand, a small Texas-based company called Organic Essentials that sold cotton products, from swabs to sanitary pads, largely under the radar in natural food stores. The company worked with regional cotton growers to source its fiber and had a turn-key line of tampons and pads that we agreed to purchase.

I wasn't entirely comfortable with the idea. Only five years earlier, we'd tried feminine care and had abandoned our attempts. The products had received more complaints than any other product and hadn't exactly been a blockbuster. On the other hand, feminine care was a potentially huge category for us, one with diaper-level potential.

These were the thoughts running through my head as I sat in my living room with LaRhea Pepper and her husband. An organic cotton farmer and the founder of Organic Essentials, LaRhea was explaining to me that the company was essentially bankrupt. If I didn't take their feminine care line, both the business and her farm were toast. In a strange twist of historical irony, Seventh Generation was now their last-chance savior, the only hope of rescuing her enterprise from certain death. It was not the best reason for such a big purchase, and certainly the fact that they had given organic tampons a go and hadn't quite succeeded gave me pause.

Though it left an uncomfortable lump in my throat, I swallowed my hesitation, and the deal went through, largely thanks to the encouragement of my wife, Sheila.* Suddenly we had our own line of feminine care products—for the most part, all we had to do was put our label on their packaging. But now the big question: How do we introduce them to the world in a way that makes a big impression?

We came up with what we thought was a novel way to give them wings. We'd apply the idea of radical transparency to both menstruation itself and the products involved, a basic women's health subject that for too long had been taboo to talk about. Ours would be the opposite approach—we'd demystify sexual wellness by creating a blog where consumers could talk openly and honestly about their periods, and we could deliver information about why chlorine and pesticide-free feminine care products were essential to women's health.

---

* Sheila was quite rightfully obsessed with the notion of avoiding the carcinogenic tampons most women were inserting into their bodies and thoroughly committed to this new venture's success. The product line went on to become part of her legacy at the company.

The project was christened Tampontification, and it launched with a website that also sought to start a concurrent conversation about homelessness. After learning a little about both issues, consumers could drag a box of tampons that appeared on the screen over to a housing icon and with a simple click "drop" it into their local women's shelter, which would trigger a real-world donation and address a critical need that often went unmet.

At first there was plenty of suspicion. It seemed too easy to be true, and it was hard to persuade people that, yes, we really were making an actual donation with every click. Once we convinced everyone of the program's veracity, it took off like a badly spooked horse. In almost no time at all, we had over 700,000 responses. People kept clicking and dropping with wild abandon, and the concept almost immediately proved way too successful.

There were so many pads and tampons being given away that the shelters didn't know what to do with them all. They started calling and asking us to stop. Which we were happy to do because we were hemorrhaging money fulfilling our obligations. Soon thereafter, facing a mountain of donations nobody wanted anymore, we pulled the plug on Tampontification and left our feminine care line alone to become a quieter success.

But now that our work had produced some meaningful progress of the only type that really matters in the corporate sphere (i.e., profit), our approach needed to be codified. We needed a guide for building on that success as we ventured further and further into uncharted realms where we could easily lose our way. So it was that we embarked on a project that I've long considered among the most important work Seventh Generation has ever done, an updated progression of mission, vision, and operating principles statements that sought to lay down our own corporate ground rules.

Though we'd had a purpose that was larger than ourselves since our inception, we'd been seeking our way in the wilderness with only a vague philosophical light to guide us. That was fine when there were just a few of us. It's easy to get the whole company on board when you can count all its employees on one hand. But now the company was growing exponentially, and our basic principles needed to be articulated more clearly to ensure that everyone was on the same page.

There was also an issue of leadership. At a time when everyone was beginning to discuss what it meant to be a responsible business,* I felt Seventh Generation should be the point person in that process and lay out the strongest possible terms for corporate social responsibility (CSR).

The effort was open-ended. As the company evolved, the scope of "responsibility" widened, and so did its ethical underpinnings. The result was not a single document set in stone, but a series of iterations, each built on those that had come before. The process wasn't difficult, but it wasn't simple either. There was no real roadmap for what we were trying to do. We couldn't just buy a textbook or hire a consultant to walk us through it. We had to figure out both process and end product ourselves, which was part of the fun but also part of the challenge.

There was no end to the places to which our imaginations would run. I'd constantly look around the company and see nothing but areas for improvement or innovation. This would lead to more work, more rumination, and the need to reflect on both our mission and vision statements. And I wasn't the only one tasked with the job. Everyone at the company had a seat at the development table, which put a lot of cooks in the kitchen.

---

* My book *The Responsibility Revolution* offers a more thorough examination of how corporate responsibility should manifest itself and how companies are breaking the boundaries of convention.

This itself was an innovation. When companies do this kind of high-level work, if they do it at all, they typically restrict it to the C-suite, which issues the resulting precepts from on high. I wanted us to take a more wholistic and organic approach and have our mission, vision, and operating principles statements "trickle up" from the people who were tasked with bringing them to life. We needed to slice through the whole onion, not just the skin.

With that in mind, we created three company-wide committees to monitor our activities, document the results, look for places we could improve, and expand our mission/vision work to embrace any new directions we found:

- The Green/Community Involvement Team ensured that we as a company exhibited "green" behaviors internally; developed resources to help employees make more conscious choices in their lives; influenced and supported our brokers, vendors, and distributors in adopting green business practices; and explored ways to contribute to community life.

- The Values & Operating Principles Committee integrated our values and operating principles into every aspect of our business and workplace community, and provided guidance for both employees and the company to operate authentically.

- The Work/Life Balance Committee focused on work/life balance issues within the company and determined ways to support employees in making choices that met their needs in both areas.

Each committee was tasked with establishing specific annual goals and meeting every month to coordinate activities and track progress. In addition to this work, every employee also developed an individual annual plan to set personal goals that would support Seventh

Generation's mission/vision as well as their own personal and professional objectives.

To keep everyone focused on this work, we based up to 25 percent of an employee's potential bonus on the realization of these objectives. It started the moment you were hired. As a new employee, your first two days at the company would be spent in training workshops that covered not just our company's history, structure, positioning, industry, and markets, but the health and environmental issues our products addressed, our mission and vision, and our values and operating principles.

Here's an example of our evolving "Values & Operating Principles." Dating from 2004, it's the third and most highly evolved version of the early 2000s era.

SEVENTH GENERATION VALUES & OPERATING PRINCIPLES

TRUST IN OUR BRAND	To provide authentic, high-quality products that build trust in our brand and in our mission.
WOW SERVICE	To provide service that delights those we serve.
SOCIAL AND ENVIRONMENTAL RESPONSIBILITY	We take responsibility for our imprint on the planet and in our communities, while producing financial results that sustain our business.
PERSONAL GROWTH AND FULFILLMENT	We are committed to personal and professional growth and fulfillment.
OUR COMMUNITY	To create a workplace community that embraces respect, dignity, trust, honest communication, open minds and hearts, fun and playfulness, and a spirit of willing participation.
LEADERSHIP	To inspire, innovate, and be a force for change in the industries, markets, and communities we serve.
LEADERSHIP, INSPIRATION, AND POSITIVE CHANGE	A company with the authority to lead, the creativity to inspire, and the will to foster positive social and environmental change.
MAKE THE WORLD A BETTER PLACE	A community in which individuals possess the resources, knowledge, courage, and commitment to make the world a better place.
SUSTAINABILITY, JUSTICE, AND COMPASSION	A society whose guiding principles include: environmental sustainability, social justice, and compassion for all living creatures.
AN EARTH RESTORED	An Earth that is restored, protected, and cherished for this generation and those to come.

TRUST & AUTHENTICITY	We are committed to becoming the world's most trusted brand of authentic, safe, and environmentally responsible products for a healthy home.
SERVICE & INSPIRATION	We are dedicated to setting the standard for superior service and to providing our customers with the resources and inspiration they need to make informed, responsible decisions.
BALANCE	We strive to achieve balance between the fiscal, social, and environmental responsibility of our company.
AN EXCEPTIONAL WORKPLACE COMMUNITY	We are committed to creating an exceptional workplace community, one that inspires honesty and trust, respect and compassion, and a spirited sense of play. A community that provides opportunities for growth and the freedom to realize our full potential.
COMMUNITY PARTICIPATION	We will fully participate in and provide leadership to each community of which we are a part.

All of this work was an attempt to inject the company's DNA into everybody's veins so that the entire staff—even the newbies—was always working cohesively from the same perspective. It was a way to keep moving forward as quickly as possible without losing our focus on what mattered most. Everyone needed to be instinctual about how they approached the choices that had to be made because the decisions never stopped coming.

In 2003, we attempted to qualify everything with our first CSR report. At the time, CSRs were leading-edge, which is right where I wanted Seventh Generation to be. But within the company, the initial response to the idea was not what I'd expected and proved highly controversial.

This was largely my own fault. I was determined that our report would not be a feel-good whitewash but an exercise in radical transparency. Not a naked PR exercise wrapped in a warm and fuzzy cloak but a reality check. Unfortunately, I sold the idea from an extreme position. I announced to the staff that our CSR report would be one that "highlights everything that is wrong with the products we sell along with all the other things that are wrong with the company."

That framing did not go over well. My newfound passion for an in-depth discussion of our failures elicited two types of general reaction from the management team: soul-crushing anxiety and heart-stopping terror.

In an era where creating a CSR report of any kind was still a relatively bold act, everyone was sure that a meditation on our faults and shortcomings would be used by our competitors to our disadvantage. We spent months talking it all over before I finally convinced everyone that a genuinely open and honest accounting of our work—even one that was somewhat brutal—was exactly what we should be doing.

To accomplish this, I insisted on using a set of guidelines and requirements known as the Global Reporting Initiative (GRI), which had been developed in the late '90s by the Coalition for Environmentally Responsible Economies (Ceres), the Tellus Institute, and the United Nations Environment Programme. This was a radical move—the GRI guidelines had been designed for and heretofore exclusively used by large public enterprise-level companies. We'd be the first private company to adopt them—and the smallest by far—which made it a somewhat square-peg-round-hole situation. We struggled to find the resources necessary to assemble the mountains of data they demanded and found ourselves highly challenged to answer the questions concerning our supply chain and other deep-level operational facets.

Yet this depth represented exactly what I felt we should be examining and addressing. The CSR report was not just about informing the public, but about enlightening our staff and guiding our agenda. The effort generated important new transparency pressures and forced us to think about everything—including what else we needed to be thinking about.

This made our lawyers crazy. "Why are you talking about all this stuff?" they yelled. "You're risking a galaxy of lawsuits!"

They saw the whole thing as one big billboard for our numerous and often undisclosed deficiencies, and they were incredibly nervous—a feeling to which the management team could definitely relate.

"Good," I said. "This should be making us nervous because that will spur us to improve and innovate. We don't want to live with products and systems that are not all they're cracked up to be. We want to be legitimately good. Rampant anxiety about how far we have or haven't come can only help."

But it wasn't all moaning and wailing and gnashing of teeth. Mixed in with everybody's trepidation was also a fairly big dollop of pride. We'd managed to capture all of our efforts in one place and produce a report we were not afraid for the world to see, and we said as much in its introduction:

> *While we are tremendously proud of what we have accomplished, some of our products are not as authentic to our environmental mission as we would like them to be. We sometimes have to make trade-offs between environmental benefits, product performance, and product cost. We have prepared a critique of our own products to deepen understanding around some of the choices and trade-offs we have made relative to specific product ingredients. It may seem a bit unusual that we've chosen to critique our own products, but we believe that a key part of being a socially responsible business is transparency—and that means sharing what's really going on, not just what we'd like people to see.*

As anticipated, our adversaries immediately tried to twist our transparency to their own advantage. One enterprising salesman from a competitor actually photocopied all of the negative things we said about our products and shared them with one of our bigger buyers in an attempt to use our own words to sabotage the account.

He essentially said, "Look, I know you love Seventh Generation, but you should know all these terrible things that they themselves have just confessed. They're awful, and you shouldn't be stocking them."

The buyer replied, "Okay, let me see the same data for your products and then I'll make a decision about who I put on my shelves."

Game. Set. Match.

Because of course the competition had no data, no report, and nothing else that even remotely resembled what we'd done, either materially or spiritually. All they could do was sputter excuses, slink away, and wish they'd never brought the subject up. Far from delivering a fatal self-inflicted blow, our CSR work had provided us with a clear mark of differentiation and a fundamentally important strategic advantage. The natural products industry and its consumers embraced our honesty in peeling back the layers.

The problem wasn't that we were confessing our sins. The problem was that others weren't—and just why was that exactly?

Where the CSR reports were problematic was how they put all kinds of pressure on us to collect more data and push more envelopes. They forced us to continually ask an immense burden of questions and track a huge amount of metrics. They put deadlines on our progress to be greener and cleaner, and provide the proof.

They were not just heaven-sent marketing. They were the planning tools from hell, a detailed year-over-year way to identify objectives and monitor results on endless fronts. They were complex, expensive, and, frankly, an enormous pain in the ass. But once we'd gotten into the game, we couldn't get out. We'd set a new industry standard, and there was no way we could retreat.

To wrangle it all, I hired old friend and brilliant wild-man Gregor Barnum to be the world's first director of corporate consciousness. Gregor had the intellect and spirit needed to both keep the company on its toes and manage its efforts to make progress. Much of his time was spent examining the impacts of our supply chain, which took some patience. He was tasked with gathering information our partners weren't used to sharing, like how much energy or water they were using to make our stuff. Typically, they had no idea, and Gregor would have to teach them how to calculate BTUs per batch, gallons per minute, and more. This was an extensive education process, and producing the actual data was no easy chore either. Our manufacturing partners often protested both. With contracts at some fifteen factories at the time, we heard about fifteen different reasons why it couldn't be done.

We persisted anyway. It was our hope that even if they couldn't or wouldn't come up with all the numbers, the process would still yield improvements in sustainability. The fact was, many vendors used production processes not aligned with our values, and many of our partners didn't necessarily hew to our ideas about enlightened management. For a host of obvious reasons, we couldn't just impose our views. What we could do was ask questions and talk to vendors about what we were doing and why it mattered. We could start the conversation, which was no small thing.

Where it got tricky was when we started talking about social policies and employee wellbeing. For our part, we were simply starting to look at everything from a larger whole-system perspective. It was no longer just about getting the highest quality product for the lowest feasible price. It was: "Can you make our dish soap and do your employees have good health insurance and adequate days off?" We were pushing our business relationships into a whole other dimension, which created decent friction. The reality is that one of the ways a supplier can make a product cheaply is not to provide benefits to their employees. We didn't want to be taking advantage of that kind of thinking, and our suppliers were unhappy about us poking into their business practices. Not only did they fervently wish we'd mind our own business, they saw this as just another crazy Seventh Generation demand they were getting sick of addressing.

"Stop giving us all this @#$%&! extra paperwork to do," went the refrain. "You're already a gigantic nuisance and a complete headache to deal with from an environmental perspective. Now you're asking us whether or not we give our crew enough breaks? Now you're handing us yet another questionnaire loaded with crap we have to look up? Don't push your luck. Don't make yourselves the customer we're trying to lose."

Yes, we were walking a fine line, but I also knew we had a little weight we could judiciously throw around. Generally, we sought suppliers where we'd be at least five to as much as 30 percent of their volume, which made them small enough to make our business meaningful and therefore worth the extra effort. But there were limits. We had to be careful not to push too far too fast.

All these measures were ahead of their time, but time quickly caught up, and a few years later, in the face of rising energy costs and increased regulation, all these factory owners and transportation companies realized they needed to be as efficient as possible. They not only started asking these same kinds of questions about their operations voluntarily, but many felt obligated to do a CSR report themselves, tracking the data for prospective clients. We resisted saying "told you so!"

In addition to scrutinizing our vendors, Gregor was also leading a review of our own products. These studies were producing some interesting results but required going down all kinds of rabbit holes. An innocent look at the ingredients in the bottle would lead to asking questions about where the bottle itself came from and who was making the label. "What's in the glue that holds the two together? How recycled is that plastic cap?" And all of that was before addressing what happens when our consumers actually used the product inside, which often required lots of hot water. "Can their scents adversely affect indoor air quality? Do the ingredients break down in the environment? How long does that take? Are there aquatic toxicity issues?" Every product was an onion with layer waiting under layer, and we had to peel them all if we were serious.

For example, we embarked on a greenhouse gas life-cycle analysis of our liquid laundry detergent, certain that we'd find the biggest environmental burdens coming from all the trucks needed to transport the product from factory to store. To say we were off the mark is an understatement. The product's largest contributions to climate change were actually produced by heating the water in the washing machine during use. We'd had no idea. It was an eye-opening surprise that not only underscored the need to conduct all this self-analysis but also suggested some startling new directions to explore in terms of boosting the impacts our products had. We rushed to develop a cold-water laundry formula as quickly as we possibly could.[*]

Suddenly, all the work we'd been doing to push the social and environmental envelopes was getting noticed, and our trophy case was

---

[*] The impacts that resulted from consumers' use of our products, which are now called Scope 3 emissions, represented a whopping 90 percent of Seventh Generation's total environmental impacts. Most of the effects we were having on the planet, surprisingly, were happening in our customers' homes. This is a crucial finding, and though we can logically expect that the situation is similar for other brands, most companies still refuse to disclose their own Scope 3 emissions, even a decade later.

getting crowded. Most of these made sense, like when our 2003 CSR report won the Ceres-ACCA North American Award for Sustainability Reporting, or when we were selected as one of the Fast 50 by *Fast Company Magazine*. These were all tremendous honors, but the biggest came from "behind enemy lines."

In December of 2004, Seventh Generation received the Corporate Stewardship Small Business Award from the U.S. Chamber of Commerce (USCC) Center for Corporate Citizenship. The honor was profoundly surprising for all kinds of reasons, not the least of which was that the USCC was the standard bearer for the sorts of corporate values we'd declared as anachronistic. We were fundamentally challenging their central paradigm of profits over everything else, and to be recognized for our rebellion by the very organization responsible for defending the status quo was mind-boggling. It was as if the Republican Party had given Bernie Sanders a medal for his work to expand government benefits, and had I not seen the press reports myself, I would have thought it was a sick joke.

Yet there I was in Washington, D.C., on a cold December night, just two blocks from the White House at the big awards dinner, invited by an organization to which Seventh Generation has never belonged— and with which it had frequently clashed. Sitting in the famous International Hall of Flags at table number one, I sipped cocktails with Secretary of Commerce Don Evans; Raymond Gilmartin, president & CEO of the Merck pharmaceutical company; Robert Nardelli, president of Home Depot; and Michael Novak, public policy scholar at the American Enterprise Institute, one of America's most conservative "think tanks." I was Daniel in the lion's den. And it was deeply surreal.

When I rose to the podium to accept the honor, I said, "We've received this award for one of two reasons. The first is that you have no idea what we're actually doing, and you've just unwittingly given an award to a company that's challenging everything you believe in. The second is that you guys are a hell of a lot smarter and much more visionary than I thought you were and have genuinely recognized that we are leading the way into a future you know you have to follow."

In truth, I'm pretty sure it was the former. I don't believe the USCC understood how radical Seventh Generation really was. They didn't seem to know much about what we were doing, and we likely received the award because Michael Porter, a rather famous Harvard professor on the committee, was really advocating for us. He probably showed them our CSR report and told them we were the only small company that had ever done anything like this, which was good enough for the USCC.

Despite the perhaps oblivious nature of the award, it was a validating moment and one of our more interesting milestones. Yet this unexpected embrace by the U.S. Chamber of Commerce also posed a big question for us: Where exactly were we going with all of this work?

Because despite all our growth and success, all our mission statements and all those awards, we didn't really know. We'd been too busy bailing out the boat to worry much about its course. It was simply enough to still be headed anywhere other than the bottom of the sea. Now that we'd demonstrated the validity of our company's proposition and made a little money, we had the luxury to contemplate what our business should accomplish over the next three, five, or even ten years. Only one thing was set in stone: Unlike many (and ultimately most) of our peers, I was adamantly against the idea of cashing in our chips and selling the company.

Though our purpose seemed obvious to outsiders, inside the company itself, it wasn't at all clear, despite hundreds of hours of work. In an effort to be inclusive, the company had increasingly pursued too many goals and projects at once, some of which were in direct conflict with others. We forgot a lesson we had learned earlier: Nothing important happens without focus and clear priorities.

There were other issues, too—me being one of them. I was increasingly creating problems for the business by defining my own complex array of objectives. Most of which were a direct outgrowth of my emerging fascination with systems thinking, which had taught me that you can't successfully tackle one thing without tackling a whole bunch of others as well. The beauty of this modus operandi is that it makes you incredibly effective. But for everyone else involved, it's complicated, demanding, and crazy-making because you're continually asking people to look in multiple directions at once. This is in direct opposition to a traditional business approach, which is to focus on two or three clear-cut priorities to the exclusion of most everything else.

Some people at the company found this "look everywhere" approach invigorating. "Thank God, we're not looking at just A, B, and C, we're finally looking at D, E, F, and even G, too!" But for others it was a complete headache. "I can't do my job because I've got so much shit to do that has nothing to do with it!"

Meanwhile, a rising number of companies had decided that they, too, would join the responsible ranks and push the envelope of possibilities themselves. On one hand, our goal had been to create a new model for others to emulate, but now that we were having some success spreading that influence, the bandwagon was getting crowded, making it much harder to innovate. To remain on the leading edge, we had to push that edge further and further out from the comfortable center. We were no longer just thinking outside the box. We were in a different building across town from the box, distancing ourselves from convention every day, which created immense friction.

From the street, things couldn't have looked better. By 2005, our sales had reached $49 million, and we were growing almost 40 percent a year. We were making money, expanding our brand, and riding a wave of acclaim for corporate responsibility work that had essentially cemented our vanguard position as both an industry and sustainability leader. We were the one to beat with a future so bright, it burned holes in the competition. But inside the company, that future was starting to feel like a scary place.

Our stratospheric growth had become a wild ride, driving us when we should have been driving it. We needed to take control and steer with the sort of dedicated intentionality that had so far escaped us. For that, we needed a roadmap. It was time to create a strategic plan with a concrete vision that, like a practical version of our mission and vision statements, would unite everyone at the company in common purpose around shared tactical goals. Yes, we had tried this before, but now it was time to try it again, this time to hopefully produce a map that led us to a clear set of destinations.

As we thought about what that map might look like, I wondered if I should be in it. Was I even the right person to lead the company through its next stage of growth? Was my vision compelling enough? And if it was, could I provide the leadership that the business needed to fulfill it?

I didn't know. What I did know was that after ten years of juggling and bailing water, I was pretty tired. As the company had grown, the stress had, too. Some of that pressure was coming from the increasingly complex challenges of managing an ever-larger business, but some was coming from more personal challenges like how to have more honest conversations and be a better manager. I was less and less motivated to deal with operational issues—the sales calls and fundraising, the quarterly reports and analysis—and more and more interested in our cultural innovations.

I was spending more time writing and more time speaking about cultural impact and discovering that what I really wanted to do was affect the world in ways beyond Seventh Generation's reach. In this desire there was a fundamental tension because it was Seventh Generation that provided the platform from which to effect change. The company and its notoriety gave me the credibility to say what I wanted to say and have it taken seriously. Unlike an academic speaking in largely theoretical terms, I could speak as a business leader who had spent years in the corporate trenches doing the actual work. I was a practitioner of the arts I espoused with expertise rooted in real-world trials, which was an incredibly effective place to pontificate from.

Unfortunately, I guess I sometimes pontificated a little too much for my own personal good, which could put a bit of a target on my back.

In spite of the occasional backlash to my extremely progressive point of view, annual sales had gone from a slim $3.2 million in 1995 to almost $50 million in 2005, a staggering growth rate of nearly 32 percent annually that was more than double that of the natural products industry as a whole. We now had seventy branded products and were the leading green brand in the U.S., with 45 percent of the country's total sales in the combined paper and plastic, cleaning, diaper, wipes, and feminine hygiene categories. The turnaround was nothing short of stunning.

The company had changed, and I had, too. Not only had I learned that turning a profit wasn't the terrible soul-sucking pursuit I'd once assumed, but I'd learned that when you play the business game, not everything has to be a home run. You have to take big swings, looking for the transformational grand slam that would blaze the way to a permanently red-hot future.

In a way, this had always been my approach—the Skills Exchange and Network for Learning, the audiobooks, and even the Seventh Generation Catalog had all been built on a meteoric rise of some kind. Now, I'd come to see anything less as a disappointment. But there's value in hitting a double or even a single. Those can and do pay off as well, and when you string enough of them together, they form a perfectly acceptable alternative route to success—a little less flashy but just as viable.

Not every product can be a new diaper line. Not every guerrilla marketing campaign is going to turn into a Tampontification. But sell enough toilet paper and you'll build an empire one roll at a time. Some layers of the onion are smaller, but they all add up.

The company's future would end up being largely formed from a series of smaller yet important victories, successes that bubbled up slowly rather than explode on the scene. I would have less and less to do with these wins over time. As the company had matured, so had I—and now I was ready to evolve to the next level. A level where I would not lead the company so much as I would endeavor to lead the revolution it started.

CHAPTER FIFTEEN

Out from Under the Table

In September of 2006, I attended a Leadership Institute retreat at the Hollyhock Centre, a wellness and personal growth organization based in Vancouver, Canada. Held at the group's Cortes Island campus, the event gathered about a hundred socially focused businesspeople to trade ideas, learn new skills, and build community to reenergize our work back home. It was to be a few days of connecting with kindred spirits, and I was looking forward to it, especially exploring the idyllic island setting of ancient forests and coastal wetlands.

My assignment was an ice-breaker of sorts, and it was a bold one. I was to give a talk about something I'd never told anyone before. It was an interesting way to start, one that certainly fell within the confines of the center's mission to "inspire personal growth," yet posed a daunting challenge for the program speakers, who were suddenly tasked with baring their souls. Uncertainty rippled through the room, but we weren't there to fake it. I decided to honor the spirit of the moment as truthfully as I could and reveal my deepest secret:

My lifelong battle with depression.

To this day, I don't know what possessed me to be so breathtakingly honest, but it was a watershed moment. Suddenly I found myself standing in front of an audience of total strangers, openly confessing something I'd never shared with anyone but my wife and a revolving crowd of therapists: How I'd spent a literal lifetime struggling to rise above a dense cloud of despair, and I'd been doing it almost completely alone, always profoundly afraid that if I spoke about my troubled mind, then the world would deem me defective, forever tainting the way others perceived me.

My confessional had been a while coming. Though I'd been silent about my own problems, I'd talked with others about their own mental health. Through these encounters, I discovered that my intimate acquaintance with depression could be a positive force to encourage people to go into therapy, consider medication, and take other steps. I'd seen how I could be more effective by sharing my own experiences. Remaining silent wasn't helping anybody, and my attitude about the secrecy I'd held for so long was changing.

Hollyhock gave me permission to take the final leap of faith, despite the paralyzing fear still beating in my heart. The words spilled across the room, carrying my truth out into the world, and in that moment of spontaneous radical personal transparency, I experienced a seismic wave of relief. As I finished revealing my most honest self, I felt freer than I had in years. It was a tremendous high to discuss my greatest challenge so openly, no longer fearing the consequences. Let them come, I thought.

I needn't have worried. My confession was affirmed by an outpouring of support from fellow Hollyhock attendees. Over the course of the next day, countless people sought me out to thank me for sharing my struggles.

"I've suffered from depression myself," so many said, "but I never talk about it. Now I think maybe I can."

This was heartening and rewarding to hear. Indeed, around 20 percent of all Americans will develop what's called "major depressive disorder" at some point in our lives. And that percentage gets even higher when you look at the statistics for teenagers.

Ever since high school, I had tried a constant stream of treatments and therapists. The first I tried was at the Areba Casriel Institute, where my brother, Peter, was already enrolled. My treatments were similar to his. In theory, they counseled that I could get to the root of my feelings through screaming and essentially shout them out of existence. But the practice was geared toward addicts, who can have quite different issues, and it turns out that shrieking into the void really isn't a particularly effective way to deal with biochemical imbalances. I tried it for a year, but all I really got out of it were strained vocal cords.

In one sense, I was lucky. Depression wasn't a constant presence in my life. It ebbed and flowed like a black tide, something that would suddenly seep in under the door and flood my life once a month or every other month. Some days, some weeks, some months I felt fine, but invariably the disease would come roaring back all over again. There was no consistency, and I never knew when or if the switch would flip. And I certainly didn't understand why these feelings ran so deep. None of it made any sense. My depression was capricious—a cruel jump-scare waiting to happen as I went about life, always fearful of the next time it would leap out of the shadows.

At the same time, it was a secret, and secrets take work to keep—and they exact a toll along the way. My depression could be raging, yet I exerted great effort to make sure no one ever knew. I was adamant that there'd be no outward sign, and regardless of how bad things might get, I refused to let it affect my functionality in the world or the perceptions people had of me.

Depression felt like a defect, an embarrassing malady that just didn't seem like anything respectable people would ever experience. My parents knew because my therapy at Areba Casriel was built around involving the family. Yet aside from informing them and confiding in Sheila and Marc, a close friend from high school, I never told another soul, and it was a mark of pride that no one had an inkling anything was wrong.

After a year of failed attempts to expel the illness at the top of my lungs, I tried Reichian psychotherapy, a treatment that seeks to lower defenses born of trauma and release trapped emotions physically stored in the body through a combination of guided self-exploration and deep tissue massage. Reichians believe that the key to positive mental health lies in freeing the buried feelings that have created these defenses. It's certainly an approach that works for some—but I had a horrible experience. My therapist would berate me for being late, and I was chastised for not producing enough painful memories on his couch. He was overly stern, medically underwhelming, and intensely dislikable by virtually every metric that mattered. Instead of curing me of my depression, he sent me running away from anything Reichian as fast as I could.

My bleakest moments came in London during my brief dalliance at the publishing firm. I fell into a place where I was truly adrift. At that bottom, I'd found the darkest thoughts of all but had fortunately sought help at the Philadelphia Association, the organization founded by famed psychiatrist R.D. Laing, where I learned how to at least manage the disease. The depression itself hadn't gone anywhere but I learned to better navigate my way by accepting it as part of life. Depression was something that could be managed rather than a terrible destructive destiny.

My condition stabilized. There were still many days when I was down, but I could count on one hand those that were so bad I couldn't function. Covering it all up had become such a well-rehearsed act that I performed my way through even the worst of it.

Finally, life landed me in Vermont, which altered the course of my inner existence, too. I found a new therapist who strongly encouraged me to give medication a try.

This was a step I had firmly resisted for years, rooted in the great conflict I'd historically had about my depression: What was my natural state? Was my depression just an inherent part of who I was? For too long, I'd felt the answer was more than "yes." Depression wasn't one tangential trait among many, but a defining characteristic. I thought a pharmaceutical intervention would just be covering that inner essence up with a synthetic veneer of manufactured happiness. I didn't want that false sense of being "okay" that I feared would lead to a lifelong dependency on drugs.

Thankfully, I was wrong. The first medication I tried, Lexapro, was a phenomenal success that largely stopped my depression in its tracks. I may not have been fully healed, but I couldn't believe how much of my life I'd spent feeling so black when the light had been as close as the pharmacy.

In addition to my overdue prescription, the one-on-one therapy itself also proved terrifically effective. My new therapist, Ray Ann Barry, used visualization as a tool to guide me to a core truth: Much of my depression stemmed from being left alone as a child. The routes I took to this crucial realization involved envisioning all kinds of scenarios.

Sometimes I was asked to picture myself hugging my children. At other points, the therapist had me visualize myself as a child in a room. I'd be instructed to go and take this child out of that room and into the sunlight, an apt metaphor for my treatment itself.

The combination of this therapy and the medication was stunningly effective. I went from being frequently depressed to experiencing the illness just a couple of times a year, and never as badly as before. My progress taught me a valuable lesson: There's no one solution to depression. You have to keep looking until you find the one that works.

It's not like heart disease, a well-understood condition whose causes are fairly singular and whose treatments are clear. Instead, depression is caused by an infinite number of highly personal mechanisms, some of which are biochemical and some of which are situational. Finding the right treatment for yourself is a process.

I'm grateful I kept going. Trying medical solutions and finding the right therapist saved me—and saved my family, too. As my depression wore on through the years, it was taking an unmistakable—and likely terminal—toll on my ability to be a good father and decent partner. Sheila and the kids put up with a pretty miserable, short-tempered miscreant for a long time, someone who hid from his illness by working too much. Setting that person aside so the real person underneath could emerge gave me a new beginning with my family.

Depression has been a humbling experience, offering me a long, intimate encounter with the power of the subconscious that is both clarifying and terrifying. Our minds are so profoundly complicated, they can defy their own attempts to understand themselves. Depression taught me how delicate this life is, how fragile we all are. We are not now nor will we ever truly be rulers of our domains. We are ships on a wind-driven sea, dodging krakens and tempests alike, doing the best we can to keep our seams in shape and water out of our holds. There are no guarantees that we'll make it to safe harbor. No promises that we'll make it out alive. I was fortunate. I'd escaped the worst of it and had survived to tell the tale.

My brother, Peter, wasn't so lucky.

Like me, Peter also suffered from depression. Unlike me, he wasn't averse to treating it with drugs, and he did so with prodigious abandon, trying anything he could get his hands on. He self-medicated through life with the kind of ruthless enthusiasm of which legendary addictions are made. There was no potential balm not worth a try, no high not worth chasing. He was addicted to gambling, addicted to sex, and addicted to drugs and alcohol. And because he was smart and charming, he succeeded in spite of all this.

After Peter left Seventh Generation, he started his own business importing inexpensive clothing from Asia and selling it in bulk to discount department stores like T.J. Maxx. For a time, the business did well, and the money flowed in. But it was never enough to dispel the anger and resentment Peter experienced, believing life had not endowed him with all he deserved. So he sought his revenge by living fast and loose.

For many years, his balancing act on that knife edge never resulted in more than a nick or two here and there. Somehow he kept his shit together, at least enough to maintain a baseline level of functionality. That changed after our father died in 1990. Though he and Peter were not particularly close, Peter and my mother were, and in the wake of our father's death, Peter assumed the role of our mother's caregiver. It was not an easy task. Despite only being in her late sixties, she was in the early stages of Alzheimer's, and the disease was progressing rapidly, which only increased Peter's pain.

Around the same time, the United States changed its tariff rules, and the import model his business depended on collapsed. Denied his birthright and left with nothing yet again, Peter turned his attention to our mother full time, and for the next five years could do little more than hold her hand as she vanished into dementia's netherworld.

It was devastating to witness, and despite the preordained nature of the diagnosis, Peter was knocked to his knees after her death in 1994. His world shattered yet again, he took his relatively modest inheritance and bought a Mercedes before moving out to the Hamptons at Long Island shore, where he proceeded to party as hard as he could—which was really saying something in Peter's case. Devastated by loss, he unraveled—blowing through all his money, indulging in wild drug and gambling binges.

He would disappear for days at a time, and we'd spend hours trying to convince his credit card company to tell us where he'd made his most recent purchases so we could track him down and make sure he was okay. During one particularly difficult period, we followed the paper trail to a hotel. When the police broke into his room, they found him overdosed on the bathroom floor in an attempted suicide.

It was not the first time he'd tried to kill himself, nor would it be the last. In the early 2000s, the cycle became a tragic routine that found Sheila and me engaged in a literal life-or-death struggle to keep him from succumbing to the monsters raging inside. There were hundreds of long-distance phone calls and countless police department wellness checks, endless sleepless nights followed by traumatic days.

Eventually, Peter ran out of money and his options dwindled. On May 1, 2000, we received a call from the local police department. They'd found him in the Mercedes parked at the beach. He'd shot himself and was gone.

It remains the most painful experience of my life, a loss I cannot quantify. It left a void that cannot be filled and brought my depression back again into a deep, pervasive, and dimensionless grief. Despite his travails and all the chaos he provoked, Peter had always been one of the greatest lights in my life. He was everything I was not, an endlessly charming daredevil, and I admired him for it. He was capable of so much I could never dream of doing, such as easily orchestrating a party for three hundred people or striking up a witty conversation with a stranger, skills my shyness would forever prevent. He put fun first, yes, but when he got down to work, he was always brilliant at whatever the job called on him to do.

As Sheila says, he lived more in his half-life than most people live in a full one; and knowing that brings comfort to our memories. But we were also left with only questions and that terrible game of second-guessing that comes in suicide's aftermath. We played the tragic history on repeat in our heads. What had we missed? What could we have done differently, faster, better? Why hadn't we saved him from this desperate madness and its catastrophic lie?

Eventually we concluded that we'd done all that we could—and sometimes even more. We'd shepherded Peter through treatment program after treatment program. Residential, outpatient, therapies for depression, counseling for addiction.

There was nothing we hadn't tried. I'd given him work. I'd given him love. I'd given him my time and tried to give him hope. Yet it was never enough, and eventually I came to understand that it never would have been. But there's no way to save a man who doesn't want to save himself. We'd thrown all the life preservers into the water, but the soul we sought to rescue refused to swim.

Peter has been gone a long time now, but the legacy he left in my world is very much alive. His passing forced me to look at how I was approaching my own life. Much as my depression found me contemplating life's inherent frailty, the loss of my brother had shown me its ephemeral essence. Too often I'd failed to appreciate the wonder that surrounded me, and I had not done the best job of honoring life's gifts with the gratitude they deserved. I took my brother's memory and turned it into a promise to myself: I would live more fully, be more present, as kindly as possible, and make it a point to enjoy every day more deeply. I'm not sure I've done a particularly good job of all of that, but I've tried my best. And when it comes to what really matters, that's all any of us can do.

The depression that Peter and I struggled with manifested in entirely different ways. Peter was always jumping from one thing to another, unable to see the light, while somehow, I could be laser-focused on a mission and able to find hope even when things were dark.

So many entrepreneurs struggle with depression silently, afraid that their investors, customers, and employees will see it as a defect, a dangerous sign of weakness. Just as many believed you can't be a profitable business AND do good in the world, some accept a myth that you can't be an effective leader AND struggle with mental health. Happily, my life has demonstrated that both are possible at the same time.

CHAPTER SIXTEEN

What Were We Thinking?

Though going public with my depression in 2005 was something I'd never intended, we all know life is a trip through the unexpected. No matter where we land at the end of the proverbial day, it's often not the place we thought we would. That's true for people and for companies, too. My own was no exception.

Seventh Generation started as a simple business selling basic products whose purpose was fundamentally ordinary. We just wanted to make things that were safer for people and the environment in ways that were healthier for both. Yet, fate warped our objective into a destiny we didn't see coming and turned the company itself into something we'd never anticipated. By the mid-2000s, we were no longer merely a consumer products company. We were a thought leader at the forefront of the burgeoning corporate responsibility movement.

"Thought leader" is a weird term. But I understand that trailblazers will find their paths followed and will be looked to for advice about navigating what comes next. In Seventh Generation's case, we didn't realize this was a function we'd assumed until we'd been doing it for a long time. To provoke change, as was core to our purpose, we need models of new possibility to follow and iterate upon. These models are often expressed through stories—excellent content that can be "marketed" to the media, potential employees, customers, even shareholders. This type of marketing is often more interesting and authentic than the typical corporate messaging that feels cold and lifeless.

From our perspective, we were simply engaging in a logical educational push to create context for what we were making and selling. We needed to build a framework in which to operate, to establish the rules of engagement, create guardrails, and set benchmarks so we could more clearly gauge our own metrics of success. This work was really self-focused until it became obvious that so many other people were watching.

We had two audiences. The first was our consumers and prospective consumers. Building the rationale for buying our housekeeping alternatives was a necessary engagement strategy because we were selling a type of product that people didn't know they needed—and then asking them to spend a bit more for that privilege. In this sense, our marketing initiatives amounted to educational outreach about the problems our products addressed and why the solutions mattered. With no one else discussing these ideas (and certainly no other consumer product companies), this learning-based sales strategy quickly turned into a form of thought leadership.

Our approach was piecemeal: a datapoint here, a factoid there, the nature of which would depend on whatever we were trying to sell in that moment. If it was paper towels, we'd make a point about deforestation. If it was laundry detergent, we'd have something to say about optical brighteners. As the millennium turned, however, our scattershot consumer education efforts coalesced into something more intentional and organized.

In January of 2001, an article in the Science section of *The New York Times* brought to light an emerging household health issue: How the air inside the average home was more polluted than the air outside—and in some cases, the difference was dramatic. In fact, studies were showing that indoor air was exposing people to levels of carcinogens and other toxins that were five to seventy times greater than those encountered outdoors. This was just one more price of living in the modern world, where energy-efficient construction techniques meant to hold down heating and cooling needs also trapped the potentially hazardous vapors, aerosols, and particulates produced by cleaning products.

Two years later, in March of 2003, a headline in the *Los Angeles Times* underscored the point when it declared "Chemicals in Home a Big Smog Source." The article highlighted new research pinpointing household products—including cleaners—as the L.A. region's second biggest contributor to smog after tailpipe emissions.

News like this didn't get much attention, but it sure caught ours. The idea that the ordinary consumer products we brought into our homes were making the air we breathe inside alarmingly unhealthy was perhaps the clearest and most urgent justification for our products yet. It put a big fat exclamation point on our company's entire raison d'être, and propelled huge product development programs like the creation of Seventh Generation's Free & Clear line. Since the story about indoor air quality remained largely out of view, we made it our job to tell the story.

In marketing materials, we crafted narratives discussing this new realization and offered examples of the real-world consequences: You spray a conventional cleaning product around your house, and it triggers your child's asthma. You have to pull them from school, miss work, see the doctor, buy medication. That all costs money, well more than the extra you would pay to purchase a nontoxic alternative. Yet all this is nothing compared to the psychological costs of fearing for your family's health. Compared to these expenses, spending a few cents more for Seventh Generation to prevent them is a genuine bargain.

It was an economic rationale wrapped in a health argument packed into a lesson on an obscure but crucial emergent environmental issue. It was Seventh Generation in a nutshell, and no one else was having these conversations. These stories began to organically take on a life of their own and exert a very different brand of influence outside of their original mission. They weren't just ads and shelf talkers anymore. They had evolved into examples of cutting-edge corporate leadership.

One of my favorite ads involved taking the actual label from a bottle of Tilex mildew stain remover, a leading brand, and turning its own self-declared warnings that directed you to open windows before use, turn on fans, avoid prolonged breathing, keep away from sick people, wear gloves, etc. into a convincing argument that you shouldn't be using the product at all. "Do you have a toxic waste site under your sink?" the copy asked in a piece that simultaneously addressed indoor air quality, family health, economic value, and conventional consumer product environmental issues.

This ad made the lawyers twitch. We were calling out a specific product for very specific dangers, and in their view, any comparison to any product was a grave mistake. Especially one from a corporation whose legal department expenditures dwarfed our entire annual budget. I resisted their attempts to muzzle us because we were just letting the competition's own label do the talking. We didn't need to say anything about the product at all when we had the criminal on tape confessing the crime.

All we did was publish the evidence. It was a bold stroke, both for its audacity and its authority.

Successes like these made it tempting to put our foot on the gas pedal, but we were always cautious and never cavalier. I was mindful of the need for caution, documentation, honesty, and transparency in all our materials. There were frequent deliberations with our marketing and PR teams. Was the evidence there? Was it defensible? Could we explain it to consumers without lawsuits or glazed eyes?

We relied on science and journalism in equal measure and always kept a library of materials to back up our claims. In hindsight, these efforts fueled our arrival as a thought leader. When your marketing materials contain citations from EPA research and references to articles in the *New England Journal of Medicine*, you're bound to be perceived as more than just another company on the block.

These perceptions were further fueled by Seventh Generation's commitment to ongoing external engagement. Our growing desire to be an activist company found us launching campaigns as we sought ways to demonstrate the highest possible level of fealty to the ideals we espoused. Pursuing these projects expanded our presence on the national stage, which increased visibility and boosted our trendsetter reputation.

One of the biggest issues we seized upon was the fact that while personal care products had to disclose their ingredients, household cleaners did not. When you brought that bottle of Tilex home, you really had no idea what chemicals it contained, nor what health hazards they might present. Under the guise of protecting trade secrets, manufacturers had long ago won the right to put some of the planet's most toxic chemicals into their formulas—known carcinogens, antigens, mutagens, and more—without saying a word. It was a deeply sickening situation. Literally. And one that would not be allowed in most other industries—think stocks and the SEC.

Our response was an ongoing right-to-know campaign in which we sought to shine as harsh a spotlight as possible on this unhealthy state of affairs. We pushed for industry and regulatory changes that would supply some badly needed transparency and let consumers know exactly what risks they were taking when they doused their homes with conventional cleaning products.

We started in a wholly obligatory way—by becoming the first consumer products company to voluntarily disclose all the ingredients in all of our products. We redesigned our labels to provide the information, published all our material safety data sheets* online, and invited customers to look. In an industry that had always treated its formulas like deep-state secrets, this alone was a profoundly subversive and highly revolutionary act.

It was also a risk because it exposed a key Seventh Generation vulnerability: We still used some synthetic chemicals in our products. It was a point that reflected the difficulty in creating 100 percent natural product formulas that worked just as well as conventional ones. Thankfully, the issue largely boiled down to a few preservatives for which no effective naturally-derived alternatives had been found yet.

Engaging with our customers on the issue and explaining the challenge we faced diffused any potential objections. Our position was hard to argue with: By definition, natural products attract mold and other

---

* A material safety data sheet (MSDS) is a standardized manufacturing industry document that summarizes any potential health or operational hazards of a chemical—from eye irritation and cancer to reactivity and fire dangers—and describes best handling practices. It's an essential accident and injury prevention tool for anyone working with dangerous chemicals. Typically, these sheets are found in the workplace as a way for employees to properly familiarize themselves with the materials they're handling. Most people will never see one.

pathogens, so in lieu of a viable organic solution, synthetic preservatives were the only way to keep them on shelves.

On one level, it was perhaps the ultimate trust-building exercise with our customers—we were pulling open the curtains on the back room to show how we made the sausage, and it wasn't on a wood-burning stove with flowers picked from the garden. On the other hand, I had confidence in our products, in our customers, and in the fact that full ingredients disclosure was the right move for our company, our industry, and public health. People were getting sick, maybe even dying, because too many companies refused to clean up their act. As the industry's leading alternative, how could we not speak up?

That's not to say it was easy. By definition, this mission meant talking about many of the individual offending ingredients themselves, which was difficult to do without people tuning out. We had to make people understand there was an important issue,* and then we had to explain it. What was really in these formulas? What were the chemicals we were worried about? What happened when you sprayed them, combined them, ingested them?

We took a shotgun approach, peppering all our marketing and communications with various pieces of the puzzle that allowed consumers to assemble a more complete picture over time. We were also unafraid to go to the other extreme and published extensive guides that contained in-depth discussions and dense glossaries of the toxic ingredients manufacturers were using.

---

* Most consumers assume that if a product is demonstrably dangerous there's a law or standard that won't allow it to be sold. The mere fact that you can buy it infers that it's safe. Yet this is hardly the case, and most are surprised to learn just what kinds of hazardous and toxic chemicals conventional household cleaners typically contain. Yes, products have to be labeled, but those laws are byzantine at best and riddled with gigantic loopholes that allow known hazards to stay hidden. Dangerous risks remain unaddressed thanks to a regulatory situation that serves corporate interests rather than consumers.

A few years later, much of this information was expanded into a full-fledged 200-page book called *Naturally Clean: The Seventh Generation Guide to Safe & Healthy Nontoxic Cleaning*, a resource that finally put all the information and guidance we'd collected about hazardous household products in one place. Think "thought leadership."

These were challenging communications packed with highly granular facts and data. Even explaining the basic concepts of toxicity was a heavy lift.* It took some work to reduce all this convoluted science into breezy English people could understand without getting overloaded, and in truth not many of our customers really cared to go that deep.† Nine out of ten couldn't explain the specific benefits of using a given Seventh Generation product instead of its conventional counterpart. "Natural and nontoxic" was all they wanted or needed to know. Yet because we had done the work, we became the resource people turned to for this obscure information, which remained hard to find, despite the advent of the internet.

Our right-to-know work culminated in 2008 with a campaign we called "Show What's Inside" that offered an entire website about the potential risks in many cleaning products and a mobile label-reading

---

* The problem with discussing toxicity is that almost anything is toxic in a high enough volume. Salt, for example, is essential to life, but ingesting too much can kill you. Toxicity is never clear-cut. Instead, it's a function of quantity over time, which makes the use of the word "nontoxic" extremely complicated. That was a critical label for Seventh Generation to deploy as one of the most powerful triggers for our customers, yet we had to be very careful about how we defined and used it because any product—including ours—could be toxic in certain amounts. What the conventional consumer product companies were saying was that their products were safe if used according to instructions. We had to discuss "toxicity" by explaining its meaning without creating any legal jeopardy for ourselves.

† During our right-to-know era, the issue of hormonal disruption became a hot topic within environmental toxicology circles. Science had discovered that certain chemicals behaved like hormones when absorbed by the body, and this mimicry was causing deleterious health effects. This remains a hugely important finding but was even harder to explain than toxicology. We tried, but the issue never generated the traction or alarm we felt it should, and we eventually gave up.

app to guide shoppers in the store. In tandem, we partnered with the Environmental Working Group and pediatrician/author Dr. Alan Greene to encourage consumers to demand greater ingredient transparency and urged Congress to pass the "Kid-Safe Chemical Act." We kicked the whole thing off at the American Academy of Pediatrics National Conference in Boston, where we hosted a panel discussion and a press conference designed to raise awareness.

Not long after, one of the biggest companies in the space, SC Johnson, cloned our ingredient-disclosure effort and called it their own. The maker of Windex, Glade, Raid, and other billion-dollar brands had followed our example almost to the letter with a campaign dubbed "What's Inside." It was plagiarism, sure, but why quibble? Industry change was the goal, and on that score, we were winning. Getting copied was the entire point.

With wins like this starting to accumulate, I focused on pushing the activist envelope as much as I could, going so far as to accept a position on the Greenpeace board of directors, a rather un-CEO-like move that broke new ground even as it got me into a fair amount of trouble.

In September of 2007, many in the company, including myself, had gathered in Baltimore for our annual pilgrimage to Expo East, a critical consumer products show. It was our industry's social and sales event of the season, a chance to mingle and meet its key players, shore up existing relationships, and forge new ones, too. Unfortunately, on its opening day, Greenpeace had scheduled a huge climate protest just down the road in Washington, D.C. The prior night, at dinner with the Seventh Generation crew, there was an intense conversation: Should we be in this convention hall tomorrow morning hawking toilet paper, or should we be out there on the front lines defending the planet?

Some said we should put up a "gone protesting" sign on our booth and abandon it entirely. Others thought that would be disrespectful to the customers who had come in from all over the country to see us. In the end, everybody was allowed to follow their own conscience. About half chose the rally. Half stayed in the hall to meet and greet stakeholders.

The next morning, we blocked the entrance to the State Department, where the Meeting of Major Economies on Energy Security and Climate Change was being hosted by Condoleezza Rice. I was rewarded for my efforts with a free ride in the back of a Metropolitan Police van to the D.C. jail, where I was locked in a cell with a bunch of much younger protesters who were seriously impressed that this old guy had gotten himself arrested too.

Back home, the Seventh Generation board of directors was not happy. At all. They expressed a supreme level of what could charitably be termed "intense discomfort" at all the attention I'd garnered and told me in no uncertain terms that extracurricular activities like this were not okay. It was an interesting moment because, from my perspective, this was exactly what the CEO of a company like Seventh Generation should be doing. This was a critical and highly effective way to communicate our values. I could write all the blog posts about climate change that I wanted but protesting to the point of civil disobedience said so much more. My arrest wasn't problematic. It was perfect.

The board was not persuaded. Most members remained resolute in their opinion that getting arrested at protests was an inappropriate expression of our concerns. They slapped my wrist as hard as they could, and I was essentially told not to do it again.

In hindsight, their reaction should have been much more of an awakening for me about the growing divide between my unconventional vision and the board of directors' far more conventional vision for running the company. This growing chasm was a symptom of changing circumstances behind the scenes. Unlike the board's earlier incarnations, by the mid-2000s, our board was becoming less occupied by progressive-leaning countercultural types and filled with traditional business types who'd "bought" their seat through big stock purchases and other connections. Many of them didn't really understand what we were trying to build. There was trouble ahead, and the board's protests about my protest were an early warning sign that I unfortunately bypassed.

Though I did make an intentional effort to engage the board on how we could best express Seventh Generation's alternative brand values, it wasn't enough. I never convinced them that putting me in handcuffs was, in fact, a fundamental part of leading our industry in a new direction.

In general, the board was queasy about our relationship with Greenpeace, an organization known for taking radical action against corporations to back up its uncompromising environmental positions. I had no such qualms. Forging strong connections with activist environmental organizations like Greenpeace, the Environmental Working Group, Friends of the Earth, the Environmental Research Foundation, and the like was exactly the example I wanted to set. These were the very NGOs that were policing the business community, and partnering with them conferred a wealth of benefits that significantly boosted both our reputation and CSR efforts. Our NGO collaborators served as advisors who guided our efforts and consultants who kept us tuned into environmental trends. But the mere fact of our mutual association conferred a huge amount of credibility that made Seventh Generation a solution within a problematic industry.

In 2006, we took things to the next level and partnered with Greenpeace for a program called "Change It." The idea was to hold an annual contest for college students and award the winners an all-expenses-paid week of grassroots education, community organizing skills building, and direct action training under the auspices of Greenpeace's own experts. The long-term goal was to seed the entire country with a new generation of environmental activists equipped with the tools needed to make a difference.

The program was a way to exert lasting influence and marked one of the few times Greenpeace ever collaborated with a for-profit company. We budgeted $400,000 dollars a year to recruit and train a few dozen applicants and went off to the races.

Change It was a huge success on all kinds of levels, generating a great story about this feisty little company in Vermont trying to change the world. The program itself had an enormous effect on its participants, who became both lifelong brand ambassadors and dedicated local environmental advocates. At the same time, it served to excite retailers and others in the trade, a crucial marketing goal. Our $400,000 expenditure may have been a big one for us, but it proved to be some of the best money we ever spent, an investment that is still generating returns nearly twenty years later.

Change It was certainly unusual. So was the time I paid $10,000 to have my blood drawn by the Environmental Working Group and examined for toxins. Despite my own "natural" lifestyle, my body turned out to contain high levels of lead, mercury, and the fragrance ingredient bisphenol-A. But neither of those was our crowning achievement. That honor goes to a roll of toilet paper.

Since our early mail order days, we'd been obsessed with chlorine, the rabidly dangerous element behind some of the devastating industrial processes on the planet and the atom responsible for the lion's share of humanity's deadliest chemicals. One of the biggest ways chlorine is bad news is the way it reacts with the lignins in wood pulp. During the paper bleaching process, dioxins are produced, poisons capable of triggering spooky health effects even at significantly lower levels of exposure than most hazardous materials. Trust me, you do not want to read the studies, nor do you want to ever buy anything made from, with, or near chlorine. It turns everything it touches into toxic waste.

Which is why we sold unbleached paper products, and to make the point as clearly as we could, we printed rolls of our toilet tissue urging consumers to "Learn facts about chlorine that will scare the crap out of you." Square after square detailed the chemical's dangers, and my guess is that anyone who worked their way through the entire roll never bought a bleached paper product again. The piece wasn't funny. But also it was. Everybody loved it, and it became our greatest promotional hit.

Consumers, however, never saw it. Like so many of our efforts, it was meant exclusively for our trade audience, because without their shelf space our cause would be lost. In this, we had no choice. Our resources were extremely limited, and we had to directly convince brokers, distributors, and retailers that we were a hot commodity. They were the gatekeepers and influencers who determined what brands consumers encountered, which conferred instant credibility. Plus, we had a sales force to excite and a supply chain to motivate, so we fired much of our marketing ammunition in places consumers never saw.

Fortunately for us, it rarely stayed there. Our fact-filled rolls of toilet tissue may have only been given out at trade shows, but they often wandered into homes as hip novelty items. Direct-to-the-trades promo pieces filled with toxicology lessons were only mailed to grocers, but they popped up in C-suites across the business world as examples of doing business differently.

We found even minor trade promotions like our environmental savings statements lasting well past their intended expiration date and wandered out into the world at large, where they took on second and even third lives that turned them into something else entirely. These statements quantified the resources a retailer was helping to conserve by stocking our low-impact products—how much water was saved and how many trees left standing, etc. They were simple and straightforward calculations meant to help our wholesale stakeholders feel good about partnering with us. Along the way, they also became a valuable tool by which we could measure our own sustainability achievements, and that spread their influence even further. Today, they've become a fundamental part of environmental, social, and governance (ESG) reporting, an unexpected rise to prominence that belies their humble beginnings and our original intentions.

We engaged in these kinds of outside-the-box exercises because the truth was that despite our growing success, we remained a very small voice in an industry filled with big players who could out-shout us any time they wanted. By every metric, we were badly outgunned, and I knew we had to do things like blood tests and novelty toilet tissue to get the level of attention we needed. This wasn't a novel strategy, though. Lots of small entrepreneurial companies resort to outlandish gimmicks just to be seen in a crowded consumer marketplace. What was unique in our case was the authority-reinforcing side effect our own stunts seemed to generate. We got noticed, but in today's social media parlance, we also got followed, which was worth much more. We weren't the industry's biggest brand, but we were becoming its most influential.

On one hand, when it came to the general public, we did indeed want to move minds and change behaviors. It was a codified part of our core mission, and we knew that assuming the role of educator was the key to spreading knowledge and bridging it to action.

Our other audience, however, was far more accidental. Here the onlookers were made up of our peers and fellow businesses, who were quietly taking notes on everything we were doing. They were following our lead simply because we were one of the few to follow at a time when there was a rapidly growing consumer preference for supporting responsible companies.

Historically, corporate responsibility had been a pretty simple proposition. It essentially meant giving money away. Companies would form a charity, host a dinner, sponsor an organization, orchestrate a fundraiser, and/or make big splashy donations and call it a responsible day. But consumers had grown savvier in the 1990s and were seeing through the "feel-good smokescreen." They'd begun insisting on more than corporate lip service to just causes. In the emerging view, old-school corporate citizenship initiatives like these were more of a distraction than anything else, an easy way to deflect criticism and avoid tackling the fundamental problems at the heart of the free market system. Tucked away out of sight in a hidden corner of northern Vermont, we'd been busy quietly building new definitions for responsibility around deeper social ideals and more responsive corporate governance that addressed our desire for genuinely meaningful business benevolence. Now the rest of the world was taking notice.

It was about time. For too long, corporations had been little more than a tool for concentrating wealth in the hands of people who already had an outsized share. There were, of course, some outliers trying to buck the trend. Companies like Ben & Jerry's and the Body Shop were exploring new ways to do business. There were also intermittent brief glimmers of sanity voiced by renegade executives like Johnson &

Johnson CEO James Burke, who declared that his first and second priorities were always for his employees and his customers, with investors coming in a distant third. But for the most part, the corporate sphere was a place where the primacy of shareholder returns was everything.

Seventh Generation was attempting to pioneer what later became known as "stakeholder capitalism." This new structure sought to benefit all stakeholders, not just shareholders and senior management. Stock ownership for all employees is a great start, ensuring they benefit from the value they create. But stakeholders also include the local community, your supply chain, customers, and of course the environment. We didn't want to be like those other companies. But now they wanted to be more like us.

That reality hit us after we'd created our first few corporate social responsibility reports in the early 2000s. They had received more attention than I'd expected and had quickly gone from being an annual internal tool to help us track our progress to something more akin to a how-to manual that other companies used to guide their own responsibility efforts.

At the same time, we were confirming the viability of alternative methods. We were showing people that change was not too difficult to engineer. Safer products were not too expensive. Natural ingredients did work. We'd adopted a larger purpose dedicated to systemic change and had inadvertently turned our marketing department into a political education wing to further that goal. In a time when consumers desired a better brand of capitalism, our efforts were thought leadership as a form of hostage taking. At a certain point, companies had no choice but to follow our example.

And that's what happened. Suddenly unbleached paper was mainstream. Indoor spaces became worthy of environmental protection.

Ingredient disclosure became a rapidly growing trend. Savings statements turned into standard operating procedure.

We were finally being taken seriously, and I eagerly leaned into our new role as a thought leader. This work would quickly become some of the most fulfilling I would ever do, boosting my own search for meaning even as it pushed the company's influence beyond environmental issues and into much broader systemic realms.

On a personal level, the timing of the shift was nearly perfect. My role as Seventh Generation's CEO had lost its sheen, and after a period of frenetic growth and all its challenges, I was feeling the heat of burnout. In response, I'd started shifting my attention away from the day-to-day management of the company to writing and public speaking, being a "thought leader" on wider stages where I could more fully explore and promote the ideas closest to my heart. This was work I enjoyed so immensely that it wasn't really work at all, and it dovetailed with Seventh Generation's rising star.

The sudden widespread interest in our ESG work was helping to drive public awareness of Seventh Generation. As the face of the company, I had also become the de facto spokesperson for the corporate responsibility movement we were leading,* which was proving profitable.

Harnessing all this energy to fuel Seventh Generation's growth was a no-brainer, and given my desire to move out from behind my desk, the change was a fait accompli. We hired Chrystie Heimert, a

---

* For a time, we considered getting an actual spokesperson as the company's voice. Some on the management team thought it might be symbolically more appropriate (and more appealing) for a young mom to represent us, but the idea never went beyond discussion. For better or worse, I was the best candidate for the job. I knew the company and its intentions inside out, and I understood the chemistry behind our products and the issues they addressed. Also, I understood the socially responsible business landscape. In the same breath, I could talk about indoor air quality, cleaning product toxicity, Seventh Generation's sustainable alternatives, and make the case for the new corporate standards they represented.

multi-talented public relations guru who had been instrumental in shepherding Ben & Jerry's own effort to incorporate broader missions into their bottom line. She would guide us down a new strategic path to leverage our new thought leadership position for the greater good and the company's, too.

I took on a new official title, Chief Inspired Protagonist, and began to write prodigiously for our new audience of executives and managers. There was a fresh blog with my byline and articles and op-ed pieces in the national press. Company newsletters hosted conversations about larger business issues, which formed key subjects for me to speak about at business-to-business venues like the Sustainable Brands convention and GreenBiz.

In 2004, I published *What Matters Most: How a Small Group of Pioneers Is Teaching Social Responsibility to Big Business, and Why Big Business Is Listening*. The book was an exercise in collecting everything we had learned about corporate responsibility, outlining its key principles, and supplying a roadmap for executing them. The idea was to make our model of doing business more accessible to anyone brave enough to walk down that road with us. It was the biggest piece of thought leadership either the company or I had ever done.

As I stepped away more from day-to-day operational management, I followed up *What Matters Most* with *In Our Every Deliberation: An Introduction to Seventh Generation* in 2009. This book was initially intended to simply be a manual for new employees, but it ultimately went so deep into our goals, methods, and madness that we decided to publish it as a de facto manual for conducting business our way. This was an outgrowth of our work with an advisor named Carol Sanford.

The following year, with the help of Bill Breen, we published *The Responsibility Revolution: How the Next Generation of Businesses Will*

Win, a broader but less meandering how-to whose aim was to guide the business community to the next level of its ongoing ESG evolution.

There were lots of stories to be told, and I had become a good storyteller whose audience was actually listening. Every company should explore unconventional avenues for storytelling, not only in marketing to customers, but also in how you engage with everyone from vendors to distributors to the public. Storytelling isn't just words, but actions. Credibility is built on authenticity, and authenticity rises from what you do, not what you say. Everything rides on making the right choices and being transparent when you make the wrong ones. But operating by one set of rules in a world that's operating by another created a tension that could make these decisions almost impossible to make. And compromise is sometimes warranted in everything other than your values, as painful as that can be.

CHAPTER SEVENTEEN

Radical Transparency

When is something toxic and when it is not?

Anything is toxic in high enough volumes, even the good stuff. Salt, for example, is absolutely essential to life, but if you ingest an excessive amount, it can kill you. It's the same with water: You won't last long without it, yet drink too much and you'll suffer fatal water intoxication. Contrary to consumers' general belief that a substance is either "poisonous" or not, many (if not most) substances are actually both. The confusion doesn't stop there. Toxicity, it turns out, is hardly black and white.

Instead, it's all gray area. In certain cases, toxicity results from a single exposure to a seemingly insignificant amount of the substance in question.

For example, the EPA and the Centers for Disease Control and Prevention consider lead unsafe in any amount, and a single gram of botulinum toxin is capable of killing 100 million people. Just 0.025 grams of sodium cyanide in three cubic meters of air is "immediately danger-ous to life and health." This is acute toxicity.

In other cases, the length of time required to produce a toxic effect can be measured in years. It's the tiny amount of dioxin encountered every day for several decades that eventually produces a tumor. This is chronic toxicity.

Ingest enough of a given material or chemical over the wrong time span, and you'll likely need the services of a good mortician. When absurd quantities are required to produce ill effects, the material in ques-tion is generally considered nontoxic (see water and salt). When more likely exposure levels can easily cause trouble, a substance is thought to be toxic, though to what degree remains a matter of how much over what length of time.

And it's this timeframe loophole that conventional cleaning prod-ucts manufacturers exploit to slip in their dangerous ingredients. Because warning label requirements only speak to issues of acute toxic-ity, chronic exposure effects go unaddressed, despite the fact that when it comes to most ingredients, this is the far more worrisome outcome.

What the conventional consumer product companies say is that their products are safe if "used according to instructions." We disagreed, but we had to explain why, and that forced us into all kinds of presenta-tions about toxicity and discussions about acute vs. chronic.

Complicating matters even further was the fact that we had to sup-ply our own definitions of "nontoxic" and other crucial marketing terms like "natural" and "safe" for ourselves and our customers, definitions that sometimes took another entire pamphlet to explain. In a world that likes its marketing reduced to pithy taglines and single-sentence claims, this was an overwhelming challenge, and it wasn't even our biggest one. Making matters worse was the fact that our definitions were often con-trary to those the industry itself used. Our "nontoxic" was not their "nontoxic," and resolving this tension was one of the greatest dilemmas we faced, because language was our greatest vulnerability—and the only one our competitors thought they could use to slow our roll.

In the early years of the company, we hadn't had much trouble in this department. To consumer product giants like Clorox, we were a fly so small we weren't worth the swatter. That changed in the early 2000s as our market share was climbing and our unorthodox approaches were being noticed by retailers and consumers alike. Now we were a rapidly growing threat that needed to be dealt with, and litigation over the language we used was widely viewed as one of the best ways to sap our resources and slow us down.

In 2010, Procter & Gamble filed a complaint with the National Advertising Division (NAD) of the Council of Better Business Bureaus, challenging our advertising claims about our diapers, specifically the use of the words "safe" and "safer." P&G argued that these terms were misleading and unsubstantiated, and therefore violated the NAD's Code of Advertising Standards. We argued right back, but in the NAD's view, our interpretation of the terms was faulty and not supported by adequate scientific evidence. Though we certainly disagreed, we lost the case, paid out a $200,000 fine, and were forced to adjust our wording in future ads.

Lesson learned. We had been careful but not careful enough. The complete absence of any standardized legal definitions or government regulations around the use of the "nontoxic" label—and other crucial Seventh Generation buzz words—left us with plenty of wiggle room,* and our instinct was not necessarily to play it safe. We sought to embrace

---

* Around this time, we attempted to create a natural cleaning product association to bring together all the companies in our industry segment—Ecos, Ecover, Method, etc.—and define a set of common terminology and standards. We had one meeting, but the project fell apart quickly thereafter. Maybe the others just didn't trust that the biggest company in the room could be a fair organizer of such an initiative, which doomed the effort.

ideas of radical transparency in all our communications that went above and beyond. We didn't want to stop at simply adhering to that letter of the law, because as far as industry regulations and standards went, that was a pretty low bar. My thinking was that just because something was legal to say or do, that didn't automatically make it morally right.

Companies are allowed to do many things that are tacitly wrong. Our idea was to create language that reflected everything we knew about toxicity in household products. But the issues that language was addressing were so complicated that it meant playing by a perilous set of rules that the competition was eager to exploit to our disadvantage.

We also found ourselves adjudicating constant conflicts between our bedrock need for safe nontoxic ingredients and creating marketable products that actually worked. In a natural products industry that was just getting off the ground, that involved many compromises. The debates were constant. How harmful would a chemical have to be to preclude its inclusion in a Seventh Generation cleaner, especially if it was the only ingredient that worked? Was it better simply not to make a product that had a "bad" ingredient than it was to make a product that was still significantly better than its conventional counterpart? Where exactly should we draw our line in the nontoxic sand?

Our chemistry wizard, Martin Wolf, helped us develop a series of guardrails we could use to keep our train from running off the toxicological tracks.

Biodegradability became mandatory. If an ingredient didn't rapidly decay harmlessly in the environment after use, it was forbidden no matter how well it worked and regardless of potential alternatives. Chlorinated chemicals were another absolute no. We would have nothing to do with anything that had anything to do with chlorine. We wouldn't use solvents that created acutely or chronically hazardous vapors, known as VOCs. Also, we forbade any chemicals that were considered toxic in Europe where there were stricter standards than in the U.S.

Outside of these ironclad rules lay a land of trade-offs and negotiations in which anything was potentially fair game and quandaries were as common as stains on a ten-year-old's jeans.

Surfactants were always a major bugaboo. These ingredients are basically soap-like compounds that lift and remove soils, stains, and grease. In the beginning, we had to rely on petroleum-based surfactants in our products. It was originally our only choice, but still it was obviously not a great one, and we rushed to find surfactants derived from natural oils like coconut and palm. Eventually, two effective naturally-sourced candidates emerged: sodium lauryl sulfate (SLS) and sodium laureth sulfate (SLES). Both cleaned quite well but each came with its own unique disadvantage. SLS was fairly harsh and could be irritating to the skin. SLES was a lot gentler but making it produced a byproduct called 1,4-dioxane, which remained behind in the finished product in minuscule amounts.

Despite some suspicions about 1,4-dioxane's ultimate desirability, we picked SLES for a couple of reasons. The first was that the jury was still out on its potential toxicity—the State of California considered it a "known" carcinogen, yet the World Health Organization had found no evidence to indicate it caused cancer. In any event, the levels of 1,4-dioxane contamination in our finished products were well within government limits and so low that they were virtually non-detectable. It wasn't an ideal solution, but compared to the much more likely risk that SLS would cause unacceptable skin irritation for many of our customers, it seemed like the right choice.

It wasn't.

In early March of 2008, the Organic Consumers Association (OCA) released a report declaring that it had found 1,4-dioxane contamination in a hundred "natural" consumer products, including Seventh Generation Dish Liquid. A big article in the *Los Angeles Times* trumpeted the news on the eve of the Expo West, the natural product industry's biggest annual trade show, and the OCA announced a press conference at the Expo to discuss its findings.

Everyone at the company was completely freaked out. Panic rose in the trenches of Anaheim as we went from joyfully setting up our booth to huddling in some anonymous conference room, wringing our hands over the sudden blindside and assessing our options.

We didn't have many. The OCA had found a level of 1,4-dioxane contamination in our dish liquid of two parts per million. This was a nearly non-detectable amount—even Johnson's Baby Shampoo had significantly higher levels. But technically, the amount wasn't zero, and we realized that was the only story that mattered. The OCA test results weren't wrong, and in a black-and-white world, there was no way to explain even the barest presence of a possible carcinogen in a product we'd boasted was 100 percent safe and healthy. It didn't matter how little there was or how nontoxic our product legitimately remained.* There was no explaining that nuance to consumers. From their perspective, our product was either dangerous or safe. The end.

Now the press had been summoned, and in less than twenty-four hours, the hammer of scandal, earned or otherwise, was not only going to fall hard, it was going to hit us while we were attending the year's

---

* Essentially, the OCA was saying that if you pulled a million random molecules out of our formula, two molecules could be expected to be 1,4-dioxane, a contamination level of 0.000002 percent, an amount sitting at the very edge of non-existence. At this percentage, you'd have to wash your dishes literally thousands of times a day to reach the State of California's danger threshold.

biggest gathering of our retail customers. It was a moment of genuine peril, one with the potential to permanently devastate our brand, destroy everything we'd built, and take my own reputation down via flames in the process—and we didn't know what to do. Under similar circumstances, when a company finds its reputation threatened, most businesses believe the best defense is to fight back and fight back hard.

I had no interest in defending the status quo. Once I saw the deeper implications of the 1,4-dioxane situation and collected my thoughts, I came to a quick decision. We'd defy tradition and do the unthinkable—the Seventh Generation way. I would go to the OCA's press conference myself and use their platform to tell the world they were right—we'd screwed up big time.

As I entered the press conference the next day, I found myself having second, third, and even fourth thoughts about this unlikely strategy. I was walking into the lion's den to confess, not contest, and the place was packed to the absolute rafters with reporters jostling for position. The OCA's representatives stood at the lectern prepping their papers and PowerPoint presentation. I was more nervous than I'd ever been. They didn't know I was coming, and I wasn't sure how my appearance would go over. And that's before we even got to the risks I was about to take with the Seventh Generation brand.

When they started taking questions, I raised my hand, identified myself, and asked if I could speak. To their credit, the OCA reps let me have the mic. I started by apologizing to all of our consumers and stakeholders. "We'd made a bad decision," I confessed. "We rationalized the presence of 1,4-dioxane in our product when we shouldn't have."

I went on to say how the OCA was correct. "No carcinogenic chemicals should be in any Seventh Generation, period. Either as an intentional ingredient or as a byproduct. It didn't matter what the levels were. It was the wrong call, and the OCA was right to call us on it."

I pledged right then and there to remove 1,4-dioxane from our dish liquid and any other product that might contain it within eighteen months and to share how we'd done it with the industry so that no product anywhere would ever again need to contain the contaminant. I promised: "We will fix this and we will fix it fast."

It wasn't just the only thing we could do. It was the right thing to do, and the response was overwhelmingly positive. For one thing, out of a hundred companies named in the report (most of which were also attending the Expo), ours was the only one with the guts to show up to the press conference. We got points for that alone, and having apologized on top of it, while making a firm commitment to change, sealed the deal.

Admittedly, no one in the company had even the remotest idea how to engineer a 1,4-dioxane-free product in eighteen months. But that was the least of our worries. We'd turned what could have easily become our greatest PR crisis into a unique opportunity to support the values and character of our company and its products. We'd maintained the courage of our convictions and stayed true to ourselves. Radical transparency made all the difference.

The incident was a perfect example of the uncommon kinds of complications Seventh Generation so often faced as a result of both our unique positioning in the marketplace and the noise we'd made to attain it. We would always be held to a different and much higher standard because we ourselves insisted on it. Invariably, this was going to lead us straight into the arms of brand-threatening dilemmas like the OCA report and company-defining moments like the Expo West press conference.

Our Albertsons conundrum was a perfect example.

Albertsons was a West Coast grocer and the first major supermarket company that agreed to give us some shelf space. That had been a big deal for us. We'd recognized that the path to meaningful profitability depended on expanding into traditional big grocery chains, and our successful relationship with Albertsons was key in demonstrating the mainstream viability of our products. It had taken immense work to get our stuff into their stores, and that work was finally paying off.

Shortly after our products made their way onto Albertsons' shelves, they declared their intention to cut employee medical insurance benefits. Theirs was a problem many businesses were facing before the advent of the Affordable Care Act—health insurance expenses were skyrocketing, rising as much as 12 percent a year. The situation was out of hand and many companies were being forced to make tough decisions.

In addition to announcing healthcare cuts, the grocer had also recently revealed record operating profits. They had the money. They just thought they could have more of it if they stopped paying for health insurance. So nobody really bought the company line about facing increased competition and a challenging economy in a difficult industry. The move looked, smelled, and sounded like a naked cash grab to goose profits and boost stock prices.

Albertsons' employees reacted as you might expect. They went on strike, and shortly afterward, the company imposed a lockout. The conflict was a bitter one, and it looked like it would last for a good long while. Initially, we didn't react because we weren't paying attention. There were a million other things happening and the Albertsons strike hadn't yet penetrated the management team's fog of retail war.

This was not the case among the staff. One of our employees immediately voiced the opinion that selling to Albertsons while its employees were striking against the company was not okay. We were in effect siding with management and crossing a picket line, and that wasn't who we were. Gregor Barnum, our director of corporate consciousness, agreed. He was deeply concerned and felt we had to take a more authentic stand. It was a serious and seriously complex situation. Gregor was absolutely right, but pulling the plug even temporarily wasn't exactly an option. We had an agreement with Albertsons. If we didn't deliver product on a continuous basis, the consequences would likely get us kicked out of the chain.

That wasn't the only factor we were juggling. There was also our nascent relationship with the entire grocery industry to consider. We were a new kid on the block, and we didn't want anyone thinking that if they did business with us and had a labor issue, we'd pull our products off their shelves. That would have been untenable for retailers and a dangerous precedent we didn't want to set.

Some inside the company thought the strike had nothing to do with us. Our obligation was ultimately to our consumers. That was the mission. The labor issues at Albertsons were irrelevant. To refuse the company's business would mean making our products unavailable to people who needed them. The other half of the company vehemently disagreed. They believed it was unethical to make money from a company that was clearly screwing their workers out of health insurance.

The problem was completely intractable, and no one in our management team had faced anything like it before. We knew we had to put our money where our mouths were, but in this case that meant most of our money, and there was absolutely no way we could do it without crippling our future opportunities. To refuse to ship would be corporate suicide and a knife to the heart of our own stakeholders. But to continue to ship would be brand suicide and spiritual death to our mission.

We were a sustainable deer caught in the socially responsible headlights. Nobody had even the slightest inkling of what move to make.

We took the issue to the entire staff. The conversation underscored a theme that kept bubbling to the surface: Where do you draw the line on corporate responsibility? How far back and forward along your supply chain should it go? What supplier and customer externalities do you factor into your decision-making? When is it your place to police your partners? And when should you literally mind your own business?

For the most part, our answer had been "when wasn't it our place?" I thought a company should take as much responsibility as possible. We didn't want to profit off the backs of workers or the environment, whether it was our workers or Vermont's environment. Now we were, but we had no idea how to stop.

The solution was brilliant, and I wish I could remember who came up with it because it played to both sides of the argument without compromising either. We would continue to sell as much as we could in Albertsons. But we'd donate every dime we made from them to the workers' strike fund that was supporting Albertsons' employees. We'd help the workers without harming our company—and keep meeting our customers' needs.*

Our ruthless adherence to higher ideals had once again backed us into an interesting corner that didn't exist at most other companies. Somehow, we'd again managed to avoid getting destroyed by it. It was becoming standard operating procedure, but even so, it couldn't prepare us for the challenge Walmart would present.

---

* I worried more than a little about the potential blowback from Albertsons, but interestingly, we never heard a peep from company management about our clever have-it-both-ways solution. I suspect they didn't want to draw any more attention to the strike and just stayed mum about it. Whatever the reason, the relationship remained solid.

For almost any business, making the choice to become a supplier to the largest consumer outlet in the history of civilization would have been the ultimate non-decision. It's just that kind of deal, one that can singlehandedly seal your success. Unfortunately, we were the kind of company for which the seemingly easiest questions were often the hardest.

In 2002, the same year as the Albertsons strike, Seventh Generation was approached by Walmart Canada. The retailer wanted to stock our merchandise. Were we interested?

Yes, we totally were.

But also, absolutely not.

In fact, the offer sent a shock wave through the company. The potential was dizzying, but the stakes were enormous, the risks unparalleled. What on Earth should we do?

On one hand, visions of dollar signs danced in our heads. Even capturing a minuscule portion of Walmart Canada's household product sales could catapult our company into semi-permanent prosperity. A deal with Walmart would double our sales and explode our market value. At the same time, selling to Walmart Canada would take our products and their much-needed health and environmental benefits into hundreds—if not thousands—of communities we'd never otherwise reach. In many places, Walmart was all there was, and if you weren't on their shelves, you weren't anywhere.

Then again, Walmart in the early 2000s was not the company it is today. Back then, it was the poster child for corporate evil. The company was a key contributor to urban sprawl and responsible for decimating countless small-town Main Street economies. It was abusing employees and squeezing vendors, environmentally laissez faire to the point of recklessness, and at times appeared committed to becoming the most irresponsible business on the planet as it pursued a merciless bottom line at the expense of virtually everything else. Supporting a company like that was a potential death knell for a company like ours.

Or maybe not. Some inside Seventh Generation made a solid alternative case for doing business with the retail behemoth. Walmart attracted large numbers of consumers to often-ignored small towns. And the appearance of a Walmart store could be counted on to bring overall local prices down by 10–15 percent, which increased consumers' purchasing power. More importantly, they asserted that this was not a boat we wanted to miss. It was a choice between revolutionizing our mission and expanding our impact at the speed of light . . . or forever remaining a niche player in the household products market.

I did not necessarily disagree. The growth argument was valid. Walmart Canada's overtures notwithstanding, it had become increasingly clear to me that, as with grocery chains, Seventh Generation would never have the impact we dreamed of without mass market retailers. We were leaders in the natural foods category, but it wasn't enough. Long-term sustainable growth meant large supermarket chains and, yes, huge warehouse stores like Walmart and Target.

Even though this was Walmart Canada and not Walmart U.S., the Walmart name and all its burdensome baggage was all most people would probably see. The question was how deep the in-bed-with-the-devil impressions would run, how long they'd last, and whether or not we could weather the storm.

There were internal issues at play, too. Would the relationship water down our cherished company values and weaken the heart and soul of the company? Would it turn us into money-grubbing hypocrites in the public eye? It had happened before to countless companies that had fallen under the Walmart spell. The mass market retail road was littered with the bones of companies that had thought they could handle it, found they couldn't, and paid the price with their very existence.

It was a question of brand equity and control. Would we be creating value for our stakeholders? Or diminishing it? How much would we have to give up and would the potential gain make up for it? It was not a simple decision.

In the end, we decided there were just too many unknowns and too much risk. After much internal deliberation within the management team and the staff itself, I made the call. The answer was "thanks but no thanks." This just wasn't the time.

That, however, was not the end of the story. In 2005, I was called out of the blue by a Walmart vendor we'd never talked to before. They'd been asked by Walmart U.S. to pass along a message that the mothership now wanted a meeting, but given our loud and proud contrarian stance, Walmart was a little anxious about approaching us directly. "Would you be interested," the vendor asked, "in talking to them?" The short answer was "sure." We'd be happy to talk, but they should know we still had no interest in selling our products in their stores.

That said, I was more than willing to have a conversation with them about corporate responsibility, and I said so in a letter I wrote to then-CEO Lee Scott. I saw it as a great—albeit surprising—way to fulfill our mission and spread our influence. Love them or hate them, there was no question that Walmart was powerful. With annual sales at the time of a quarter of a trillion dollars (yes, that's a "T"), the retailer was so big that it functioned as a de facto private sector regulatory agency setting global standards. If they wanted a product this way or that, then the manufacturer just had to do it, and that's how they'd offer it to everybody else, too.* If I could convince Walmart not to sell items

---

* For example, when Walmart decided in 2007 to sell only concentrated laundry detergents, every major detergent maker jumped on that previously ignored bandwagon as fast as possible to avoid being removed from the retailer's shelves. As a direct result, these once hard-to-find formulations instantly assumed mainstream and ubiquitous prominence, which created significant positive environmental impacts.

with certain toxic chemicals, maybe those chemicals would disappear from consumer products overnight. Yes, engaging with this corporate giant in an attempt to meaningfully bend its trajectory toward equity, justice, and environmental sustainability was definitely a tall order, but I was willing to try.

So on an early morning in December, I found myself on a plane to Bentonville, Arkansas. My first stop was an actual Walmart Supercenter outside of town. Andy Ruben, the company's VP of sustainability, met me inside, along with a collection of buyers responsible for infant and toddler products, from diapers and wipes to clothing and furniture. We walked around the store, looking at various products with various problems, most of which they seemed genuinely surprised to learn about.

Still, to their credit, they were taking me seriously. They were listening, and I gave them what amounted to a Seventh Generation primer, a quick lesson on chlorine and dioxins, phthalates and PVC, organic cotton and household cleaners, toxic chemicals, the precautionary principle, and the power Walmart held to change the world. We spent so much time talking that when we finally stopped, I was already fifteen minutes late for my meeting with Lee Scott. This didn't help my nerves, which were already twitching.

Dressed in a dark gray jacket and a black sweater, Lee was standing at the front door, holding it open for me as we pulled up to the company's headquarters. It all seemed so unlikely, I checked his name badge to confirm it was actually him. We exchanged the usual small talk about flights and weather as we wound our way through a warren of offices and cubicles to a nondescript conference room where the senior management team was immersed in a conversation about holiday sales.

The discussion ran the gamut of customer problems, a disappointing sales update, and a recap of an unhappy call from the chairman of the board. The conversation dragged on for several more minutes of daily decimal percentages and dollar amounts, the men alternating between handwringing analysis and cautious congratulations. As a consumer products company CEO myself, I understood a focus on sales, but this seemed excessive. It also felt a little too personal. "Why in the hell," I wondered, "are they discussing all this in front of me?"

Lee must have seen my confusion. He stopped the sales chatter and admitted that the conversation about sales never stops this time of year before casually mentioning income streams so far beyond what my little company was generating it was like comparing the sun to a lit paper match.

Finally we got down to our own business, and immediately I was caught off guard. Lee said he didn't know that much about me and asked for a quick bio. I found it an odd request—I figured surely someone had prepared the equivalent of an FBI dossier on me and that Lee had read it weeks ago. But I seized the opportunity and after a short self-introduction, I asked Lee to describe the legacy he wanted to leave.

He struggled with the question, falling back on the Sam Walton story and describing himself as continuing a tradition rather than designing a new purpose for the company. I was a little uncomfortable doing it, but I felt his response was a cop-out, so I pressed him. But still, he wasn't expressing anything about a purpose, a mission, the things he wanted to do, or the kind of company he wanted Walmart to become. He was just giving me a list of diversity programs and environmental initiatives. We weren't getting anywhere.

I threw caution to the wind and took a more direct tack. "I have plenty of my own opinions about Walmart," I admitted, "but I also have a lot of thoughts about how I'd change the company if I was king for a day. Do you want to hear them?"

Lee kind of shrugged. "Why not," he said. "Everyone else comes down here and tells us what they think we should do. We're used to it!"

I didn't hold back. I spoke about the possibilities that could emerge from real transparency and honest self-criticism. I urged him to engage with the company's toughest critics, listen to their advice, to go deep and think big. But Lee knew the drill—in a recent speech he'd talked about being the best company possible and using Walmart's clout to make the world a better place. He'd touted commitments to renewable energy, zero waste, and sustainable products, and had done so enthusiastically.

"That all sounds great," I responded. "The problem is, nobody believes you guys."

I told them it was an issue of transparency. "You're not credible because you're not really being truly open and honest. You don't really ever offer any meaningful social or environmental information about your company and its impacts, and that effectively forces people like me to go to the opposition to get it. That means your critics are telling your story, not you, and you're seen as less than forthright on top of it all—a perception that all the initiatives in the world can't fix."

A pregnant pause birthed a sudden wave of understanding around the conference table. I could tell I'd struck a chord. There's transparency and then there's radical transparency, and the latter is the only kind that really works.

Lee sighed and talked about the company's many issues: trouble with the labor community and civil rights groups, with activist organizations and environmental NGOs. Even the federal government was starting to pile on. The company had tried to engage, but fearing the fallout, not even politicians wanted to meet with them. Whenever anyone did agree to talk, they insisted the meetings be clandestine. He talked about entering buildings through secret entrances for conversations that never happened. The secrecy sounded painful.

Lee was humble and self-critical but also embattled and defensive. No longer suspecting me as a wolf in sheep's clothing and sensing my genuine desire to help, a more passionate and authentic man emerged. One who was starting to consider the challenges and opportunities with fresh eyes.

"Look," I said, "the opportunities are endless. Imagine a Walmart committed to ending poverty, to revolutionizing the U.S. healthcare system, to providing legitimate transparency on its products' social and environmental impacts, to supporting a sustainable U.S. agriculture system. What would people think of a company like that?"

"Take household cleaners," I continued. "You could revolutionize my industry with the stroke of a pen. If Walmart required full ingredient disclosure on the label of every cleaning product it sold, the entire industry would redesign its labels overnight and most of the toxic chemicals its formulas contain would be gone before it had finished. This is not some kooky impossible dream," I told the room. "You can do this. You guys actually have the power to change the world."

Then I asked if they wanted my help. They did!

We parted as friends, and every three months or so for the next few years, I traveled back to Bentonville to coach and critique. Lee and I made an odd couple to be sure, but our relationship had its impacts. Helping him and his team see all the possibilities and understand how to achieve them remains among the most important things I've ever done.

The meeting was not, however, the end of the story.

Three years later, we hired an intern to conduct an in-depth analysis of Walmart and the eighteen other mass market retailers operating in the U.S. and create an index rating them on their social and environmental performance—everything from average hourly wages and the percentage of employees covered by health insurance to carbon-reduction goals and green building commitments. There were fifteen criteria, and lo and behold, although Walmart had a terrible reputation, our results not only found the company doing much better than the general public was giving it credit for, but Walmart's final score was higher than some of the retailers with whom we were already doing business. It was either stop selling to them or start selling to Walmart. We really didn't have any other ethical leg to stand on. Strangely, the Walmart argument was suddenly about our fairness and hypocrisy.

Nevertheless, entering Walmart on any basis wasn't a simple decision. The prior November, I had floated the idea in an interview I'd given to *Fortune* magazine. I followed up with an article in our newsletter, the *Nontoxic Times*, and many of our customers had responded to these trial balloons with thoughtful and often impassioned letters and emails. The feedback was a critical part of our decision-making process, as were the debates at staff meetings and other internal venues where pros and cons ricocheted around the office like pinballs. In the end, the pros won. Walmart had made social and environmental commitments that were specific enough for accountability and had made significant verifiable progress toward becoming a better corporate citizen. Walmart had changed.

Any one of these dilemmas—and there were many more—could have been a fatal blow to our hard-won Seventh Generation brand. Again, we were quite publicly holding ourselves to a much higher standard, and our attempts to become a new kind of more responsive and accountable corporate entity had, in effect, painted a neon bullseye on our back that dared the world to take aim. Yet ironically, the radical transparency that was largely responsible for this scrutiny was also what continually saved us.

Typically, companies only want to share what they've already figured out. They love talking about their solutions and hate discussing their problems. The last thing most businesses want is to have customers peeking behind the curtain because maintaining and growing a business is full of misses and mistakes. What this approach fails to see is that creating full transparency and open dialogues with your stakeholders establishes a foundation of reciprocal trust. When you aren't hiding anything, you don't have anything to hide. It's never the crime that gets you. It's always the coverup.

I've often put it this way: If you were to date someone who behaves like the average company, they'd spend the whole evening telling you how wonderful they are and how terrific their products are and what a great staff they have. They would continually present themselves as the ideal partner, but who wants to be in a partnership like that? The fact is nobody wants to spend any significant amount of time with someone who's constantly going on about how great they are. That's not real. Nobody's perfect.

If you're going to enter into a relationship, it's going to be with someone who's honest with you about their strengths and weaknesses, about who they really are, warts and all. Without that kind of interpersonal transparency, there's just nothing to build a future on.

Companies continually fail to understand this fundamental truth. If anything, most businesses seem congenitally unable to be honest about who they are, and it's constantly getting them into more trouble than they realize. In fact, all too many public relations crises are rooted in a basic, historic lack of radical transparency. This lack creates a vacuum that consumers fill with their own interpretations of situations and events, perceptions and suspicions, all informed by the fact that the company in question hasn't been forthcoming in the past. When trouble strikes (and it will), companies in this position are left trying to "spin" the narrative.

By the time we'd grown big enough to get noticed, we'd already spent years constructing a platform of radical transparency. Unlike the typical corporation, we were deep into a dialogue with consumers about the choices we faced and the compromises we had to make. Our position was never to deny these compromises, but to explain that every company had to make choices and trade-offs. Consumers just weren't usually aware of these concessions. Yet at least when you supported Seventh Generation, you knew what those concessions were—and why.

That openness fostered some very strong consumer loyalty that allowed us to weather the 1,4-dioxane incident. We had brought a much deeper level of integrity to the table, which gave us valuable room to maneuver through controversies when they struck.

When most people think about Seventh Generation, they think of environmentally friendly products, but in reality, our most important product was radical transparency. We framed all our decisions with this bedrock idea, especially the difficult ones, and used it to guide our conversations with our consumers. How would they feel if they were sitting in the conference room with us? What questions would they want to ask? What would they want to know if they knew enough to ask?

Most companies take the opposite position. "Well, nobody's asking about issue X or subject Y," they say. "Why should we worry about it? Let's not."

It's a common perspective but a hazardous one because it sets up a dynamic of subterfuge, whether directly intentional or not. Over time, a company's secrets will have a corrosive effect on the elements its brands are counting on for success—trust and fealty, faith and forgiveness.

Such external transparency, however, wasn't our own exclusive savior. We also found salvation through internal openness and engagement. We invited our staff not only to chime in and opine on the decisions Seventh Generation faced but to push back when they disagreed with whatever the management team might be contemplating. We had created a culture in which people felt safe to challenge me and everybody else, and we had made the input we collected via employee candor part of our decision-making process.

Frequently, as in the case of Walmart and Albertsons, the stakes were high enough that it was essential for the entire company to weigh in. In those not uncommon cases, we took the conundrum to staff meetings and opened the floor for comments and suggestions. These staff meetings would frequently grow very interesting (and very long!) as various debates could become quite energetic. The discussions were not only fascinating but typically yielded fresh ideas and perspectives I hadn't considered.

Some were more comfortable than others when it came to voicing their concerns so publicly—we had certain employees who relished their contrarian points of view and were never hesitant to speak up, and others whose shyness I could relate to. But even when views were expressed in private conversations, these dialogues were invaluable. In some ways, we even made the people with the most controversial perspectives the heroes of the hour. Their maverick opinions were, after all, truly embodying the Seventh Generation zeitgeist.

Admittedly, opening up debate about key company decisions to employees and seeking their input can be potentially problematic. You must ensure that your staff is genuinely and meaningfully aligned with your mission, vision, and values. Otherwise, staff meetings could easily veer from the ethical path and stray toward the usual corporate impulse to maximize financial gain as the prime overriding directive. This was why we made personal beliefs and philosophies a cornerstone of our hiring process—we needed everyone navigating with the same compass.

Our Walmart puzzle was a case in point. In advocating a negative position, management was basically saying no to expanding our sales and creating more short-term value for our shareholders, which included employees. In the end, our choice was ultimately a financially deleterious decision. But we were comfortable debating it with our staff because we knew everyone would approach the issue from at least a general vantage point where money wasn't the only object worth discussing.

Done right, the best safeguard your brand can have is your own employees, but for them to be able to offer that protection, they have to do more than understand the company's culture and embrace its ethics. They have to know it's okay to hold you accountable. They can't be scared to open their mouths or worried about repercussions when they do. When they aren't, great things happen. In our case, employees' perspectives were a key part of helping steer Seventh Generation through a constant minefield of potentially explosive issues and represented a fundamental rejection of Milton Friedman's belief in shareholder primacy. Being publicly and privately open about our dilemmas and soliciting alternative viewpoints guided us through it all.

Now the only question left was how far could we go?

CHAPTER EIGHTEEN

What's the Point?

As Seventh Generation headed toward the back half of the 2000s, everything was a rosy shade of brilliant green. Our suite of sustainable household products had evolved to the level we'd long envisioned and at last worked as well as—if not better than—some of their conventional counterparts. From both environmental and performance perspectives, they were the best they'd ever been, and this progress was reflected in growth on the company's ledger, which for the first time, traded red ink for black.

In 2006, the company's annual sales reached a high watermark of $63 million, a significant 28 percent increase over 2005.* Better yet, we were actually making money. Our operating income was $1.8 million, more than double what it had been the year before. After years of

---

* From 2000 to 2010, Seventh Generation's sales grew at the rate of about 30 percent annually. Though that may not seem as extraordinary as the kind of explosive growth you hear about in the tech sector, it's a fairly astonishing pace for a consumer products company that has to physically produce, ship, and retail every individual item it sells versus a software company that makes something once and then sells it via frictionless digital channels. The two business models couldn't be more different, which makes our decade of double-digit annual growth much more impressive.

constant losses, we had arrived at profitability, a paradisiacal place we were not 100 percent sure we'd ever see. Seventh Generation was not only viable but thriving.

I liked the profit, but I loved the sales. While the growth in income was no small thing, the growth in sales meant we were reaching ever more people and dramatically increasing our effect on the world, which was always more exciting to me. We had never wanted to simply make money. We had wanted to make a difference, and now we were. It was an incredible high, but like many highs it was also extremely addictive. Instead of relaxing and resting on our hard-won laurels, I found myself thirsting for more. More sales, more growth, more impact. We were on a roll.

At least that's how it looked to outside observers. Inside the company, it was a different story. Behind closed doors, we were slowly but inexorably devolving into a red-hot mess. There were a couple of factors at play. The first was directly related to the aforementioned explosive growth. Managing the growth meant hiring people with actual consumer packaged goods experience, which forced us to recruit new staff members who came from traditional companies like Arm & Hammer and S.C. Johnson. Their hearts were in the right place, but there wasn't much time for retooling their conventional thinking. If we wanted our company star to continue its meteoric rise and successfully challenge the primacy of our mainstream competitors, the people we needed to help us had to hit the ground running.

Our hiring drive had essentially created a whole new company, one where fully half of our staff had only been at Seventh Generation for two years or less. As we integrated a more traditional class of employee, it was putting immense pressure on the company culture we'd spent so much time nurturing. There were increasing amounts of friction as that culture bumped up against individuals for whom it was utterly alien. These were staff members who in many cases weren't there primarily because of our mission but because we were a good stepping stone for their own career development. While they were great people, we worried that their orthodox operating modes could water down our mission over time.

Second, we were going in a hundred different directions at once. As part of our intention to be as philosophically inclusive as possible, we had unwittingly become a bit schizophrenic. We were pursuing a broad spectrum of goals and projects, many of which were in conflict with each other. We were trying to create the best place on Earth to work, save the planet, and make the world a better place while setting sales records, revolutionizing the consumer products industry, eliminating toxic chemicals, and changing the fundamental nature of business itself. It was an ambitious agenda to say the least. Too ambitious, actually.

The result was a serious identity crisis with more questions than answers. What kind of company did we see ourselves becoming moving forward? Our efforts to create a new strategic plan that would guide us hadn't worked out, and we were back at square one. Successful from a conventional point of view but rudderless from our own maverick perspective. And with so much going on, there wasn't much time or space to consider if we were doing the right things.

With our staff getting larger by the month, our offices in the old Burlington icehouse were feeling the strain. I loved the building, but it just wasn't made to hold a company our size. The process of creating our new headquarters was a true labor of love. Gregor Barnum, our director of corporate consciousness, led the work to ensure the space would align with our culture and its values. LEED standards were just the start.* There were dozens of other factors to consider, and he brought in a simpatico Arizona design firm to help guide our thinking.

As luck would have it, that design firm had been working with a consultant named Carol Sanford, who'd been helping them grow their business. Gregor kept hearing good things about her work, and his curiosity was more than a little piqued. He thought she might have insight we needed, so he arranged for Carol and me to meet in Burlington.

I was greeted by a real character—a small, older woman who gave off waves of warmth in between great tides of passion. Despite a fairly astonishing surfeit of luggage (and no shortage of health issues), she was a bright-eyed bundle of wit and energy who blew into the room and promptly blew me away.

The first thing she said was that we shouldn't ever have brought someone in to write our strategic plan for us. We ourselves were the only people capable of creating a plan that would genuinely reflect the essence of our true identity and beliefs. She told me she would teach us everything we needed to know to design an intentional path forward to grow the business the way we wanted. Based on employee development and personal growth, she would show us how to strategically position ourselves as an indispensable partner for our stakeholders and help us redesign structures, systems, and processes so they embedded regenerative practices into our daily work.†

---

* Leadership in Energy and Environmental Design (LEED) is a certification for buildings designed with environmentally sustainable materials and technologies. In our case, that meant an energy-efficient geothermal HVAC system, water-conserving plumbing, rainwater capture, recycled construction materials, indoor air quality features, and other eco-friendly strategies that reduced our environmental footprint significantly.

† Regenerative practices serve to repair damaged systems and further improve those that are currently undamaged. The idea is to operate in a way that makes things better than before. For example, regenerative agricultural strategies seek to rebuild damaged soils, further enhance healthy soils, restore lost biodiversity, and enhance the land's ability to absorb atmospheric carbon.

I was completely excited by everything she had to say. For too long, it had felt like Seventh Generation was just aimlessly slogging through an endless, albeit responsible, swamp. Saving the world was no small endeavor. Carol was offering a focused map out of that morass, and the relief I felt was palpable. She was surprising because her résumé hadn't exactly been the kind that ordinarily gets my attention. For twenty-five years, she'd been consulting for Fortune 500 companies, and her client list included many of the companies that Seventh Generation considered part of an axis of corporate evil: firms like DuPont, Weyerhaeuser, Clorox, Colgate-Palmolive, Warner-Lambert, and Scott Paper. She'd built a career out of sleeping with our enemies, yet here she was advocating an approach that was completely far-out, even for me. She seemed to really get us right off the bat, and that alone felt like a tremendous breakthrough.

I was ready to sign up right then and there. But Carol would have none of it. "Don't hire me," she said. "It'll set up the wrong dynamic if the CEO brings me in on his own. Put together a group of people, I'll audition, and you can put it to a vote."

It was wisdom from the very start, and I followed her advice. We assembled a group of sixteen people from different departments and every level of the company—administrative assistants all the way up through senior staff—and I made sure the roster included our most outspoken internal critics as part of the process. We set aside an entire day so the group could meet with Carol, hear what she had to say, and make a decision.

It wasn't even close. Everyone was as enthusiastic as I was and the vote to move forward with her was unanimous. It was the first of many times the sixteen of us would gather together under Carol's auspices, and our group would become pivotal as the work progressed. The members of what became known as our Core Team would be Carol's advocates within the company and disseminate her work, acting as coaches guiding the rest of the company.

We began what turned out to be an intensive process that would last three years. The overarching idea was that Carol would teach us how to answer an essential question: "What does the world most need that we are uniquely able to provide?" And then, how to use this new knowledge to craft a strategic plan that represented the company's true nature.

Three days a month, Carol ran full-day workshops with the Core Team. If you were interested, you could double down on that with smaller weekend personal development sessions. On our off days, we had reams of reading assignments to dig through, papers she'd written with arcane titles like "Psychological Aspects of Language: The Epistemology, Ontology, and Paradigm of Our Language" and "Levels of Energy from the Perspective of Decision-Making and Behavior," all of which had at least twenty pages.

The reading itself was incredibly dense and difficult, and her instructions more so. We were to digest the papers whole, in one sitting, and without taking notes or marking up the papers themselves. Worse, Carol told us she had deliberately written them to be hard to digest, a strategy meant to force people into the acute level of focus needed to actually change the way they think. There certainly was some truth to this—she wrote in a way that fundamentally disrupted conventional modes of thought. Sometimes I would read one of her missives and think to myself that it made no sense at all. You really had to work at it. Which was the point.

Yet while some of this work was arcane, much of it was not. We learned, for example, to master the art of designing and then executing how to have a difficult conversation. To become a company that didn't avoid them but instead confronted the challenges they presented in ways that left everybody feeling okay. Our assignment here was both simple and daunting: We were to hold three of these conversations and then report back on how they went. (I can report that it wasn't easy!)

In another workshop, she taught us what she called "the law of three," the idea being that if you were faced with two bad choices—as in the case of our Albertsons dilemma—how can you create a third path that resolves all of the issues with the first two?

The practice we used most often was called a "task cycle." This was a game plan for organizing a meeting or a project that forced everyone to consider in advance what they were about to do and why they thought they should do it. It looked something like this:

1. **Start with Essence and Purpose**

   a. Before designing a task, we must first identify the essence (unique potential) of a person, team, or organization.

   b. Then we have to ensure the project aligns with the core purpose of the company, not just its operational goals.

2. **Integrate Regenerative Principles**

   That means we must ensure that the task:

   a. develops capability, not just gets the work done.

   b. requires our staff to engage with wholes, seeing systems and patterns.

   c. is tied to value-adding processes that benefit stakeholders beyond the immediate team or company.

3. **Structure as a Developmental Learning Loop**

    The task cycle is meant to be:

    a. self-reflective—staff must evaluate how their own thinking and effectiveness evolve through the task.

    b. iterative—not a one-and-done, but part of a growth loop.

    c. individually owned—accountability is intrinsic, not externally enforced.

Five Phases of the Task Cycle Include:

1. **Framing**—Define the task in terms of outcomes and principles, not steps.

2. **Engagement**—Execute while reflecting on one's own patterns and the evolving system.

3. **Integration**—Draw learnings from the experience into self-understanding and team development.

4. **Renewal**—Re-design future work with new capability and insight.

Over time, Carol taught us an invaluable series of frameworks like these to use in our daily office life. Collectively, these strategies helped the company act together in a much more aligned and purposeful manner, organizing our thinking and actions.

Much of this work was related to elevating our relationships with our retail customers. Her view was that much of our business was actually being conducted in a very traditional way, and that this conformity represented a huge missed opportunity. For example, when she looked at our relationship with Whole Foods, she said we weren't adding anywhere near the value we could be.

Yes, we had a solid partnership, and it was growing like crazy, but it was almost entirely transactional. We weren't really doing anything meaningful to help Whole Foods become who they wanted to become. Instead, our relationship with the company was based largely on sales per square foot, and while we were generating more than anybody else in the category, that was but a beginning, not an end. If we could also help Whole Foods fulfill its purpose and mission, we would be valuable to the company in a very different and far more important way than any of the other brands with which they were doing business, which would simultaneously help us fulfill our own purpose.

So we came up with a project to redesign Whole Foods's entire household products aisle. At the time, it was something of a jungle, with every brand vying for itself, and each one focused solely on its own product presentation and assortment. We came in with fresh eyes and an intention to double sales in the aisle, which meant boosting our competitors' numbers as well as our own. The intention was to create a new higher value for our relationship by growing the category versus just growing our own fortunes within it—and it worked! We doubled sales and turned the category into a big winner in five test stores, which earned us more than a little admiration from Whole Foods. Unfortunately, internal issues at the retailer prevented a national roll-out of the concept, but we'd at least demonstrated our unique worth as a supplier—and the validity of Carol's approach.

In her view, this idea of adding value to create exceptional relationships should extend all the way down the chain, from the overall company's relationships with its stakeholders to the level of the employee's relationship to the company. Success was rooted in knowing who you intended to become. When your aspirations were clearly understood, you became far more valuable to others because you were now working from a much more energized and enlightened place. When everyone at the company achieved this self-awareness, the company could work together to find its own true purposes and accomplish almost anything.

For me, this was a surprising but invaluable learning experience, and it forced me to realize that a trait I had long considered one of my greatest strengths was actually a weakness. I had always been proud of my problem-solving skills and typically showed up at meetings ready to play the role of the fixer. What I'd failed to see was how that didn't provide any space for anyone else to create solutions. Instead of running a company full of people capable of resolving difficult challenges, I had unwittingly cultivated a culture in which everyone relied on me while their own potential rusted away. I may have been good at getting us out of tight spots, but I was restraining staff development when I should have been feeding it. Talk about an eye-opening moment.

For months, I had a Post-It note stuck on my computer: "Ask questions. Don't provide answers." It was my daily reminder to butt out and give others some room to cultivate their own problem-solving talents, which was a new way of operating for me. Indeed, it was new for the entire senior staff because when we sat down to analyze a situation, it turned out I wasn't the only one sucking all the developmental air out of the room. Every member of our senior team thought they themselves possessed all the unique know-how the company needed. As C-suite situations go, this was hardly atypical. Most companies have just a handful of upper management stars who are considered the main breadwinners. Carol's job was to help us to see that this was not an effective way to lead the business. We had to give everyone ample chances to shine.

Staying out of the way had other benefits, too. I could focus on my own growth, which was particularly important. Carol and I embarked on a coaching process, an inner exploration of who I really was and how I could best express this "essence," as she called it. Achieving this awareness was crucial because, in many respects, the essence of Seventh Generation was a reflection of my essence. To understand the company's "soul," I would first have to search for my own.

Carol's process led to my reevaluation of my own core values, which were predictable and straightforward. They focused on honesty, transparency, and authenticity. This means telling everyone the same story and using that narrative to reveal both the good and the bad—which is why if a friend doesn't tell me the truth, I am relentlessly unforgiving. And it's why when I speak publicly, I take an almost perverse pleasure in disclosing everything I'm doing wrong via "radical transparency."

Carol also encouraged me and the whole team to explore what she called our "core purpose." I discovered mine to be creating a world of justice and equity. This, however, is not something that business is very good at. In important respects, the concepts go against capitalism's short-term, hyper-competitive, winner-takes-all grain. Justice and equity were not something that Seventh Generation had historically been very good at either. Yet as we learned from our imperfect attempts to achieve sustainability, it was essential that we continued to try until we got it right. Simply put, justice and equity are linked to almost everything from healthcare and education to living wages and environmental quality.

These revelations were as fascinating to me as the way in which Carol guided me to them. My experience during this process is well represented by the book *Presence*,[1] which describes how most of our life experiences fall within the pre-established patterns we tend to follow over and over. For whatever reason, the possibility of doing things differently just doesn't occur to us. Yet it is outside these patterns and behavioral norms that all possibility lies. If we can slow down our minds enough to intentionally watch how we think, to become conscious of how we generate our thoughts and question whether there is another way, a whole new world opens up.

Making the shift to this better way of moving through the world involves embracing systems thinking—understanding how all the pieces of a given system relate to and depend upon each other to enable optimal healthy functioning of the whole. Too often, we consider these various elements in isolation and approach each part of the system individually when, in fact, everything in the world is deeply interconnected.

Much of what goes wrong in the world happens because we fail to see these connections and therefore can't anticipate the unintended consequences of our decisions. The choices we make are vastly improved when we appreciate how inseparably integrated everything is.

For example, ethanol, which is essentially energy derived from natural vegetable sources—mostly corn—not fossil fuels, seems like a great idea until you look at the ethanol production system as a whole. Then you realize how much total energy it takes to grow, ship, and process that corn, which turns out to be an amount of energy greater than that which the ethanol itself actually provides. This hidden net negative benefit becomes even worse when you look at the larger "corn system" of which ethanol is part and discover that turning corn into ethanol decreases the food supply and drives up the price of corn to unaffordable levels for people in Mexico, which then creates a measurable increase in childhood hunger. From a systems perspective, ethanol fuels are not the great panacea everybody thought they were. Rather, they are a dreadful idea that many of us end up unwittingly supporting whenever we fill our tanks with gas.

Carol correctly believed that this sort of systems thinking was foundational to both Seventh Generation's operational functioning and success. Plus, our product development program, our staff equity efforts, and all the rest. Learning to see the world in this new way was as exciting and powerful as the new growth it was helping us achieve. There's no question the process was difficult, and even if I ultimately failed to master much of what Carol was teaching me, the return on the investment in trying was still impressive.

That wasn't the case for the company as a whole. Over the course of Carol's time at Seventh Generation, much of the initial rabid enthusiasm slowly turned to mild interest, faded to grim determination, and finally decayed into mute surrender. As the work progressed, it became a chore for many. Some were still all in, but over time, the company grew divided on the wisdom of continuing.

For one thing, too many people found Carol's program too complicated to understand without a nearly religious level of dedication. No matter how hard we tried to make the path clearer, it remained a bit too murky and was too challenging for too many.

In some ways, this was just the nature of the beast. The journey to any undiscovered destination will always be fraught with peril of one kind of another. Machete in hand, you have traveled off the edge of the map and are blazing a trail into what can sometimes be a daunting unknown. Such experiences will always be marked by fear and confusion.

Another issue was just the sheer amount of time the whole process required. It devoured long stretches of hours and was diverting a significant amount of energy from the significant task of actually running the company, which was growing like crazy and already over-working people past their limits. That was especially true where the Core Team was concerned.

After three years, we reached a breaking point. I convened a staff meeting about the "Carol Process," as we called it, and posed the question: Was it worth continuing at this point? We'd been doing it a long time. It was costing us time and money in appreciable amounts. Were we still getting what we needed as individuals and as a company or had the project run its course? I called for a show of hands: "Who wants to keep going?" It was under half the company. The people had spoken.

Despite my own enthusiasm for the work, ending our relationship with Carol was not as difficult a call as you might imagine. I could see the majority's point. Three years was more than enough, and we had failed to get enough people deeply engaged to justify continuing. That doesn't mean there wasn't value for everyone. But moving forward, the overall value was no longer worth what it cost us.

That said, the progress we had already made was tremendous, and I considered the Carol Process an outsized success. For me personally, it had been a transformative experience, one that had triggered a huge evolution both in my thinking and my sense of who I wanted to become. She had provided me with badly needed clarity about my own role in the next stage of Seventh Generation's journey. Now I knew with certainty that I was no longer interested in selling more toilet paper and laundry detergent. My own essence laid out a leadership path as an educator and activist, helping others reconcile what appeared to be irreconcilable differences within the company and in the business community at large.[*]

It gave new impetus, for example, to my innate fixation on wealth inequality, but now I could bring that obsession to bear on the company itself. Why is wealth accumulation so lopsided in the United States? Is it because there just isn't enough money for everyone to have a decent life free of poverty and want? No, it's not. There is, in fact, plenty of cash to

---

[*] For example, Carol was instrumental in helping me prepare for my meeting with Walmart CEO Lee Scott. She made me understand how I couldn't do the meeting off the cuff but had to design the conversation in an intentional way. It was her idea to ask Lee what he wanted his company legacy to be, a question that opened the door to possibility.

go around. This is not a math problem where the sums just don't add up. This is a capitalism problem where the businesses, the system, and our public policy create a funnel that accumulates wealth into the hands of a very few people at the very top of the corporate and investment food chain. If, on the other hand, businesses were reshaped as engines of equity that more widely shared this wealth through worker ownership, you would begin to eliminate economic inequity in a meaningful way.

On the ground, lofty ideas like this turned into practical brand-defining projects like Seventh Generation's own employee stock ownership program, which distributed a 1 percent ownership interest in the company to the staff every year. This totaled up to 20 percent over the twenty years I was CEO, representing a materially significant amount when the company was ultimately sold to Unilever. This was money that represented college tuitions, down payments on homes, and nest eggs for retirement. Research has shown that employee ownership also creates greater loyalty, less turnover, more innovation, and better financial performance.

Creating this wealth for our employees also added a whole dimension to the success and impact of our business itself, which I would list as one of our greatest accomplishments. In most companies, the idea of employee ownership simply doesn't even exist. And if it does, it certainly can't be found anywhere among the firm's self-declared metrics of success. Seventh Generation, however, put it at the top of the list and made it a primary feature of the more highly evolved business model we were creating. In doing so, we set a new ethical standard. Even though our employee ownership initiative was ultimately crippled by a board of directors who were not nearly as progressive as they should have been, the program was definitive proof of what's possible when you choose to think differently.

This was but one example of how my personal work with Carol yielded material rewards for the company. Now we constituted a company empowered to respond to the world much more consciously and with new and far more expansive ideas about its possibilities.

Suddenly, the strategic vision with which we'd once wrestled with so much frustration didn't seem so far out of reach. Though Carol was departing, she was leaving us with a roadmap and a single question to carry us forward: What did the world need most that Seventh Generation was uniquely able to provide? From this line of inquiry would grow our new purpose and what Carol called our "global imperatives."

Though they essentially replaced our strategic plan, our global imperatives were a concrete manifestation of both my own and the company's essence, designed to represent the future world we dreamt of building. The global imperatives reinforced our belief that the corporation is the most powerful global institution in today's world and that the role of business in society is one of the most important levers for change.

The global imperatives had a short-term purpose to raise the bar of possibility as an example for other companies to follow. But at their core, they were big-picture objectives that could take twenty-five, fifty, even a hundred years to achieve. This alone made them a much different sort of document since that's generally not a comfortable timeframe for most companies. Trying to get a business world focused obsessively on quarterly returns, stock buy-backs, and annual reports to think in terms of decades (if not centuries) is itself a radical act, which made the pursuit of these global imperatives so challenging. They required a complicated mix of many elements: a long-term commitment, cooperation with other businesses and organizations, our own ongoing education and development, and the need to look systemically at everything we do—a herculean task in a world that compartmentalizes almost everything.

As you can imagine, creating such a document wasn't simple. There was a lot of ground to cover, and we had a lot of cooks in the kitchen since everyone in the company was involved. We discussed our global imperatives in staff meetings and company-wide retreats. We circulated text and elicited feedback. We went through dozens and dozens of iterations before settling on a "final" set of global imperatives:

1. **As a business, we are committed to being educators and to encouraging those we educate to create with us a world of equity and justice, health and wellbeing.**

Our first imperative was largely drawn from my own personal endeavors in continuing education. It also expanded that mission to include social justice concerns, our way of saying that nobody wins unless everybody wins. Seventh Generation had shown it was an excellent educator. Now we had to encourage those we educated to go educate others and become co-creators of the healthier world we sought.*

2. **To achieve that, we must create a world of more conscious workers, citizens, and consumers.**

Again, we were good at part of this, but the overall idea needed work. We had very intentionally and successfully established a company full of exceptionally conscious employees. But the rest of humanity? Not so much. Then again, creating a world of more conscious citizens and consumers was a pretty high bar. Consciousness

---

* Not to say we didn't try. One manifestation of this directive was *Planet Home*, a how-to book on maintaining a nontoxic home published in 2010. As an attempt to write a book with our customers, we tapped the community of Seventh Generation fans for new ideas and practices they themselves had discovered.

requires intention, which is hard to achieve in a mile-a-minute world that's throwing out constant distractions. It demands that we objectively observe ourselves and purposefully break our own patterns to develop new ones that bring purpose into our thoughts and meaning to our actions. That's challenging to do since it's incredibly difficult to get people off the hamster wheel of life. We often become so caught up in what we are doing that we lose sight of the effect we seek to have.

3. We are committed to creating a world that is rich in value as contrasted to a world that is rich in artifacts.

A fundamental conundrum of our business is how it's based on making highly disposable products that create lots of waste and have a short lifespan. This is not good, but it's what both our company and the entire economy excels at doing. Such a business model has created a world filled with things that are consuming the resources of the planet faster than they can be regenerated. This is supported by the hopeless and desperately ironic promise that the accumulation of these artifacts will replace the richness that's being lost in our increasingly isolated consumerist lives—relationships, community, nature, connection.*

Yet still we pursue them in a vicious downward spiral of disappointment and decay. It's a problem, and Seventh Generation is a part of the problem. We sold paper towels because they generated a lot of income when, from an environmental standpoint, we should have sold reusable cloth towels instead. Yet we couldn't bring ourselves to make the

---

* In his 2003 book *Growth Fetish*, Clive Hamilton wrote that "at the beginning of the 21st century . . . despite high and sustained levels of economic growth in the West over a period of 50 years—growth that has seen average real incomes increase several times over—the mass of people are no more satisfied with their lives now than they were then. If growth is intended to give us better lives, and there can be no other purpose, it has failed . . . The more we examine the role of growth in modern society, the more our obsession with growth appears to be a fetish—that is, an inanimate object worshipped for its apparent magical powers."

switch because it would have been financially painful. We didn't have an immediate solution, but at least with this imperative, we were declaring our intention to figure it out and do better.

4. **We will work to create governance and social systems that increase the capacity for understanding differing perspectives and points of view.**

For me, this was a no-brainer. Our system of government has long since been overrun by businesses imposing priorities through expensive lobbying that narrowly focuses on their own objectives to enhance short-term profits. This isn't good for anybody other than large shareholders and senior management. We need new governance and social systems that ensure the physical and economic wellbeing of all citizens, which requires the willingness to listen to other voices and appreciate their perspectives rather than an obsessive battle for "winner takes all."

One essential aspect of this work is inviting those with conflicting beliefs to sit at the table with us—something that we need now more than ever. By bringing together business, government, labor, NGOs, religious organizations, and community groups to discuss problems in a multi-stakeholder dialogue, we create possibilities that simply don't exist when we approach issues from a silo, and this was a role I wanted Seventh Generation to play.

5. **We believe that our business and all businesses should engage in the personal development of everyone who works for them.**

Looking back, I suppose one could call this the Carol Sanford imperative. Under her wing, we had devoted considerable time and money to growing each other so that we could grow our company through the act of fulfilling our own possibilities. And no matter what any of us thought about Carol's process, most had accepted that this kind of personal development was essential to any company's real success, albeit a success defined by some pretty unique metrics.

6. We are committed to approaching everything we do from a systems perspective.

Much of what Carol's work at Seventh Generation was teaching us was to think in a deeply systemic way, to understand that everything was endlessly interconnected. Even pulling one apple out of the cart could upset the whole pile. This consciousness of the world's innate interconnectivity became the signature driver of our entire operation, which made this imperative a prime directive of sorts.[*]

7. We must ensure that globally, natural resources are used and renewed at a rate that is always below their rate of depletion.

As an "environmental company," the concept of using less natural resources than the Earth can reasonably replace was perhaps even more central to our business model than systems thinking. Despite the naysayers, the concept here is pretty simple: We are rapidly depleting the vital

---

[*] In the ensuing years, much of what the Carol Process gave us slowly ebbed away, a function of company leadership (or the lack thereof). Yet her influence was such that traces remained, especially regarding systemic thinking. As of this writing, for example, Seventh Generation's 2022 sustainability report suggests using "handprints" to reconsider its CO_2 emissions. The idea is that you check every place the company leaves a "handprint" for hidden climate burdens. One's own goods and services are an obvious area to examine. For example, we'd long ago discovered that the biggest environmental impact of doing laundry was heating the water. The result was a reformulation of our products to work in cold water. Also, consider your business's financial system. Which bank is the money sitting in? What are those banks doing with that money? Are they investing it in fossil fuels or solar panels? It's not a small question, and Seventh Generation knew to ask because of systemic thinking.

support systems that sustain life on Earth, and it has to stop or there will not be clean air, fresh water, healthy food, and all the rest for the next generation, let alone the following seven. Full stop.

8. We are committed to creating a business which is not just sustainable but restorative.

That means products that are not "less bad"—as almost all of the products we sell today are—but actually "good." This idea was far ahead of its time. Today it seems that everyone is trying to jump on the regenerative bandwagon without any clue of what it really means.

For me, the final imperative was the most important and would shape the next decade of my thinking. This commitment framed my growing concern, not just about the future of responsible business, but about the whole sustainability movement itself: that both were headed toward ultimate failure and in urgent need of a firm recalibration. Both were focused on developing goods, services, and behaviors that were merely "less bad," and that is not an approach that will repair the damage we have done to our planet nor lessen societal challenges from hunger to social inequality. "Less bad" only slows the rate of environmental and social destruction when we need to be restoring and regenerating all that we have harmed. We must create solutions that don't harm less but that actually leave the world better off than it was before.

For Seventh Generation, that meant the entire life cycle of our products must produce a positive, regenerative effect on a net-basis— an engineering objective that can only be accomplished with systems thinking. This is no small challenge. To this day, none of our current products come close to meeting this standard. That, however, doesn't preclude the possibility that they can. This dream starts with acknowledging that a much different approach is now required.

An example would be a laundry detergent that goes beyond being nontoxic, vegetable-based, cold-water appropriate, and highly concentrated to reduce packaging waste to also become a product that leaves the laundry water cleaner that it was before and actually makes textile fibers stronger so your clothes last longer.

Joseph Jaworski, co-author of *Presence*, once said that "when all is said and done, the only change that will make a difference is the transformation of the human heart." After fifty years of working to make the world a better place, I have come to the conclusion that he's right. We're not going to solve the challenges we face without a dramatic increase in both loving kindness and human consciousness.

This is the only way we can fundamentally change the nature of business and transform it into a global force for human and natural systems restoration and protection. We have to not only change the way we think, but also the way we feel. We must move from intellectually understanding the need for a dramatic course correction to believing it deep inside our souls, where our power to genuinely impact the world is born. Our system of business and commerce is designed in such a way that it is rapidly killing our world. Its purposes and objectives are errant, and so are the mindsets that manage them. Most of enterprise is a self-reinforcing feedback loop of bad behavior that does little more than encourage and reward the absolute worst human instincts. And the only way to change it is through a change of heart.

At Seventh Generation, we codified this belief by creating a position we called the director of corporate consciousness. The goal was to have someone on the staff whose sole responsibility was to promote systems thinking and deploy our global imperatives in their decision-making. In effect, the role was to change the hearts and minds of the company so that everyone was moving in unison toward all the right goals.

The person we picked was Gregor Barnum, my former Hampshire College roommate and longtime friend. Gregor was a philosopher, a dreamer, and a schemer. He didn't think outside the proverbial box. He lived so far beyond its margins that you couldn't see the box from his position on the intellectual spectrum. Gregor was a mad man, a wild man, a sweet man, a brilliant man, and a magnificently beautiful one, too. To be in a room with Gregor was to be joyfully carried away to a place of hope and possibility. Gregor hoped and believed more than anyone.

In many ways, he was born a man out of time, someone from a future that didn't yet exist, and so unconventional in the modern context. Most companies would never have considered him for such a key management position. That, of course, made him the perfect choice to become Seventh Generation's new director of corporate consciousness, for his mindset was naturally and instinctively attuned with the business we wanted to build and the world we wanted to inspire.

Gregor loved revolutionary thinking, and the farther out on the vanguard it was, the better. In conversation, he could weave Buckminster Fuller, biomimicry, Hegel, and systems thinking into a single idea that left me in awe. Gregor was so far out on the cutting edge that the cutting edge was in his rear-view mirror. All you could do was follow or get out of the way.

Much of his role revolved around helping people learn about systems thinking and apply its modalities to everything they did at the company. There were no other directors of corporate consciousness at any other companies and no templates to follow. He was the world's first, which made the job his to create from scratch. This he did almost effortlessly.

Mixing humor with mindfulness, he did these things in a way that endeared him to the entire staff, which proved to be the key to his effectiveness.* Everybody loved him, and he loved everybody right back, a quality of personality that should be a key qualification for such a position. It was as much about vision and knowledge as it was about having a certain sensibility of generosity and spirit that Gregor himself embodied. There was no one like him, and Seventh Generation—from its imperatives to its products—was much, much better for it.

---

* When we were building our office on the Lake Champlain waterfront, there was a lot of work to be done and not enough time to do it before leases expired and our company became, in effect, homeless. That winter, the construction crew had to work on Thanksgiving. It was not the most benevolent state of affairs, so Gregor took it upon himself to cook an entire Thanksgiving feast and brought it to the office to serve everyone who had to work.

CHAPTER NINETEEN

Falling Out & Rising Up

Our multi-year engagement with Carol Sanford left Seventh Generation in a good position to enter its third decade of life. We had made a long and careful study of both ourselves as individuals and our company as a whole, and completed a clarifying process that helped us hone who we were and what we wanted to accomplish. Through that work, we understood our motivations in ways we never had before and had achieved a new awareness of how best to express them through the business we were cultivating.

A long and occasionally dark period of uncertainty had ended, replaced with good feelings about the future. With $150 million in sales, year-over-year growth in 2010 now stood at an astonishing 50 percent. At last, we had a strategy to guide this meteoric ascent in the form of our global imperatives and a director of corporate consciousness who would help us manage these collective intentions in a systemic way. We still had issues, and they weren't minor, but I had confidence that we could deal with them quickly and move forward. I believed the company was ready for whatever was next, eager to explore the possibilities waiting there. I was, too.

Unfortunately, the Seventh Generation board of directors did not agree.

Which brings us back to where we started—Saturday, October 23, 2010, the morning after that tumultuous board meeting. I was fired in a terse phone call and told not to return to the office. After twenty-one years of blood, sweat, and tears, it was over.

Back home in northern Vermont, sitting in my dining room on what should have been a pleasant late autumn day, I was in a state of complete shock. I simply could not wrap my head around my sudden reversal in fortune. Twenty-four hours earlier I'd been leading the company I'd run for the last twenty years. Now I was persona non grata, an exiled enemy of the corporate state who wasn't even allowed back in the office to collect his things and say his goodbyes.

I plunged headlong into the stages of grief, starting with a deeply immersive experience of total denial. *This isn't happening*, I thought. There was just no way it could. The idea of actually being fired (fired!) by the company I'd birthed and raised lay completely outside the bounds of all possibility. Clearly, there'd been a mistake. We'd fix it on Monday and get back to business. It was beyond inconceivable that I would so permanently and summarily be dismissed without even a back-channel warning.

Except that it wasn't—and for reasons I couldn't do a damned thing about.

For one thing, I didn't control the necessary 51 percent of the company's stock that would have kept me in the driver's seat. Over the years, we'd sold so much of the company to outside investors that

I was no longer the majority shareholder. This was the price we'd paid for thirteen years of operating losses that had required us to constantly raise capital just to keep the ship afloat. It didn't matter that I was a founder with over two decades of service on the books and the CEO who'd just engineered the most successful year in Seventh Generation's history. The dilution of my ownership effectively rendered me an employee serving at the will of the board. And that board was no longer filled with like-minded souls focused on higher objectives. Too many seats had been awarded to outside investors who were chiefly concerned with their own financial returns, which they now believed I stood in the way of maximizing.

In hindsight, I should have seen it coming. Situations like the board's reaction to my Greenpeace arrest and their inability to grasp the value of the Carol Process were clear warning bells that big trouble was brewing. Too many of my fellow board members were not kindred spirits in it for the long sustainable haul. They were "all business" on every level, and as I sat at my dining room table that morning, I realized this epiphany had come too late.

That's not to say I didn't try. In fact, I immediately went out and wasted a lot of good money on a lawyer, thinking I might have some kind of case against the company. Eventually, he told me I didn't. I'd lost the company I'd built, if not fairly at least squarely. My hands were tied, and he recommended I keep them that way to protect my employment contract.

Whether it was out of some kind of vestigial kindness or due to a legal concern, the board hadn't fired me for cause. There were other conditions laid out in the contract that allowed them to terminate employment, and they used one of these reasons instead. For the board, it was a double-edged sword—there would be no "cause" for me to potentially legally contest, which was good for them. Yet at the same time, cause was required to cancel the contract, which was good for me. Yes, I could definitely be fired, but if it wasn't for cause, the contract itself would remain in force for four more years during which the company would have to continue to pay me. It was a dim silver lining. But one that was difficult to glimpse amid the sea of emotional black clouds churning with waves of shock and loss that stretched past the limits of my own horizon.

In many ways, Seventh Generation had been one of my children, a living, breathing being that was made from a big part of me and that existed in my heart as much as it existed anywhere else. Having the company ripped away from me so suddenly left a wound whose pain was exceeded only by the anguish I experienced in the wake of my brother's suicide. I was incredibly hurt and profoundly sad, and not just for a couple of weeks. It would take years for me to recover from the events of that autumn weekend—and scars would always remain.

In the meantime, there was no place to hide. My termination was an intensely public event. "A Pioneer in 'Green Business' Is Fired," read the headline in *The New York Times*. "Jeffrey Hollender Forced Out of Seventh Generation," shouted *Vermont Business Magazine*. The news spread from media to our dismayed retail customers[*] and the socially responsible business community, where it was greeted with disheartened surprise and prompted a truly incredible tide of support. I can't even recall how many people reached out to let me know that they were there if I needed anything. I received dozens of calls and messages from old friends, passing acquaintances, and sympathetic peers alike.

---

[*] In later conversations with contemporary members of Seventh Generation's sales team, I learned that Whole Foods was especially appalled and ultimately made Seventh Generation pay a price where the relationship was concerned. Apparently, we were never again favored the same as before.

Unfortunately, there wasn't much I could say. The same contract that continued to pay me would be null and void if I disparaged the company. Not only were my hands tied, but my mouth had been taped over.* For its part, Seventh Generation had nothing more to officially say about the matter either. After releasing a fairly backhanded statement that paid lip service to my legacy while insinuating ultimate failure,† the company had gone silent. In the informational void that followed, people were free to make their own assumptions. Naturally, many assumed I'd gone rogue and done something seriously wrong.

This was especially hard on my family. Here in our tiny little state where almost everyone knows nearly everyone else, it was the big news of the week. From the local evening newscast to the front page of the *Burlington Free Press*, I was a top story, and speculation ran wild. At school, my kids were peppered with questions they didn't know how to answer. "What happened to your dad? Was it sex? Was it drugs? Were there bloodstains on the walls and bodies in the basement?" Everybody from the classmates in homeroom to our friends in town had questions. And despite our innocence, we weren't able to answer any of them. All we could do was shrug.

---

* I did eventually broadly talk about what happened as a precautionary tale, advising other entrepreneurs of the risks they face when raising money and which governance practices to consider enacting to protect themselves from what had happened to me. The company wasn't particularly happy about this because it wasn't good for the brand, but because I never discussed specific details, there was nothing they could do.

† "As the leader of the company since its very earliest days and its philosophical guiding light for over two decades, Jeffrey has been an integral part of our brand and an obvious lynch pin [sic] of our success, our unique corporate spirit, and our much acclaimed emphasis on equity and justice in the way we conduct our business . . . His is a legacy worthy of the highest respect and admiration, and nothing in our recent decision should dim that in any way," read the statement. It then went on to declare, "As organizations grow, so do their managerial requirements. Eventually these increasing layers of complexity demand the recruitment of experienced professional leadership whose abilities and experiences are required to move forward. This is the crossroads at which Seventh Generation now stands."

Sheila had it worst of all. She remained an employee and refused to resign her board seat in order to maintain some influence. We were still big shareholders with the vast lion's share of our family's financial skin in this game, so she needed to keep her eyes and ears on the inner corporate sanctum. She had to return to the lion's den, now as a hostile party, and the environment there was toxic. It was a horrible situation and very difficult to steer through. But she'd been a New York City lawyer and was used to the sort of enmity she now faced. She soldiered on, doing an amazingly brave job.

The strain my family was under only added to my anger, which had risen significantly as the initial sting faded. I felt wronged in the worst ways, held hostage by the unholy priorities of a system I'd spent twenty years working to change and, even worse, betrayed by friends. All this after I'd engineered ten straight years of at least 30 percent annual growth against long odds. It was a spectacular run by any measure and one that was just now culminating in a historic year where sales had risen to a record level. Who did they think they were, and, more importantly, what did they think they were doing? From a shareholder perspective, it seemed remarkably short-sighted to fire the person responsible for creating this kind of stratospheric business value.

I was furious at the many people who had participated in and supported this coup. People who had turned on me, despite our close relationship. And I was generally mad at the rest of the staff for not walking off the job in protest.

The latter wasn't necessarily a rational feeling. I came to terms with the lack of a staff rebellion as it was really just a reflection of my own failure to develop a company culture that felt sufficiently empowered to take that kind of dramatic action in a moment of crisis. For another, the board had clearly communicated they would not tolerate any sort of insurrectionist behavior in the wake of my firing, and people were worried about their jobs. They had kids to feed and mortgages to pay. What else could they do?

In the end, we all had to get on with our lives the best we could. My firing had been a seismic event both personally and professionally, but like any earthquake, all you can do when the shaking stops is sort through the rubble for whatever's left, pick up those pieces, dust off your faith, and move on toward what you hope will be happier days.

I retreated to an office with a phone and a desk that my dear friend Yoram Samets had set up for me in the immediate aftermath, which was somewhat ironically located in the old icehouse Seventh Generation had once shared with his marketing firm. Seeing my despair, Yoram made sure I had a place to go and pretend I was working on some purposeful new project. It was a great comfort and one that went a long way toward helping me to recover from the trauma.

For the most part, I ignored Seventh Generation. For a while, the company didn't stray from the course that had been set prior to my departure. Turmoil in the C-suite notwithstanding, it was business as usual with nothing to irk my ire or tank the stock I still owned. I projected a sense of outward calm, a capability honed through years of masking my depression, but inside, my mind was reeling and all was turmoil. There were two things I was desperate to figure out: Why did they fire me without warning or negotiation? And what had I done to contribute to their adversarial attitude and decision?

The first question was pretty easy to answer. My position on ending Chuck Maniscalco's relatively new tenure as CEO had combined with my wholesale rejection of any kind of employee stock give-back and created a bridge too far. Add in the slow burn of my fundamentally nontraditional approach to management—from the arrest record on my corporate résumé to my constant public confessions of the company's sins—and I'd obviously used up all my get-out-of-jail-free cards. I'd finally succeeded in making the board a little too uncomfortable and unwittingly forced them into a proverbial corner.

Recognizing this meant also acknowledging my own mistakes in the affair. If I hadn't been so impatient about Chuck and so adamant about the employee stock situation, I likely wouldn't have been sent to the gallows. It was classic me—insistent to a fault about my own perspectives, especially when they involved ethical or moral principles. The reality is, I wasn't incorrect. But I was being right in the wrong way. Upon reflection, had I just had a little more patience with the board where Chuck was concerned, I believe that everything could have been resolved. Just six months later, the board came around to my reasoning and replaced him. Another example of me being a little far ahead of the curve for my own good. And for that, I paid the price.

The company did, too. Growth slowed dramatically after my departure. In fact, the company never again came close to generating the pace it had known in the 2000s. How much of that decline was due to the loss of my leadership and almost pathologically relentless drive to achieve ever more success? How much was due to market forces? I'll leave it to others to decide.

Whichever it was, I was no longer there to keep the pressure turned up high or to course correct for changing conditions. Nor was I able to keep the company innovating on a brand level, and I suspect that in my absence, this crucial element of company development faltered. The business stopped doing the kinds of work that had defined its leading edge initiatives like Change It, Tampontification, and educational toilet tissue—fell by the wayside. Media coverage suffered, too. When Seventh Generation fired me, the company lost its chief storyteller and brand zealot. Without an iconoclastic founding father at the microphone, interest in the company as a source of quirky media fodder quickly faded.

In the meantime, I nursed my wounds, pondered the meaning of it all, and did what I usually do when the excrement hits the whirling blades of business—I got back to work.

Happily, there was plenty to do. My new book, *Planet Home*, was launching, which meant a book tour and interviews. I studied large-scale worker cooperatives overseas with the thought that maybe I'd start one here. I founded Jeffrey Hollender Partners, a consulting firm that didn't do much consulting but still managed to keep me occupied. Most of my time, however, was spent reflecting on my evolving vision of the future purpose of business and sustainability.

After many months of introspection, I recognized that I'd come away from Seventh Generation with three fundamental realizations and now had a rising desire to put them into practice. The first was that, as valuable as it was for the world to have companies like Seventh Generation serving as exceptions to the rules, at the end of the day, having a few renegades around wasn't going to move the needle. We needed to rewrite the fundamental rules of the game and institutionalize positive change through regulation. It was clear to me that voluntary action wasn't going to be enough to save us. Nowhere near enough companies were stepping up to the sustainability plate, willing to go to bat for the idea that financial gain isn't the only bottom line that matters. From putting a price on carbon emissions to setting a livable minimum wage, public policy needed to establish new standards to level the playing field and demand a far more equitable and environmentally benign game. Perhaps most importantly, we needed new rules that prevented companies from externalizing their negative impacts onto society and the natural world.

The second realization was the need to overcome the premium pricing that green products had traditionally had. Sustainability was just too expensive. The people who would benefit most were usually the least able to afford it. Part of my mission moving forward needed to involve democratizing access to healthier, safer consumer goods, which would be much easier to do if full-cost accounting prevented companies from artificially lowering the prices of their "bad" products by shifting the environmental and social costs to the public.

Finally, as solid as Seventh Generation products were, they still weren't "good" in the way they ultimately needed to be. They were simply not as bad as the competition, which was better than nothing but hardly enough. Recycled, chlorine-free paper towels and toxin-free cleaners created fewer environmental impacts, but they didn't create zero negative environmental impacts, and that, too, was a problem that needed solving.

After looking around the consumer product landscape, I landed on starting a condom company with my wife Sheila as a good way to demonstrate this new brand of deeper sustainability and what has come to be known as regenerative or "net-positive" products. Condoms could be made from the sap of the rubber tree, a renewable regenerative resource, and we would manufacture them in a solar-powered plant that reduced their impact even further. The trees themselves would sequester CO_2 out of the environment to mitigate climate change. They could be grown on a fair-trade plantation, which would fuel equity and justice by providing much more livable wages for the people working there. And we could arrange the plantation in such a way that it boosts biodiversity rather than destroys it.

From a social perspective, condoms made the world a healthier place by preventing HIV and STD infection as well as unwanted pregnancies.

They lowered birthrates and helped keep an increasingly environmentally burdensome human population in check. And we would make sure they were free of nitrosamines, a carcinogenic byproduct found in almost every other brand. To top it all off, we decided we would turn the condom industry on its head by marketing our product to women instead of to men, who had traditionally been the target audience. The new brand was named Sustain, and eventually we even roped in my daughter Meika to lead our marketing. Our message focused on an empowerment conversation with young women about the importance of taking control of their sexual health and shifting the dynamic around responsibility for condom use.

Condoms checked all the boxes I had been thinking about in my post-Seventh Generation life, and I plunged into this brave new world with the same enthusiasm I'd brought to natural cleaners and unbleached facial tissue. I read every book I could find on the rubber industry, traveled across continents to visit rubber plantations, and studied condom displays in drug stores. I bought so many boxes that the local clerks probably thought I had a crippling sex addiction.

Though I'd certainly been there before, starting a company from absolute scratch is not for the faint-hearted. It requires a huge amount of focus to envision a product, bring it into being, and build its brand visibility to a level that can sustain lasting success. Such a project was just what my overly idle hands needed. Starting Sustain gave me a place to channel all my energy at a time when I needed the diversion most. It created a new identity for my wife and myself as the founders of a company that wasn't the one from which I had been unceremoniously fired.

In the middle of this effort to put the past behind me and generate a new future in its place, I received a call from John Replogle, the former

Burt's Bees CEO who had replaced Chuck Maniscalco at Seventh Generation. John had actually been one of the two finalists when Chuck had been hired, so we weren't strangers. Still, his call was a surprise. He'd correctly perceived that having an unhappy founder wasn't a great look for the company and wanted to mend the fence. Enough time had passed to take the sting out of the whole sordid affair, and I agreed to get together.

Being back in the office for the first time since that dismal October night so many years before was surreal. An instinctual familiarity mingled with that disorienting sense of foreignness one gets in a place that was once a second home, but now no longer is. I recognized the spaces but no longer knew all the faces. Instead of being one of the team, I was an object of curiosity and abstraction, the old soldier coming back for a ceremonial tour of a fort now filled with new recruits fighting a different war. Weird doesn't even begin to describe it.

At the same time, it was a huge relief to finally put the whole thorny and unpleasant situation behind me. Though my initial meeting with John covered the normal pleasantries—it was nonetheless cathartic and liberating. Between John's overtures and the new path Sustain provided, I felt free to finally move on. To this day, I remain deeply appreciative of his proactive efforts to extend the olive branch and rebuild the fractured relationship. It was key to helping me drop a ton of emotional weight from my soul and move on into the next era of my life, and I will always be grateful for that gift. To top it all off, John also became an investor in Sustain, a deep vote of confidence and a greatly appreciated gesture.

Between starting Sustain and being welcomed back to the Seventh Generation fold as a friend, I started feeling both useful and hopeful again. There was still a role for me to play in the world, and as I cleared away the wreckage of what had been, a path to that positive personal future emerged. It had been a long dark night of uncertainty, but now a new era was dawning. I had no idea, however, just how new it would ultimately be.

For the next several years, Sheila and I nurtured Sustain with crucial help from Meika, and I found myself back in the public eye again as the architect of a much different kind of company providing a novel new spin on an essential class of consumer product. That story is another book entirely, but suffice it to say it was as exhausting as it was exhilarating.

In September of 2016, I was in a taxi coming home from the airport after a Greenpeace board retreat in Costa Rica when, out of the blue, I got a phone call from a Seventh Generation board member. I hadn't exchanged a single word with anyone on the board since my firing, and it was a total shock. What could they possibly want? Hesitantly, I answered.

"I have some big news for you," he said. "And I hope you'll be okay with it."

Uh-oh, I thought. What fresh hell is this?

"We've made a deal," he continued. "We're selling Seventh Generation to Unilever."

There was an exceptionally pregnant pause as I absorbed the monumental news. While he waited for me to explode in anger, instead, to his great surprise, I told him I was thrilled. I was a big supporter of Unilever and their sustainability mission. I thought they were a perfect choice.

"If the board wants to sell," I said aloud, "then Unilever is the best possible buyer and a great fit. They'll honor the company's values and mission."

When I learned of the stock price they'd offered, I was happier still. My twenty-six-year investment of time and energy was finally going to pay off and in a big way. And that wasn't the end of it. If the deal went through, Unilever wanted me back on the board of directors, which would become a "social mission" board guiding the company's efforts to remain a leader in the world of sustainable business in all the ways we had practiced it for decades.

There was very little not to love. Most of the existing board members, the sharks who had so ruthlessly shown me the door, would lose their seats in the deal. I would cash out in a life-changing way.* And a deal with Unilever would allow Seventh Generation to fulfill its potential in ways it could never engineer on its own, while allowing the company to pursue a triple bottom line. All while giving me a renewed say in what that looked like.

To top it all off, I got a call from Paul Polman, Unilever's CEO at the time, which I thought was remarkable. Despite the $50 billion global empire he had to run, he took the time to congratulate me on my return to the company. He said he was looking forward to working with me and that Unilever believed in everything Seventh Generation stood for. They had the same commitment to sustainability and corporate responsibility and saw the company as a model for the kind of business they wanted to become.

It was big talk, but I believed it. I'd been aware of Polman's work,

---

* Despite growing up the son of wealthy parents living on Park Avenue, my parents didn't leave much behind when they passed. The truth was they weren't great with money, and when my father stopped making it, retirement used up what relatively little they had saved. There wasn't much of an estate for Peter and me to inherit, other than mostly ancient furniture. Though it always surprises people, I was not particularly wealthy after getting fired from Seventh Generation. (Hence my enthusiasm for the continued income my contract would provide—it kept us afloat!) Certainly, I was better off than many other people, but I was hardly what one would consider "rich," and what I had was largely tied up in Seventh Generation stock.

and I was fan. Under his leadership, Unilever had become a legitimate social and environmental leader. They had one of the first and best sustainable business plans and had made some bold commitments to have a positive impact on consumer health, fair trade, organic and regenerative agriculture, ingredient sourcing, and a host of other goals. I knew there were huge possibilities in terms of helping Seventh Generation do so much more. Paul let me know that Unilever management not only knew it, too, but that they recognized there were things Seventh Generation could do for them, too.

It was, I thought, a fittingly sustainable conclusion to the story of the little environmental company that could. Seventh Generation had come a long way from that tiny mail order catalog and its tumble-down storefront on an obscure South Burlington back street. It had endured two bitter divorces, several major surgeries, multiple near-death experiences, and more twists of fate than I could count, and yet remained unbowed. Now it earned its reward for all those trials and tribulations and stood on the brink of a brand-new era of once unimaginable prosperity and an ever more impactful future that seemed permanently secure. Against all odds, Seventh Generation had survived. And I had, too.

CHAPTER TWENTY

The Future of Sustainable Business

As of this writing, it's been thirty-five years since Alan Newman and I sat down to figure out what to make of a misbegotten mail order mess. In my own case, literally half a lifetime has passed between then and now, a great weft of ages stained by loss, and anchored by love. A lifetime woven between a sometimes-knotty warp of chaos and calm that has carried me from newlywed to grandfather, from serial entrepreneur to sustainability leader. To say the very least, it has been an extraordinary odyssey.

There's still much to do, and the world needs help from all of us now more than ever. Fortunately, I've got ample time to figure out once again, "what the world most needs that I'm uniquely able to provide."

There are things that I'm proud of and much that I've learned, and some of it is worth sharing if only as a cautionary tale. With Seventh

Generation as a central crucible, I was able to conduct two decades of experiments in corporate sustainability science, some of it by measured design, some of it by just throwing the works against the wall and surviving long enough to see what stuck. The results were always instructive, and the conclusions tell us much of what we need to know if we're going to genuinely advance sustainability's cause.

I think the record will ultimately show that before the company settled into a perhaps too-comfortable middle age, Seventh Generation achieved three major breakthroughs in its first twenty years on the planet.

The first was delivering the green products industry from the womb into the world.

There were certainly green products before we showed up, but they were relatively few in number and largely technical in nature. They existed on the fringes of the marketplace down back alleys where mostly only ex-hippie back-to-the-landers and survivalists were found. Seventh Generation brought these environmentally friendly alternatives out of the basement and into the bright light of day where mainstream consumers could see them. We took them to every room in the house and taught ordinary people in city apartments and suburban households to not only appreciate their purpose but actually bring them home from the store. We showed consumers how to care and why they should, and that work made a significant contribution to the mainstreaming of sustainability, a critical first step toward a much healthier and far more rewarding economic model.

Just as the company pioneered the idea of responsible sustainable products for everyone, so too was it a pioneer in the idea of responsible sustainable practices that should be embedded into every business. Again, there were certainly companies practicing various levels of sustainability before we arrived, but they were few and far between. They mostly operated on the consumer margins in smaller niche businesses, dwarfed by the sheer scale of their conventional competitors. Along with a handful of other forward-looking companies, we pushed the idea of socially and environmentally focused responsible governance out into the business ecosystem at large. Indeed, we refuted the unholy capitalist ideal foisted on the world by economists like Milton Friedman that the sole responsibility of a business is to make as much money as it can for its shareholders, no matter the cost.

Seventh Generation laid waste to that ugly notion and demonstrated not only how to engineer the shift to a far more wholistic and sustainable triple bottom line—from focal areas and achievement targets to systems and reporting—but why it mattered more than anyone realized. As one of the original founders for what ultimately became the B Corporation movement,* we built the business case for corporate sustainability from the ground up and proved that all kinds of significant rewards were waiting for those companies that changed their ways. In effect, we broke the mold and made money doing it, which was an eye-opener for business traditionalists. While those winds of change may seem to be blowing in a different direction, I have no doubt that these practices will stand the test of time and reward the brave entrepreneurs who continue to pursue them.

The third thing Seventh Generation brought to the table was a buffet of innovations in how a brand could express its own essence and how a company could manifest its commitment to social and

---

* The "B" in the B Corporation label stands for "benefit." Certified by the non-profit organization B Lab as having met high standards of social and environmental performance, public transparency, and legal accountability, "benefit corporations" build sustainability into their charters and governance to mandate that the company's social and environmental impacts are on par with the imperative to generate profits.

environmental sustainability. Whether it was our partnership with Greenpeace, our public conversations about menstruation, or any of the other outside-the-box promotions and initiatives we executed, we were always pushing the branding envelope into new—and often surprising—territory that greatly expanded the universe of possibilities, while confirming the financial and marketing benefits of unconventional thinking. Most businesses are good at innovating their products and services. We taught them how to get good at innovating the expression of their values.

These were things that really hadn't been done before, and when history advances enough to properly assess the last forty years of corporate progress (or lack thereof), I think these accomplishments will stand as the company's ultimate legacy.

I'm also extremely proud of Seventh Generation's previous commitment to employee ownership. Although it didn't get the same amount of attention as some of our other projects, our original dedication to this idea was a major part of our social mission to address the social and economic inequity plaguing the United States. When employees are owners, they share in the financial success of the company's value that they helped to create. They care more, work harder, and enjoy a richly deserved return on those investments that, unlike today's disparate wages, is enough to build a decent life, support a healthier family, and establish a more resilient nation.

If I'd had more time, I would have eventually turned a 30 percent stake in Seventh Generation over to its employees, and in the process, transformed the business into an ESOP (Employee Stock Option Program) company that ultimately let them run the show together with management. As it was, I was at least able to plant a flag on that hill and distribute a 20 percent ownership stake in the company (1 percent for each of the twenty years I was CEO), an act that declared the issue was one worth fighting for.

Lastly, I believe that my commitment to community will be counted among my successes at Seventh Generation. It was always my goal to create the best working experience anyone had ever had. It was an intention that went way beyond perks like free on-site massages three days a week and a freezer full of ice cream. I sought to empower the staff so that everyone felt not just employed by the business but an essential part of its purpose. I wanted the world inside the company's walls to be one where everyone was valued equally and individual contributions to the greater whole were always acknowledged and appreciated. I worked constantly to draw a straight line between that better place and a more vibrant business, to cultivate a happy working community that possessed a strong and positive self-reinforcing sense of itself. At the same time, I tried to make sure that the company remained ever mindful of the needs of the greater stakeholder communities in which it operated. From our supply chain to our customers, I was determined to enhance these interdependent relationships and support the needs of everyone involved.

As I enter the last chapter of my own tale, it's unlikely I'll start another company or even a non-profit. I no longer possess the energy or will. I've begun teaching at the Stern Business School at New York University and have established a mentoring practice as a way to pass the torch to younger people who do. There's a proverbial personal groove that I've found, one I had at Seventh Generation, where I believed I was making the greatest difference in the world that I could possibly make. That's my sweet spot, the source of my life's satisfaction and contentment.

At the same time, my fears for the world and the fate of humanity and the planet have not abated. If anything, current conditions have only amplified the urgency that drives me. From the climate crisis to economic inequality, all kinds of red flags are waving in front of us, but we're not paying attention. And I'm deeply concerned about what kind of future is coming if we don't. Now more than ever, in this moment of unparalleled existential threat, Carol Sanford's fundamental question haunts me: What does the world need most that I am uniquely able to provide?

I'm still not sure I know the answer. But I believe I've found the place to find it.

How to *Really* Make the World a Better Place

Nearly fifty years in the trenches of entrepreneurship brings with it many things you wish it didn't—stress and heartache, unfortunate events and ugly surprises, an overabundance of exhaustion and an excess of cortisol. But the long winding of time also offers rewards you just can't get any other way, and they are worth the cost. Done right, summoning companies out of the economic ether can advance the human cause and even change history itself. Creating wealth boosts one's fellow human beings and lifts the world they share. To find myself at the fulcrum of such things has been as humbling as it is gratifying. I'm grateful for all that that life has given me, and now I savor its culminating gift: turning knowledge into understanding.

Having seen the eras unfurl, I can now see a few other things, too. And I think that perhaps my next role is to help everybody else see them as well.

As befits the past, that future begins with a roll of toilet paper.

Seventh Generation's customers always wondered why our toilet paper (not to mention a good deal of our other products) cost so much. Because it seemed like it shouldn't. The product, after all, was made from post-consumer 100 percent recycled fiber—essentially its only ingredient was paper that was not only already paper but wastepaper at that—and we didn't put it through any chlorine treatments either. Shouldn't it have actually cost less than traditional brands made from living trees logged in forests, transported to mills, processed into pulp, and bleached to within an inch of their dioxin-tainted lives?

That whole process, after all, is a lot more involved and expensive. Was our higher price tag simply due to the fact we were a small company that lacked the leverage needed to negotiate reasonable costs? Was our supply chain a clumsy model of waste and inefficiency? Our overhead way out of whack? Did we pay our employees too much? Or were we just simply being greedy?

The answer is none of the above. In fact, our bath tissue should have been cheaper.* It cost more for one simple reason: because our company existed in our economic system of rules, regulations, and subsidies that was rigged to make sure the product cost more.

Bleached virgin pulp made from trees absolutely should be more expensive to produce than recycled fiber. And the toll it takes on the planet—the CO_2 releases, toxic pollution, biodiversity loss, and other burdens—should make it even pricier still. But the paper industry's playing field is hardly level. Some teams are given advantages. Others aren't. And the rules of the game when they all compete together have largely been written by the reigning champs.

---

* The fine print here is that it would have been cheaper eventually. In the beginning, those supply chain and buying power issues increased our costs, sometimes significantly, until we outgrew their impact.

Paper companies, like most businesses, have used their financial clout to arrange the world to their benefit. They receive a constant stream of gifts from the federal government, such as below-market-price timber sales and publicly funded road construction in national forests.* They're largely let off the hook for the waters they poison and the air they pollute. They don't have to replace the habitats they destroy. In short, they receive many serious subsidies in one form or another, and every one artificially lowers the costs of virgin fiber paper and makes the cost of our healthier, safer, and ultimately cheaper recycled-fiber alternative appear more expensive.

The free market, it turns out, isn't free at all.

Instead, Seventh Generation, like all of its competitors, conducts its business in what is actually a highly engineered marketplace created out of hundreds of thousands of rules and laws, most of which were birthed behind closed doors and midwifed by corporate interests who stood to greatly benefit from every last comma and conjunction they contained. Though its proponents tout it as laissez-faire, this operating system is actually highly structured.

It's been deliberately designed to deliver certain results via a host of tools—the tax code, appropriations bills, governmental regulations, court rulings, executive orders, administrative guidance, and more— and for the most part, the intention is not to level the playing field, promote new ideas, or improve social outcomes. It's not to help consumers or support a healthy environment. It's not to advance equity and deliver justice. It's to grant favors to the friends and supporters who have lawmakers' ears and to the lobbyists and industries who cut the checks. It's to prop up fading industries and obsolete products, and maintain

---

* Friends of the Earth, an environmental non-profit, once calculated that the federal government spent over a billion dollars a year subsidizing the virgin timber industry.

share prices. It's to maintain the profitable status quo, and it sticks the rest of the world with the bill.

The result is a game the rich and powerful have long since learned how to manipulate and play to win. The rules of that game, in effect, are the economy, and they only change when their beneficiaries see a new way to further their own already significant advantage. As historian Karl Polanyi recognized in his book *The Great Transformation*, when politicians argue for "less government," they're really just arguing for different government. The calls for "deregulation" that have come from the American Right since at least the age of Reagan are simply demands for re-regulation.

We have the freest marketplace that money can buy, and it has been a disaster for people and the planet. The world's modern economic system, built on an ideological foundation of unrepentant greed and sculpted to malignant efficiency by money and power run amok, supports the desires of a very few at the great expense of both the remaining many and the biosphere they depend upon for survival. If allowed to persist, it will shackle our future to a grim set of unthinkable eventualities.

I have seen this system in action. Ever since my adman father drafted me for my first Saturday morning cartoon focus group, I have been watching the system's gears spin and its purposes play out. And I have spent five decades of my life trying to change the way it worked and lead us away from the so-called free market toward a new democratic marketplace that manifests the wishes of the majority and operates in the best interests of the commons, an economy based on justice, equity, sustainability, and the wholistic wellbeing of all.

Seventh Generation aspired to be the model for this vision and my own tool to change a rigged system from the inside out. From a more objective distance, I can see just how effective that tool was, and I find that I'm a little disappointed.

The truth is, Seventh Generation was not all it could and should have been. Some of that can be blamed on the forces aligned against us. There was a lot of friction thrown up against our ideas. "Business as usual" proved to be a force to be reckoned with. To the extent we succeeded, it was in spite of these roadblocks. And in many ways, we did succeed in setting a valuable example of doing things differently, which influenced the journey of thousands of businesses. But at the end of the day, that example was not the revolution it needed to be. Yes, our products were safer and healthier than the competition. Yes, our employees were treated better than most. Yes, our company's environmental impacts were less than everybody else's. By every measure, we were behaving better than those that had come before. But that's just another way of saying we were less bad. And that is not good enough.

Don't get me wrong—being less bad is always good. It's just not as good as it needs to be, given where we need to go. To be content with "less bad" is to remain part of the problem, when what we all need to be is part of the solution. Achieving that kind of deeper and far more meaningful success requires that business become "net positive."

Net positive is the future for which we all now need to fight. This new operational framework calls for companies not only to have fewer negative effects on the world but to have an overwhelmingly positive influence instead. *The Guardian* describes net positive this way: "Businesses have impacts on the environment and society. Some are negative, some positive. For a company to be net positive, the latter need to outweigh the former. To put it another way: The natural world and society should be better off with companies than without them."[1]

In the decades since I co-founded Seventh Generation, the future we've been hoping for has become increasingly elusive, all because we've been going about getting there the wrong way. Today, we primarily aspire to decrease harm and inequity by degrees rather than build a brand-new world where all have the opportunity to express and experience the full potential of our humanity. We have so fundamentally confused being genuinely good with merely being less bad that we no longer know what "good" even means. A "good" future has primarily come to mean the reduction of only the most disastrous effects of climate change, waste, overdevelopment, injustice, inequality, and all the rest. It just means failing future generations at a slower speed.

For the most part, business organizes its goals and behavior around the fulfillment of legal and regulatory requirements and the need to maximize short-term economic gains for its shareholders and management. It's the tension Seventh Generation faced: an exclusive focus on profits produces little motivation for change, fails to account for impacts on people or the planet, offloads the real costs of negative externalities onto the public, and undercuts anyone trying to do better by ruthlessly leveraging these and other systemic advantages against them. That which is currently required to avoid global ruin—regeneration and enrichment—is completely misaligned with these purposes and objectives. In effect, the game of business is played by rules that not only permit but even reward the destruction of individual lives, communities, and the planet.

As individuals and organizations, we need a new vision of the future—one driven by what we actually want rather than what we just want to avoid. One focused on what we aspire to become rather than what we seek to prevent. A place where doing good means "we" rather than "me" and where decisions are based on what will be best not just for today but for tomorrow. We must become committed to creating a world that is rich in value rather than artifacts. This is what it means to be net positive, and to get there, we have to rethink the business of business so dramatically that it will make the progress Seventh Generation achieved look like baby steps.

The principles that must guide this revolution include:

- The purpose of the corporation is to harness private interests to serve the public good by maximizing the health, wellbeing, consciousness, and potential of all of its stakeholders.

- Corporations shall distribute the wealth they create equitably among those who contribute to its creation.

- Corporations shall operate in a participatory, radically transparent, ethical, and accountable manner.

- Corporations can earn reasonable profits only by fulfilling long-term objectives, but not by externalizing their costs or using their power at the expense of other stakeholders, which include employees, customers, the community, its supply chains, and the environment.

With Carol Sanford, Seventh Generation developed what we call "global imperatives," which detail a few additional ingredients to add to this recipe:

- Business must approach everything it does from a systems perspective. It must renounce the typical compartmentalized approach that embraces only individual points of view and private realities.

- Business must adopt a brand of sustainability redefined to mean that the rate at which we use and consume our natural resources globally is never greater than the rate at which those resources can regenerate themselves.

- All products and services must become restorative and enhance the potential and resilience of all life's natural systems. They must go beyond simply repairing our planet's natural systems and seek to make them healthier and stronger.

- Business must commit to a new set of basic operating principles that fulfill the needs of the common good above all else. Morality and ethics must become primary organizing values.

For a business community that prioritizes wealth creation over all else and largely, if not exclusively, measures success in private not public terms, this is a tall order. And the dominant neoliberal ideology of the "free market" only makes it harder.

We must banish the dubious tenets of capitalism gone wild that include:

- All growth, measured as GDP, is good.

- Inequality and the unlimited accumulation of wealth by a tiny percentage of society will trickle down to the masses and not pose catastrophic risks to business, social, and environmental wellbeing.

- Technology alone will rescue us from the impacts of pollution and the unlimited consumption of non-renewable natural resources.

- Democracy can coexist with the unlimited influence of money in politics.

- Short-term decision-making frameworks won't lead to long-term negative consequences.

That's quite a belief system. And it's time we asked: "How's it working out for everybody?" Because by virtually every measure, the objective answer is "not great."

Here in the U.S., as of the fourth quarter of 2024, the top 10 percent of U.S. households controlled approximately 67.2 percent of the nation's total net wealth (MarketWatch, 11/23/24) while the bottom 50 percent of earners own just 2.4 percent of the total wealth (Federal Reserve, 3/20/25).[2] One in eighteen people live in a state of "deep poverty," including 5 million children* (UNICEF USA Innocenti Report), and some 25 percent of American adults are food insecure (CBS News).[3] All told, racial and ethnic health disparities now cost the U.S. economy $451 billion a year,[4] and global cases of early onset cancer have mushroomed almost 80 percent in the last three decades while cancer deaths for adults under fifty years increased by 27 percent.[5]

In the natural world, wildlife populations plummeted an average of 69 percent between 1970 and 2018. Out of 147,500 studied species, 41,000 or almost 28 percent are threatened with extinction.[6] Earth's atmosphere now contains as much CO_2 as it did three million years ago, and extreme heat events that once occurred every ten years now occur with almost three times the regularity[7] while extreme rain and drought have occurred more often in the last eight years than in the previous decade.[8] In 2022 alone, America experienced six "1,000-year" rain events in a single month![9]

Does this sound like a system that's working? It does not. And I hold business, the largest, richest, most powerful, and omnipresent force on the Earth, largely to blame. This makes revolutionizing the "free market" beliefs on which capitalism is based humanity's most urgent task. Simply put, without a new set of operating principles, we're doomed.

Business must change the rules of its game or it's game over, which means challenging the policy, legislative, tax, legal, and accounting rules

---

* Defined as people who make less than $6,380 a year, or families of four living on less than $13,100, per Annie Nova, "5 Alarming Stats on U.S. Economic Inequality in Pulitzer Prize-Winning Author's New Book," CNBC, March 28, 2023, https://www.cnbc.com/2023/03/28/5-alarming-stats-on-us-economic-inequality.html

that together constitute the "free market" system,[10] then replacing them with incentives and disincentives rooted in the "net positive concept," which now must become the dominant economic paradigm.

What would such a reinvented system look like? Based on my own experiences, here's an 18-point blueprint:

1. Stop transferring the cost of product externalities from business to society and the environment. Whether it's the cost of cleaning up the pollution they produce or the health impacts their operations create, companies don't pay it. The public does. And we shouldn't. Including those costs in product pricing and in companies' profit and loss statements and balance sheets is called full-cost accounting. Companies don't currently use this accounting practice, and until they do, they will never willingly make choices that are aligned with the best interest of future generations.[*]

2. Tax and stringently regulate waste, carbon production, pollution, and all other forms of environmental damage. It's pretty simple: When an activity costs a company too much money, they stop doing it as quickly as they can. Our entire tax system should be repurposed to disincentivize any and all forms of social and environmental harm to the point of extreme corporate financial peril while rewarding efficiency, sustainability, and resource conservation with prizes that business can't resist. Regenerative practices should supply the greatest financial advantages. Where taxes aren't enough, regulations that essentially mandate clean production, zero waste, and environmental regeneration should be established.

---

[*] For more information about full cost accounting, see: The Impact Institute, "The Current Field of True Cost Accounting," February 2023, https://tcaaccelerator.org/wp-content/uploads/2023/03/The-Current-Field-of-True-Cost-Accounting-Final.pdf

If and when penalties like these fall into place, you can expect better air, cleaner water, less illness, and a cooler climate to follow.[*]

3. Support renewable energy and energy efficiency. Similarly, the tax code and regulatory environment should be reinvented to promote the production and use of renewable energy and the adoption of practices that increase energy efficiency. The less energy you use, the greater the reward should be. Go the other way and the economic and legal hammers should come down hard.

4. Use tax and regulatory mechanisms to create and promote a circular economy. A circular economy is one in which production and consumption keep materials in use for as long as possible by reusing or repairing them when that useful life ends. Instead of making a product from virgin raw materials, turning it into trash at end-of-life, and buying a brand-new replacement made once again from virgin materials, this system seeks to keep the things we make and need in service as long as possible and then recycle all their components into new products following "disposal." The waste of every system is used to feed another so that there's very little garbage and far fewer extractive activities like mining, logging, and drilling.[†]

5. Restrict the extraction of virgin raw materials to sustainable levels. No company should be allowed to use more than its share of whatever the planet can sustainably produce and regenerate over time. Much in the same way that an annual report is mandatory

---

[*]   For more information about regenerative business, see: Oliver Dudok van Heel, "Let's Talk About 'Regenerative Business,' Not Sustainability," *World Economic Forum*, March 27, 2023, https://www.weforum.org/stories/2023/03/regenerative-business-sustainability/

[†]   For more information about the circular economy, see: "What Is a Circular Economy?" Ellen MacArthur Foundation, https://www.ellenmacarthurfoundation.org/topics/circular-economy-introduction/overview

for all public companies, we should require the annual production of third-party-verified corporate sustainability reports of all companies with sales in excess of $10 million. That must include Scope 3 impacts of corporate impacts on people and planet.

6. End all corporate financial subsidies that don't support sustainable business. Every dollar the federal government gives away to support a national forest timber sale and every dime it allows oil companies to deduct for their drilling costs is money we don't have for environmental protection, healthcare, and other essentials. There's no reason any company should get handouts of public funds to boost its private profits, and political pressure is the only reason they do. We must amp up our own pressure to end this absurd practice. No more taxpayer largesse to corporations and industries simply because they're big enough and powerful enough to get them.

7. Redefine our ideas about capital gains. To reverse the business community's unhealthy short-term, profit-driven mentality, long-term capital gains could be redefined to mean those realized over a twenty- to thirty-year time horizon instead of twelve months. And we should tax gains on short-term investments earned in less than twelve months at more than 80 percent.

8. Close the revolving door between government service and employment in large corporations. Public confidence in the integrity of the federal government is alarmingly low. Currently, fewer than two in ten Americans trust Washington to do what is right "just about always" or "most of the time" (16 percent).[11] One of the most potent factors contributing to this phenomenon is the fact that powerful special interests have taken over. Large corporations and their trade associations spend huge sums

on campaign contributions and lobbying. But business also exercises its influence in moving certain people into (and out of) important policymaking posts in government. This "revolving door" increases the likelihood that policymakers are sympathetic to the desires of business, either because they come from that world or plan to move into it.

9. Get serious about preventing and eliminating monopolies. In the early 1900s, government effectively regulated monopolistic businesses, but since then we've failed miserably. The societal and economic dangers of that inaction are clear. Our failure to regulate monopolies, whether it's Google, Amazon, or Monsanto, results in higher prices, lower-quality service, unfair supply-chain pressure, lack of innovation, and reduced competition. Limiting market control by any single company to less than 33 percent would begin to correct this imbalance.

10. Set a corporate flat tax at 25 percent. Despite the fact that most small and medium-size businesses pay corporate taxes at a rate of 35 percent, most large companies pay nowhere near that amount. Twenty-six Fortune 500 companies, including FedEx, Duke Energy, and Nike, reportedly paid no federal income tax over the three-year period from 2018 to 2020, despite a combined income of $77 billion.[12]

11. Increase funding and tax benefits available to Employee Stock Ownership Plans and build greater incentives for other forms of employee ownership. Job security, satisfaction, and productivity are significantly higher in employee-owned businesses compared to traditional companies. Also, research has shown that employee-owned businesses are more flexible and resilient in times of economic crisis, fostering greater employee

commitment and engagement, reduced absenteeism, superior attraction and retention of talent, lower turnover, and improved consumer confidence. All while giving employees some well-deserved skin in the game and tilting the economic playing field toward sustainability. They even perform better financially.[*]

12. Transition to a living wage. Today's minimum wage is a cruel joke that fails to consider many of a family's basic expenses. Consequently, many working adults must seek public assistance and/or hold multiple jobs to provide even the barest of basics for their families. Establishing a living wage would enable the working poor to achieve financial independence while maintaining housing and food security. And it would go a long way to help companies achieve a net-positive social impact. On the other end of the spectrum, a CEO at a major U.S. company now makes in one year what it would take a typical worker 320 years to earn.[13] The time has come to cap senior management salaries to more reasonable levels.

13. Expand the definition of unionized labor to increase the number of workers that unions represent. The percentage of union members in the labor force is 10.1 percent,[14] down from a high of 30 percent in the 1950s. We must pass the Employee Free Choice Act, which is designed to make it easier for workers to organize with a proposed "card check" system that allows them to call or

---

[*] The Employee Ownership Index (EOI), compiled quarterly by the equity incentives team at law firm Field Fisher Waterhouse, compares the share price performance of companies that are more than 10 percent owned by employees or employee trusts with the performance of FTSE All Share companies. Since 1992, the EOI has outperformed the FTSE All Share by an average of 10 percent annually, per Kristin Tingle, "The Power of Shared Ownership: How Employee-Owned Businesses Achieve ESG Goals," Wharton Business School, September 5, 2023, https://esg.wharton.upenn.edu/news/the-power-of-shared-ownership-how-employee-owned-businesses-achieve-esg-goals/

not call an election for union representation by simply checking off their preference on a card. And we must unionize the labor force to the greatest extent possible. Union representation and collective bargaining, as evidenced by the success of the 2023 SAG, Writers Guild, and autoworker strikes, greatly strengthen workers' hands when it comes to negotiating fair net-positive compensation and reversing economic inequality.

14. Replace the payroll tax with a wealth tax. Payroll taxes are the largest tax most Americans pay and the most deeply regressive—a tax that penalizes productivity and produces the greatest negative impacts on the lowest wage earners. An annual wealth tax, as Thomas Piketty suggests in his groundbreaking 2014 book, *Capital in the Twenty-First Century,* could be paid annually at a rate of 1 percent on individual assets of $1 million and at 2 percent on assets above $5 million. Given that assets of the rich grow annually at an average rate of more than 5 percent, this tax would slow the rate of wealth accumulation and concentration, and shift the tax burden from the economically disadvantaged to those most able to afford it.

15. Improve representation of employees, women, and BIPOC communities. Despite the recent attacks on DEI, diverse businesses perform better than their non-diverse peers.[15] Mandate that one woman or minority is included on the board of directors of all public and private companies. In 2012, the Credit Suisse CS Gender 3000 study, which tracked the financial performance of 2,400 businesses worldwide since 2005, showed that shares of companies whose boards include at least one woman outperformed those of companies with all-male boards by 26 percent.[16] And companies where management is made up of 15 percent

women in senior management positions had more than 50 percent higher profitability than those companies with less that 10 percent representation.

16. Provide universal access to contraception, reproductive, and abortion healthcare. We've fallen into a terrible and dangerous pit having lost the right for a woman to control her own body. Join the fight to bring back women's rights at

17. Get money out of politics. The single greatest threat to our democracy is the ability for wealthy individuals and corporations to dump unlimited amounts of money into the election process. The 2010 Supreme Court decision Citizens United v. FEC swept away a century of precedent that barred corporate money in our elections and endorsed the dangerous fiction that corporations have the same constitutional rights as human beings. We must overturn Citizens United.

18. Clean up our electoral system. Democracy that functions fairly and results in an accurate representation of Americans' views—and not just those of rich and powerful—is essential to a net-positive future. All elections from town animal control officer to president of the United States should be publicly funded. Term limits should be established to avoid political "lifers." And gerrymandering that encourages extremist positions should be banned, along with political action committees that promote a pay-to-play system of government.

This is a rough sketch of what a net-positive world would look like. And yes, building that world gets complicated fast. It's not going to be easy, and we don't have much time. But that's no reason not to take action.

As a veteran of the business sustainability movement, I'm no stranger to naysaying. "It can't be done" has been the refrain that's greeted almost everything I ever did. I understand that it's hard for people to think outside the box, and I know it's even harder to convince them to come together to make the ideas a reality.

Yet I've also seen the powerful results that can happen when they do. If I've learned one lesson after nearly half a century of starting businesses that defied the "norm," it's this: The trick is to simply believe that you can get there and refuse to take no for an answer. When the mission is righteous and our faith in it is unshakeable, there's very little that can keep us from the destiny we seek. Attitude is how you win the day, and with enough of it, the world can get wherever it chooses to go. The only thing that can possibly stop us is ourselves.

As I think about what's next, in both my own life and in the future humanity is creating for itself, I've come to see that much work remains undone. Seventh Generation wasn't the end. It was the beginning, and now the time has come to join together, harness our collective belief in a better world, and finish the job. A bright and prosperous future is ours if we want it. We just have to decide that we do.

This is the work I have yet to complete and the task to which I believe all our hands should now be set. The final adventure awaits, and I hope you'll join me in bringing the extraordinary dream it holds to life. The next seven generations—and all those beyond—are counting on us.

Acknowledgments

I have had a life full of amazing mentors who have guided my journey and helped me to become who I hoped to be. With great love and appreciation to Ivan Illich, Marshal McLuhan, Carol Sanford, Gregor Barnum, Marc Vahanian, Wilson Alling, Khanda Sundram, David Levine, and all the others who have shepherded me forward.

Notes

CHAPTER FOUR

1. Kevin Scanlon, "His Success Was Illegal," *Toronto Sun*, May 19, 1978, 2.

2. John Doig, "All Metro Is a Campus in New Adult Program," *Toronto Star,* n.d.

3. William E. Farrell, "About New York; A Neo-Classical, or Earthy, Approach to the Humanities," *The New York Times*, November 8, 1980, 27.

4. "Education: Fast Food for the Brain," *Time* 118, no. 4 (July 27, 1981). See: https://content.time.com/time/magazine/0,9263,7601810727,00.html

5. Trish Hall, "Course Merges Financial Planning With the Art of Spouse Selection," *Wall Street Journal*, August 25, 1981, 33.

CHAPTER SIX

1. Right Livelihood Foundation, "Herman Daly," accessed August 2025, https://rightlivelihood.org/the-change-makers/find-a-laureate/herman-daly/

CHAPTER EIGHTEEN

1. Peter M. Senge, C. Otto Scharmer, Joseph Jaworski, and Betty Sue Flowers, *Presence: Human Purpose and the Field of the Future* (Crown Currency, 2008).

FINAL THOUGHTS

1. Oliver Balch, "Can a Business Really Be Net Positive, and If So, How Do We Judge Success?" *The Guardian*, June 19, 2013, https://www.theguardian.com/sustainable-business/business-net-positive-how-measure

2. Abigail Tierney, "Wealth Distribution in the United States in the Second Quarter of 2024," *Statista*, October 29, 2024.

3. Aimee Picchi, "Nearly a Quarter of U.S. Adults Sometimes Don't Get Enough to Eat," *CBS News*, March 21, 2023, https://www.cbsnews.com/news/one-in-four-americans-food-insecure/

4. National Institutes of Health, "NIH-Funded Study Highlights Financial Toll of Health Disparities in the United States," NIH.gov, May 16, 2023, https://www.nih.gov/news-events/news-releases/nih-funded-study-highlights-financial-toll-health-disparities-united-states

5. Andrew Gregory, "Cancer Cases in Under-50s Worldwide Up Nearly 80% in Three Decades, Study Finds," *The Guardian*, September 5, 2023, https://www.theguardian.com/society/2023/sep/05/cancer-cases-in-under-50s-worldwide-up-nearly-80-in-three-decades-study-finds

6. Patrick Greenfield, "The Biodiversity Crisis in Numbers—a Visual Guide," *The Guardian*, December 6, 2022, https://www.theguardian.com/environment/2022/dec/06/the-biodiversity-crisis-in-numbers-a-visual-guide-aoe

7. Sabrina Weiss, Matt Reynolds, Maria Paula Escobar-Tello, "10 Facts That Prove the World Is in a Climate Emergency," *Wired*, August 17, 2023, https://www.wired.com/story/climate-change-facts/

8. Kasha Patel, "A Warmer World Causes Extreme Drought and Rain. 'Indisputable' New Research Proves It," *Washington Post*, Updated March 13, 2023, https://www.washingtonpost.com/climate-environment/2023/03/13/drought-rainfall-climate-hottest-years-extreme/

9. Scott Sistek, "6 Rare '1,000-Year' Rain Events Within a Month? Climate Change May Force NOAA to Update Criteria," *Fox Weather*, August 23, 2022, https://www.foxweather.com/extreme-weather/5-rare-1000-year-rain-events-within-a-month-climate-change-may-force-noaa-to-update-criteria

10. Jeffrey Hollender, "Net Positive: The Future of Sustainable Business," *Stanford Social Innovation Review*, April 29, 2015, https://ssir.org/articles/entry/net_positive_the_future_of_sustainable_business

11. "Americans' Dismal Views of the Nation's Politics," Pew Research Center, Sep 19, 2023, https://www.pewresearch.org/wp-content/uploads/sites/20/2023/09/PP_2023.09.19_views-of-politics_REPORT.pdf

12. Patricia Cohen, "No Taxes for Dozens of Big, Profitable Companies," *The New York Times*, April 2, 2021, https://www.nytimes.com/2021/04/02/business/economy/zero-corporate-tax.html

13. David Gelles, *The Man Who Broke Capitalism* (Simon & Schuster, 2022), 184.

14. Bureau of Labor Statistics, U.S. Department of Labor, "Union Members—2024," January 28, 2025, https://www.bls.gov/news.release/pdf/union2.pdf

15. David Rock and Heidi Grant, "Why Diverse Teams Are Smarter," *Harvard Business Review*, November 4, 2016, https://hbr.org/2016/11/why-diverse-teams-are-smarter

16. Credit Suisse AG, "Large-Cap Companies With at Least One Woman on the Board Have Outperformed Their Peer Group With No Women on the Board by 26% Over the Last Six Years, According to a Report by Credit Suisse," PR Newswire, July 31, 2012, https://www.prnewswire.com/news-releases/large-cap-companies-with-at-least-one-woman-on-the-board-have-outperformed-their-peer-group-with-no-women-on-the-board-by-26-over-the-last-six-years-according-to-a-report-by-credit-suisse-research-institute-164409706.html

About the Author

JEFFREY HOLLENDER is the cofounder and former CEO of Seventh Generation, which he helped build into a leading natural product brand known for its authenticity, transparency, and progressive business practices. While Seventh Generation was sold to Unilever in 2016, Hollender remains on the Board of Directors. Hollender is also the founder and former CEO of Sustain Natural, which developed and marketed sustainable feminine care products for women. He is the Executive in Residence and an adjunct professor of sustainability and social entrepreneurship in the Stern Business School at NYU. Hollender also serves as an advisor and mentor to numerous small business and business school students through SKU and Unreasonable.

Hollender is a former board chair for Greenpeace US and the cofounder and former CEO of the American Sustainable Business Network, a coalition of business leaders committed to progressive public policy. He currently serves on the boards of Vermont Businesses for Social Responsibility, Aquavitea, Vermont Cheese Products, Nude Foods

Market, and the Sustainability Advisory Board at Morgan Stanley. He is the author of seven books, including his most recent publications, *The Responsibility Revolution* and *Planet Home*.

Visit him at JeffreyHollender.com or MadeForABetterWorld.com